CIVILISATION

AND

THE GROWTH OF LAW

CIVILISATION

AND

THE GROWTH OF LAW

A STUDY OF THE RELATIONS
BETWEEN MEN'S IDEAS ABOUT THE
UNIVERSE AND THE INSTITUTIONS
OF LAW AND GOVERNMENT

BY

WILLIAM A. ROBSON

PH.D., LL.M., B.SC. (ECON.); BARRISTER-AT-LAW
OF LINCOLN'S INN; READER IN ADMINISTRATIVE LAW
IN THE UNIVERSITY OF LONDON

NEW YORK
THE MACMILLAN COMPANY
1935

12062

PRINTED IN THE UNITED STATES OF AMERICA
BY THE POLYGRAPHIC COMPANY OF AMERICA, N.Y.

"Les combinaisons des choses qui paraissent éloignées servent souvent à produire des effects extraordinaires, et c'est encore les raisons pourquoy ceux qui se bornent à une seule recherche manquent souvent de faire des découvertes qu'un esprit plus étendu, qui peut joindre d'autres sciences à celles dont il s'agit, découvre sans peine."

LEIBNITZ

"Despite all their differences, the thoughts of men form a more living unity than their empires or even their roads."

J. N. FIGGIS

"The difference between the two . . . types of mentality may be roughly described as that between speculation and scholarship. For progress, both are necessary. But, in fact, on the stage of history they are apt to appear as antagonists. Speculation, by entertaining alternative theories, is superficially sceptical, disturbing to established modes of prejudice. But it obtains its urge from a deep ultimate faith, that through and through the nature of things is penetrable by reason. Scholarship, by its strict attention to accepted methodologies, is superficially conservative of belief. But its tone of mind leans towards a fundamental negation. For scholars the reasonable topics in the world are penned in isolated regions, *this* subject-matter or *that* subject-matter. Your thoroughgoing scholar resents the airy speculation which connects his own patch of knowledge with that of his neighbour. He finds his fundamental concepts interpreted, twisted, modified. He has ceased to be king of his own castle, by reason of speculations of uncomfortable generality, violating the very grammar of his thoughts."

A. N. WHITEHEAD

TO

CHARLES AND DOROTHEA SINGER

CONTENTS.

ix

INTRODUCTION

THE writing of this book has been a strange and exciting adventure, and I hope the reader, whatever his other grievances, will not complain that I have led him into tame and well-trodden paths.

Let me assure the unfriendly critic that I am fully conscious of the good and sufficient reasons which might have deterred me from embarking upon so ambitious an enterprise. He can tell me nothing that I do not already know about the danger of attempting to take the whole world for one's parish; of the difficulties a single mind must encounter in endeavouring to grapple with all the several fields of knowledge necessarily touched upon in the following pages; of the impossibility of dealing fully with so vast a subject within the limits of a restricted space.

These and other objections were, however, over-ridden by two considerations of compelling force. One was that I felt an irresistible desire to write the book, no matter what the voice of caution might say. The other was that I am convinced there is a definite need to make our thinking more comprehensive than for the most part it now is in these days of minute specialisms. Hence every tendency towards drawing together the disparate threads of our compartmental knowledge ought to be encouraged.

The object of the present work is to depict the interactions between people's ideas about the universe on the one hand and the laws and government of mankind on the other. I have endeavoured to show

how legal and political institutions have been influenced by magic, superstition, religion, and science; and how these great forces have in turn been influenced by the law. The essential aim throughout has been to present a synthesis. I have had recourse to a vast store of illustrative material, and have drawn on the experience of civilised and primitive peoples, in both ancient times and modern. But at every point I have sought to subordinate the multitudinous details to the main outline of the picture I have been trying to paint. Hence, the book is not intended to be cyclopaedic. It aims at illuminating the subject-matter rather than exhausting it—or the reader.

Whether the book achieves its object is a question for others. But I may confess that the work of producing it has been a fascinating and refreshing experience. When one has been closely preoccupied with contemporary studies and immediate practical problems for some years, the contemplation of long stretches of history and remote stages of human development brings an extraordinary sense of satisfaction and release. The turmoil and conflict of our own age seem more incidental and less senseless and overwhelming when seen in perspective against the slow march of events through long periods of time.

I have made what is doubtless the common discovery that no matter where one starts out, nor in what unlikely direction the path seems to go, sooner or later it invariably leads back to the contemporary scene. In the present work, however, this has been borne in upon me in a very striking way.

The earlier part of the book is concerned to a considerable extent with the intimate liaison which existed for many centuries between law and religion,

and the causes and consequences of that connection.
The influence of religious beliefs in secular affairs
was gradually supplanted during the past century
or two by the rational element. The rise of reason
played an important part in abolishing many of the
most ancient and deeply rooted evils such as slavery,
serfdom, persecution for heresy, burning for witchcraft, the suppression of free speech.[1] We are now
witnessing a widespread revolt against reason. In
Germany and Italy the foundations of government
rest on a purely emotional appeal and the secular
authority relies upon a dogmatic creed against which
no word may be uttered. The totalitarian state thus
restores the sacrosanct basis of society. A symptom
of this is Bishop Mueller's statement that Herr Hitler
has told him that he considers the Nazi revolution to
be God's work, so that he feels himself in his high
office to be responsible to God.[2] In Soviet Russia the
anti-God campaign formed part of the official policy
of the Government for years; and one hears continual
references among sympathetic observers to the resemblance between the Communist party there and a
religious order.

In these circumstances a return of the old abuses
of which mention has been made, or others of a
similar character, would not be surprising in those
communities which prefer sacred and inviolable
creeds to the life of reason as a foundation of the
social order.

The point I now wish to make, however, is that
contemporary phenomena of this kind can only be
fully understood if they are seen in relation to the

---

[1] Morris R. Cohen, *Reason and Nature*, p. 9.
[2] *Daily Telegraph*, 28th September 1933.

developments described in this book. No one who bears these contemporary applications and conflicts in mind will fail to comprehend the practical significance which is implicit in what follows.

It remains for me to acknowledge the help I have received from various quarters. Professor H. F. Jolowicz and Professor T. F. T. Plucknett read through the first draft of the manuscript and gave me the benefit of their great learning on a number of matters. My best thanks are due to them for this friendly service. They are, of course, in no way committed to my views. Professor Jolowicz was kind enough to let me see the unpublished notes of his lectures on Greek law, which I found of great interest. Professor Charles Singer also read through the manuscript and made several useful suggestions.

My obligations to literary sources will, I believe, appear from the footnotes and the text itself.[1] But in case I have inadvertently omitted to record them in any instance, I hasten to declare that I lay no claim to originality of knowledge or primacy of learning. Any merit which my work possesses lies entirely in its conception, arrangement, and method of treatment. It is essentially an experimental study in the borderland between law, sociology, political science, and certain other sciences.

I have endeavoured elsewhere to pay my tribute to the work of that great pioneer Sir Henry Maine,[2] who may be regarded as the father of the sociology of law.

[1] One compilation I have found very convenient are the three volumes edited by Professors Albert Kocourek and John H. Wigmore entitled *Evolution of Law: Select Readings on the Origin and Development of Legal Institutions*.

[2] See my essay on "Sir Henry Maine To-day" in *Modern Theories of Law* (Oxford, 1933).

In conclusion, I must express my thanks to Miss D. W. Young, B.Sc.(Econ.), who acted as my research assistant for six months after the first draft of the work had been made. Miss Young possesses in an unusual degree the qualities required for research work, and I am greatly indebted to her help.

My thanks are also due to Miss B. Buckingham, who kindly undertook the task of making the Index.

WILLIAM A. ROBSON

London School of Economics
    and Political Science

PART I

THE ORIGINS OF LAW

I

WHAT IS LAW?

For at least twenty-five centuries, and perhaps for hundreds of years before that, men have discussed the nature of Law. The question "What is Law?" has been asked by all sorts and conditions of men: by priests and poets, by seers and kings, by the masses no less than by the prophets. Many different kinds of answer have been given; yet the question remains one of the most insistent and elusive problems in the entire range of thought. The whole gamut of human life, both in thought and in action, is comprised within the simple word Law.

Let us glance at a few of the answers which have been propounded at different times by various thinkers. Cicero, purporting to state the opinion of the wisest men of his day, observed that Law is neither contrived nor decreed by man; it is an eternal principle which rules the whole universe, commanding what is right and prohibiting what is wrong. Hence Law is no mere artefact but is the divine reason bestowed by the gods on the human race.[1]

St. Thomas Aquinas declared in the 13th century that "Law is an ordinance of reason, for the common good, promulgated by him who has care of the community".[2] Elsewhere he suggests that Law is a rule or standard, which in its most simple and universal

---

[1] Marcus Tullius Cicero, *De Legibus*, II, iv.
[2] *Summa Theologica*, I, ii, 90. 4.

3

form measures actions.[1] The views of St. Thomas
have exerted an immense influence on Catholic
thought throughout the world. An authoritative
Catholic work recently issued almost repeats his pronouncement word for word by defining Law as "a
regulation in accordance with reason promulgated by
the head of a community for the sake of the common
welfare".[2] The emphasis which Aquinas laid on the
rational and ethical aspects of Law is pushed to extreme lengths by the same authority, who go on to
state that, strictly speaking, laws are the moral norms
of action, binding in conscience, set up for a self-
governing community.[3] The late Father Bede Jarrett
attempted a more plausible and comprehensive solution by postulating that Law is the reign of order.
Law, he said, implies the acceptance by a group of
people of certain common regulations: it presupposes
that they are conscious of their unity, and that they
submit themselves not only to a ruler but also to rule.[4]

To Richard Hooker (1554–1600) Law appeared
as "that which reason in such sort defines to be good
that it must be done".[5] Among several definitions of
Law given by Immanuel Kant (1724–1804) perhaps
the most characteristic is the one in which he describes
it as "the sum-total of the conditions under which the
personal wishes of one man can be reconciled with
the personal wishes of another man, in accordance
with a general law of freedom".[6] Savigny, the great

---

[1] Bede Jarrett, *Social Theories of the Middle Ages* (1926), p. 12
et seq.
[2] *Catholic Encyclopaedia*, "Law", vol. ix, p. 53.
[3] *Ibid.*; R. W. and A. J. Carlyle, *A History of Medieval Political
Theory in the West*, vol. v, ch. iv.
[4] Bede Jarrett, *op. cit.* p. 1.   [5] *Ecclesiasticall Politie*, i, c. 3, c. 8.
[6] *Rechtslehre: Werke*, vii, p. 27.

historical jurist of the 19th century, defined Law as "the rule whereby the invisible border line is fixed within which the being and the activity of each individual obtains a secure and free space".[1]

If we turn to the later English jurists, we find them struggling to divest the conception of Law of its metaphysical and moral implications and yet to avoid discarding altogether the use of the term in connection with man's wider relations with the universe. Blackstone, for instance, starts out by saying that Law, in its most general comprehensive sense, signifies a rule of action; and that it is applied indiscriminately to all kinds of action, whether animate or inanimate, rational or irrational. Thus there are the laws of motion, of gravitation, of optics or mechanics, as well as the laws of nature and of nations. But shrinking from the implications of this unseemly flight of fancy, he retreats hastily to the position that Law is a rule of action which is prescribed by some superior, and which the inferior is bound to obey.[2]

John Austin defined a law as a rule laid down for the guidance of an intelligent being by another intelligent being having power over him. This includes both laws set by God to human creatures and laws set by men to men. Without pausing to consider the attributes of the intelligent anthropomorphic deity to which he was committing himself, Austin observed that the divine precepts are properly termed laws because they contain the essential elements of a law —namely, a command, a duty to obey and a sanction to compel obedience. Laws observed by the lower animals, those regulating the growth or decay of

[1] *Systema des Rechts*, i, p. 332.
[2] *Commentaries*, Introduction, § 2 (1st ed. p. 38).

vegetables or the movements of inanimate bodies, could in Austin's eyes be regarded as laws only in a metaphorical or figurative sense.[1]

T. E. Holland follows the Austinian conception so far as to declare that laws are propositions commanding the doing of or abstention from certain classes of action, disobedience to which is followed by some sort of penalty or inconvenience.[2] He then attempts to infuse a little life into the dry bones of Austin's "command" by stating that Law is "formulated and armed public opinion, or the opinion of the ruling body". It announces not only that certain states of things and courses of action are viewed with favour, but that if any attempt is made to contravene them, it will actively intervene on their behalf.[3]

Sir Frederick Pollock avoids the stumbling-blocks of command and obedience by describing Law as a rule of conduct binding on members of a commonwealth as such.[4] We can, he says, better realise the fundamental character of Law by trying to conceive its negation or opposite. This will be found in the absence of order rather than in the absence of compulsion.[5] Mr. Sidney Hartland, concerning himself as an anthropologist chiefly with primitive society, is not far from the developed view of Sir Frederick Pollock when he says that Law may be defined as a set of rules imposed and enforced by a society for the conduct of social and political relations.[6] We cannot regard the test of sanction as satisfactory, he points out; we are driven back upon that of recognition.

[1] *Lectures on Jurisprudence*, Lect. I.
[2] *Jurisprudence*, p. 23.   [3] *Ibid.* p. 90
[4] *First Book of Jurisprudence*, p. 29.   [5] *Ibid.* p. 34.
[6] "Law (Primitive)" in *Encyclopaedia of Religion and Ethics*, vol. vii, p. 811.

Professor G. C. Lee, in his *Historical Juris-prudence*,[1] declares that Law is that body of customs, enforced by the community, by means of which man's gross passions are controlled and his conduct towards his fellow-creatures regulated. This exclusive concentration on custom leaves out of account the formal enactment, the statute that is "laid" or "fixed", which seems to have been the essential meaning of *lex* and its equivalents in other languages.[2]

These few specimens taken from a vast literature on the subject suffice to illustrate the laborious efforts which have been made through the ages to answer the question "What is Law?" There is infinite diversity among the answers and no fundamental agreement between the writers. Much of the difficulty and confusion is no doubt due to the desire to give a single answer to a complex question. In the Greek City-State, Dean Roscoe Pound reminds us, the exigencies of the social order led to a distinction between Law and the rules of law;[3] and on the continent of Europe to-day the expression Law is commonly used in two senses, one objective and the other subjective, the former denoting all the principles of law enforced by the State, the legal ordering of life, the latter denoting the concrete legal right of a particular person. But despite these and other attempts to partition the territory, it is possible to trace through the long centuries an almost universal assumption that Law in all its shapes and forms is at bottom one and indivisible, like the Republic of France.

---

[1] P. 5.

[2] Sohm, *The Institutes of Roman Law* (1892), p. 28 n. The derivation of *lex* is doubtful. See *infra*, pp. 234-5.

[3] *Introduction to the Philosophy of Law*, p. 24.

To employ the word Law in such phrases as the laws of nature, the laws of God, the laws of morality, the laws of beauty, and so forth, is, in Holland's view, to introduce confusion. But, he continues, wonder at this misuse of terms decreases when we recall that in the ancient world the separation of the sciences from one another was unknown. "The world with all its varied phenomena was originally studied as a whole. The facts of nature and the doings of man were alike conceived of as ordained by the gods. The constitutions of states and the customs and laws of all peoples of the earth were as much of divine contrivance as the paths of the planets. The great problem thus presented for the study of mankind was gradually broken up into a number of minor problems. There occurred a division of the sciences. A line was drawn between those which deal with external nature . . . and those which deal with the actions of man."[1]

In what follows I shall endeavour to discover, among other things, whether it indeed implies a confusion of thought, and if so in what sense, to use the same word to denote the order of the physical universe and the order of human society. The idea of Law grew up historically as the opposite of fortuitous occurrence on the one hand and of arbitrary occurrence on the other. In the one case the opposition led to the idea of physical law, in the other to that of civil law.[2] A thousand objections can be ranged in protest against the persistence of error merely because it can produce historical justification; and that particu-

---

[1] *Jurisprudence*, p. 23.
[2] John Dickinson, *Administrative Justice and the Supremacy of Law in the United States* (1927), pp. 110-11.

lar pitfall at least I shall avoid. But I must confess
at the outset that, no matter how grave the heresy
may be in these days of ever-increasing specialisation,
I shall not hesitate to study the world "as a whole"
whenever the purposes of my enquiry demand it.

II

THE ORIGINS OF LAW

IF it is difficult to define Law in a satisfactory manner, a still harder task is to find the beginnings of it. The origins of Law are shrouded in obscurity and are, perhaps, impossible to discover. However far back we go into the twilight of history, there is always some form of law in existence. It does not assist our search to say that Law originates in custom.

The oldest written code is that promulgated by Hammurabi, King of Babylon 2123–2081 B.C., whose rule extended over the whole of Mesopotamia from the mouths of the Tigris and Euphrates to the Mediterranean coast. But the state of society revealed by the code of Hammurabi is an advanced one, and the law itself exhibits signs of mature development. Vengeance has been replaced by a system of justice; self-help is restrained, if not suppressed; wrong must be redressed at law. Protection is afforded to the weak, to the widows and orphans, and women are placed in a position of freedom and independence of their husbands such as they have only enjoyed in England since the passing of the Married Women's Property Acts in the 19th century.[1] Hence we are still completely in the dark concerning the rise of Law in

---

[1] C. H. W. Johns, *The Oldest Code of Laws in the World* (1903), Edinburgh; *The Relations between the Laws of Babylonia and the Laws of the Hebrew Peoples* (1914), p. 516. Cf. Sir J. G. Frazer, *Folklore in the Old Testament*, iii, p. 95; S. A. Cook, *The Semites* in *Cambridge Ancient History*, i, p. 211.

Babylonia. However far back we endeavour to trace its history or its monuments, we never reach a point in time of which it can be said "As yet there was no Law".[1] There were probably laws and even codes for centuries before Hammurabi, and the code that has survived is doubtless but a compilation made from pre-existing material.[2]

In primitive societies now existing the problem of discovering the nature and origins of Law is complicated by the fact that there is frequently no public authority capable of formulating legislation or of declaring the existing law. The absence of any definite machinery for the enactment, enforcement and administration of Law in savage society[3] has led many writers to suggest that the savage knows nothing of Law in any true sense, but is enslaved in a vast mesh of custom which dictates every act, every thought, every word he utters. "The savage", writes Mr. Sidney Hartland, "is hemmed in on every side by the customs of his people, he is bound in the chains of immemorial tradition, not merely in his social relations, but in his religion, his medicine, his industry, his art, and every aspect of his life."[4] In the more primitive forms of social grouping, remarks Professor C. K. Allen, habit is very nearly automatic. "There is not", he continues, "a very vast difference between the automatism of the ant and the tribal

---

[1] C. H. W. Johns, *Babylonian and Assyrian Laws, Contracts and Letters*, p. 39, in the "Library of Ancient Inscriptions" (Edinburgh, 1904).

[2] S. H. Langdon, *The Sumerian Revival: the Empire of Ur*, in *Cambridge Ancient History*, i, p. 461.

[3] E. Sidney Hartland, "Law (Primitive)" in *Encyclopaedia of Religion and Ethics*, vol. vii, pp. 812-13; B. Malinowski, *Crime and Custom in Savage Society*, p. 14.

[4] *Primitive Law*, p. 138.

habits of an Australian aboriginal; the ant, indeed, in many respects has the better of the comparison."[1] In the 18th century Rousseau declared that "Man is born free; everywhere he is in chains". These writers of the 20th century assert, on the contrary, that it is the savage who is born in chains.

Against this view Professor Malinowski has entered a vigorous and effective protest, based largely on an exact first-hand study of certain primitive peoples. We must, he says, abandon the idea of an inert solid crust or cake of custom pressing rigidly on tribal life from outside.[2] Law and order arise out of the very processes which they govern. The assumption of mechanical and slavish obedience to custom by savages is entirely false.[3]

It is true that among primitive peoples there is no single source from which the law is derived, nor are there all-powerful organs expressly charged with applying or enforcing its provisions. But the absence of legislative, judicial, and executive institutions corresponding to those we are accustomed to find in developed societies should not blind us to the fact that savage societies recognise a body of binding legal precepts.[4] The laws are tolerably well observed in such communities, despite an absence of written codes, courts of law, judges and policemen.[5] The failure to perceive the existence of authentic legal systems among retarded peoples, save perhaps in the case of repression against violence, is in large measure due to the fallacious habit of identifying a legal

[1] *Law in the Making*, p. 26.
[2] *Crime and Custom in Savage Society*, pp. 122-3.
[3] *Ibid.* p. 30.
[4] H. Ian Hogbin, *Law and Order in Polynesia* (1934), p. 290.
[5] B. Malinowski, Introduction to H. Ian Hogbin, *op. cit.* p. xxv.

system with the person or organ possessing power to make law.[1] If the latter cannot be discovered the existence of the former is thereupon denied.

There must be, observes Professor Malinowski, in all societies a class of rules too practical to be backed up by religious sanctions, too burdensome to be left to mere goodwill, too personally vital to individuals to be enforced by any abstract agency. This is the domain of legal rules.[2] Civil law, the positive law governing all phases of tribal life, consists of a body of binding obligations, regarded as a right by one party and acknowledged as a duty by the other, kept in force by a specific mechanism of reciprocity and publicity inherent in their society. These rules of civil law are elastic and possess a certain latitude. They offer not only penalties for failure but also premiums for specially zealous fulfilment. Their stringency is ensured through the rational appreciation of cause and effect by the natives, combined with a number of social and personal sentiments.[3]

The rules of law in primitive society stand out from other norms of conduct in that they are felt and regarded as the obligations of one person and the rightful claims of another. They are sanctioned not merely by psychological motives but also by a definite social machinery of binding force.[4] Thus among the Melanesians, the economic arrangements connected with the native canoe are supported by law, order, definite privileges and a well-developed system of obligations. Each canoe is owned by one

[1] H. Ian Hogbin, *Law and Order in Polynesia* (1934), p. 77.
[2] *Crime and Custom in Savage Society*, pp. 67-8.
[3] *Ibid*. p. 58, also Introduction to H. Ian Hogbin, *Law and Order in Polynesia*, p. xxxvi.
[4] *Crime and Custom in Savage Society*, pp. 55-6.

man, the others who work with it forming the crew.
All are bound together and to their fellow-villagers
by mutual obligations. The owner cannot refuse the
use of his canoe. The crew in turn is under obligations: each must stand by his task; each receives his
fair share of the catch.[1] The fishermen exchange their
fish for vegetables with inland communities, and here
again these economic arrangements have a legal
aspect involving mutual obligations. Professor Malinowski declares that the whole structure of Trobriand
society is founded on the principle of legal status,
which extends right up to the chief.[2] A similar system
of mutual obligations, interlocking division of functions and reciprocal rights and duties, is to be found
in Polynesia.

Among the Australian aborigines, as in all forms
of social organisation, there are norms and rules
regulating all the social relations. Those which
have organised, regulated, and active social sanction
may be called legal.[3] Unlike the Melanesians, the
Australian aborigines have centralised organs of
government consisting of headmen and a tribal
council composed mainly of the old men of the tribe,
skilled magicians, and experienced warriors.[4] One of
the chief functions of these authorities is to decide
cases of difficulty in tribal affairs and to pronounce
sentence. They possess rudimentary forms of legislative, executive, and judicial power.

On the whole, Professor Malinowski tells us,
everyone in a primitive tribe tries to fulfil his obligations, for he is impelled to do so partly through

[1] *Crime and Custom in Savage Society*, pp. 18-22.
[2] *Ibid.* pp. 46-7; Introduction to H. Ian Hogbin, *op. cit.* p. xl.
[3] B. Malinowski, *The Family among the Australian Aborigines*,
p. 9-11.   [4] *Ibid.* p. 12.

enlightened self-interest, partly in obedience to his social ambitions and sentiments. "Take the real savage, keen on evading his duties, swaggering and boastful when he has fulfilled them, and compare him with the anthropologist's dummy who slavishly follows custom and automatically obeys every regulation. There is not the remotest resemblance between the teachings of anthropology on this subject and the reality of native life."[1]

It is no longer possible to accept the suggestion that primitive communities move about in a sort of custom-bound trance, dazed by the traditional practices which they accept without question. Nor can we believe that Law is the exclusive possession of societies who have acquired the mature apparatus of thought and action which we term civilisation. More truly might one assert that whenever men have managed to live together, there shall we find the rudiments of Law. Without Law, indeed, men cannot live together. This, we shall see later, is its essential justification from a functional point of view. That is not to say, however, that Law was not embedded for long ages in the history of mankind in a morass of superstition, mythological belief and religion from which it has even now not completely emerged.

[1] *Crime and Custom in Savage Society*, p. 30.

III

MEN LIKE GODS

SIR HENRY MAINE pointed out half a century ago
that it is easier to find the origins of lawyers than the
origin of Law. The first lawyers were invariably endowed with supernatural powers bestowed on them
by the divine origin which they claimed or which was
accorded to them.[1] The ruler or king is always associated with the administration of justice. He may be a
military chief or general; he is frequently a priest or
chief priest; but he is always a judge.[2] "Whatever
else he may have been, the old King seems commonly
to have been a magician."[3] The idea that the first
king was simply the strongest and bravest man of his
tribe is utterly false. Like most purely rationalistic
speculations concerning the origin of society, it takes
no account of the fact that primitive men are devoid
of any conception of an essential rational order, and
hence are subject to superstition, a force which has
exerted an immense influence on the development of
social organisation.

In the early stages of society, men who are
ignorant of the processes of nature arrogate to themselves functions of a superhuman or divine character.
The order and uniformity of nature, recurring events
in the physical world, such as the cycle of the seasons,

[1] *Early Law and Custom*, pp. 26-7.
[2] Maine, *Ancient Law*, p. 160. For an example from modern Hawaii
see H. Ian Hogbin, *Law and Order in Polynesia* (1934), p. 247.
[3] Sir James Frazer, *The Magical Origin of Kings*, p. 36.

16

impress the primitive intelligence and delude man
into the belief that he can affect them. He foresees
them, and mistakes their recurrence, if desired, for an
effect of his own will; while any departure from the
regular order, if dreaded, is ascribed to an effect of his
enemy's will.[1] He fancies that the forces of nature are
within reach of his power, and that he can touch them
and work good for himself and evil for his foes.

Thus arose magicians or medicine-men. They are
the most ancient professional class of which we have
any knowledge, and sorcerers are found in every
savage tribe of which there is any record.[2] In the
course of time medicine-men become differentiated
into more specialised classes such as the healers of
disease, the makers of rain and so forth; while the
most powerful member of the order wins for himself
the position of chief and gradually develops into a
sacred king. His old magical functions fall more and
more into the background and are replaced by
priestly and even divine duties as magic is slowly
ousted by religion.[3] So long as men regard their gods
as beings akin to themselves and not raised to an
unapproachable height, they conceive it to be possible for outstanding members of the community to
attain divine rank in life and after death.[4] Not only
does the king possess divine powers, but he is very
often regarded as a veritable god.

Human gods have been found all over the world.[5]
The King of Sofala, a French missionary observed
in 1843, "is a woolly-haired Kaffir, a heathen who
adores nothing whatever . . . he esteems himself a
god of all his lands, and is so looked upon and

---

[1] J. G. Frazer, *ibid.* pp. 278-9.   [2] *Ibid.* pp. 150-51.
[3] *Loc. cit.*   [4] *Ibid.* p. 279.   [5] *Ibid.* p. 133 *et seq.*

reverenced by his subjects".[1] In the Makalaka hills,
to the west of Matabeleland, there lives at the present
time a human god who dwells in a cave and is never
seen. Food is placed outside the cavern by his subjects to appease him and obtain his favours. The
Peruvians formerly believed that their Inca was
descended from the sun, whence he united within
himself all civil and religious power, and was regarded as perfect.[2]

Similar phenomena are found in the East. The
laws of Manu lay it down that the King is created by
eternal particles of Indra, of the wind, of Yama, of
the sun, of fire, of Varuna, of the moon, and of the
Lord of Wealth. Then Manu goes on to state that
"because a King has been formed of particles of
those lords of the gods", he therefore surpasses all
created beings in lustre. "Even an infant king must
not be despised [from an idea] that he is a [mere]
mortal; for he is a great deity in human form."[3]
According to Manu every Brahman is also a great
divinity; or as the Law-Book of Vishnu puts it, "the
gods are invisible deities, the Brahmans are visible
deities".[4]

In Islam, the most conspicuous fact about
Mahomet is that he was not merely a divine prophet
but also a temporal ruler who governed, judged,
punished, and legislated. After the great flight in
A.D. 622 to Medina, where Mahomet acquired political power, he was sovereign as well as divine prophet,

[1] Missionary Chevron, *Annales de la Prop. de la Foi*, xv (1843),
p. 37, quoted by Frazer, *op. cit.*
[2] Louis H. Gray, "Law (American)" in *Encyclopaedia of Religion
and Ethics*, vol. vi, p. 816.
[3] *Laws of Manu*, Book VII, pp. 4-8.
[4] Main, *Early Law and Custom*, pp. 45-7.

but only sovereign because of his prophetic office.
The mosque was his council-chamber and hall of
audience; the Friday sermon his chief opportunity
for declarations of policy; and when he uttered his
most far-reaching injunctions he spoke as the very
mouthpiece of the deity.[1]

In Japan the Mikado is regarded as a divine
and mysterious personage descended from the sun-
goddess Amaterasu Omikami, the deity who rules
the universe. The modern constitution of Japan, promulgated in 1889, explicitly declares in Article III
that "the Emperor is sacred and inviolable". In
a recent treatise on the Japanese constitution, the
learned Dean of Nihon University informs us that
the Imperial line is "eternal, coeval with heaven and
earth".[2] Emperor-worship exists as a definite fact in
Japan to-day.[3] The portrait of the Mikado is kept in
the schools and public offices for the express purpose
of worship. In ordinary times it is stored carefully in
a holy place especially consecrated to receive it, and
is brought forward on national holidays or important
occasions in order that profound obeisances may be
made before it. "We keep the name of the Emperor
sacred and do not mention it in ordinary conversation," writes Dean Matsunami. "When we wish to
speak about the Emperor we use the words 'His
Majesty' just as social etiquette in the West decrees
that in secular conversation God shall be known as
'the Deity' and Christ as 'Our Saviour'. No Japanese
dare doubt the divine origin of their Mighty Ruler.

[1] Sir Roland Knyvet Wilson, *Introduction to the Study of Anglo-
Muhammadan Law*, pp. 11-15.
[2] N. Matsunami, *The Constitution of Japan* (Tokyo, 1930), p. 38.
[3] *Ibid.* p. 40.

He is in our eye the Son of Heaven. He is in our politics utterly sacred."[1]

In China, under the Emperor, there were so many human gods that a register of all the incarnate gods in the Empire was kept in the Colonial Office in Peking. Something like 160 gods took out a licence in this manner, of which 30 dwelt in Tibet, 19 in North Mongolia, and 57 in South Mongolia. The greatest of all the human gods was the Emperor himself, who was believed to wield supreme power not only over mankind but also over the gods themselves.[2]

Perhaps the most thoroughgoing manifestations of human godhood were those which existed among the ancient Egyptians. In the course of his existence the King of Egypt exhausted all the possible conceptions of divinity which the Egyptians had formulated for themselves. A superhuman god by his birth and his royal office, he became the deified man after his death. Thus all that was known of the divine was summed up in him. The official worship of Pharaoh in the temple did not in itself suffice; even beyond the limits of the sanctuary he remained the "good god" to whom all owed perpetual adoration. In particular the King of Egypt in olden times was identified with Ra, the great sun-god. "Son of the Sun, decked with the solar crowns, armed with the solar weapons, gods and men adored him as Ra, defended him as Ra from the attacks which menaced in him the divine being who, in his human existence, knew the glory and the dangers of being 'an incarnate sun' and 'the

---

[1] N. Matsunami, *The Constitution of Japan* (Tokyo, 1930) p. 38.
[2] J. J. M. de Groot, *Sectarianism and Religious Persecution in China*, i, p. 17 *et seq.* (Amsterdam, 1903), quoted by Frazer, *op. cit.* p. 147.

living image on earth of his father Tum of Helio-
polis'."[1]

In ancient Greece and Rome the royal office had a
sacerdotal character which made it necessary for the
holder of it to possess special attributes; and the same
applied to some of the lesser positions of authority.
The ancient Kings of Greece and Italy were priests.
Aristotle records that the care of the public sacrifices
of the city belonged, according to religious custom,
not to special priests, but to those men who derived
their dignity from the hearth and who in one place
were called kings, in another presidents and in a third
archons.[2] The Kings of Sparta, we learn again from
Aristotle, had three attributes: they performed the
sacrifices, commanded in war and administered
justice.[3] Homer and Virgil depict the kings as continually engaged in sacred ceremonies, and we know
from Demosthenes[4] that the ancient Kings of Attica
performed in person all the sacrifices required by
the religion of the city. An ancient King of Sicyon
was deposed because, having soiled his hands by a
murder, he was no longer in a condition to offer the
sacrifices. Having become unfit to be a priest, he
could no longer remain a king.[5]

Tradition represents all the Roman kings as
priests. The first was Romulus, who was learned in
the science of augury and who founded the city
in accordance with religious rites. Under the monarchial constitution, the king was both military chief

---

[1] A. Moret, *Du caractère religieux de la Royauté Pharaonique*
(Paris, 1902), pp. 278, 313, quoted by Frazer, *op. cit.* p. 149.
[2] Aristotle, *Politics*, vi, 5. 11-13; Fustel de Coulanges, *La Cité antique*
(17th ed.), p. 203. Cf. Xenophon, *The Polity of the Lacedaemonians*, 13.
[3] *Politics*, iii, 9. 2.   [4] *In Neaer.*
[5] F. de Coulanges, *op. cit.* p. 204. Cf. Euripides, *Orestes*, 1605.

and head priest, assisted in some of his functions by the Senate and the popular Assembly. The revolution which established the republican régime did not dissolve the union of political authority with the sacred office, for to some extent the magistrate who replaced the king was, like the latter, both a priest and a political chief.[1] There was no magistrate who had not some sacred act to perform, since all authority derived from religion. The first act of the Roman consul was to offer a sacrifice with his own hand in the forum. The victims had first to be declared by the pontiff to be worthy of being offered up. At Rome it was believed that no one could be a good pontiff who did not know the law, and no one could know the law who did not understand religious questions.[2] When we examine the character of the magistrate among the ancients, said Fustel de Coulanges, we see how slightly he resembles the chief of state of modern societies. "Priesthood, justice, and command are confounded in his person. He represents the city, which is a religious association at least as much as a political one. He has in his hands the auspices, the rites, prayer, the protection of the gods. A consul is something more than a man; he is a mediator between man and the divinity."[3]

Belief in the godlike character of princes and rulers prevailed in Europe until modern times. The Kings of England and France exercised miraculous powers of healing from the 11th century onwards.[4] They were able to do this because they had for long been

[1] F. de Coulanges, *op. cit.* pp. 204, 210-11.
[2] *Ibid.* p. 219.   [3] *Ibid.* pp. 211-12.
[4] Marc Bloch, *Les Rois Thaumaturges* (1924), pp. 31, 41-2. Philippe 1 was the first French king to touch for scrofula and Henry II the first English monarch.

regarded as sacred persons. Their dynasties were descended from the ancient Germans, who considered kings to be of divine origin and hence endowed with special powers over nature in regard to such matters as harvests.

With the spread of Christianity, the temporal ruler at first ceased officially to be a divine person, although a belief in his sacred attributes no doubt lingered on in the minds of the people for centuries. But the sacred quality of the king was soon re-established in a new form by means of the religious ceremony of consecration, and, in particular, through the essential rite of anointing.[1]

The potent force of the royal holiness which was thus symbolised is well illustrated by the utterance of Frère François, ambassador of Edward III, who in 1340 presented himself to the Doge of Venice in search of support for his English master in the war against France. He is reported to have stated, in order to show the efforts which Edward had made to prevent war, that the English monarch had written to Philippe de Valois suggesting various methods of settling the dispute. One of these was that if Philippe de Valois were indeed the true King of France, as he claimed, he should demonstrate the fact either by exposing himself to hungry lions, "for lions never wound a true king"; or better still, that he should accomplish the miraculous cure of the sick, in the manner of other authentic kings.[2] There is some doubt as to whether Edward actually wrote the alleged letter—it may have been invented by his envoy for diplomatic purposes. But there can be no

[1] *Ibid.* pp. 54-60, 65. Pépin was the first King of France to have the rite. [2] *Ibid.* pp. 15-16.

doubt whatever that such an epistle would not have been even invented by the zealous François if educated men of the day had not firmly believed in the sacred character of the king.

Nearly two centuries later, in 1626, the Bishop of Chartes drew up a State paper, afterwards ratified by the Parlement in Paris, which declared that "The Kings are gods, not by nature but through grace . . . blind obedience is a holy duty".[1] Later, in a similar vein, Bossuet wrote, "*le prince ne doit rendre compte à personne de ce qu'il ordonne . . . [O rois] vous êtes des dieux, c'est-à-dire: vous avez dans votre autorité, vous portez sur votre front, un caractère divin*".[2] The touching of persons to cure them of scrofula, performed by the Kings of England until comparatively recent times, clearly reveals the modern sovereign as the successor to the ancient medicine-man or magician. Pepys saw the king "heale" on 13th April 1661, and Dr. Johnson was touched by Queen Anne when he was a child. There was even a curious revival in France in 1825 under Charles X.[3] The process of deifying human beings could actually be witnessed in India so late as the second half of the 19th century. "Not long ago", wrote Lyall in 1872, "the Bunjâras turned General Nicholson into a new god, to be added to the many at whose tombs sacrifice and worship were regularly offered."[4]

    [1] Iv. Döllinger, *Akademische Vorträge* (Nordlingen, 1888), i, p. 275.
    [2] J. B. Bossuet, *Politique tirée de l'Écriture-Sainte* (1709), pp. 103, 210.
    [3] Marc Bloch, *op. cit.* pp. 391, 401-4. The practice really ended in France with Louis XVI, and in England with Queen Anne.
    [4] *Fortnightly Review* (1872), xi, pp. 121-40, quoted by A. H. Sayce, *Science of Language* (1880), ii, p. 298.

IV

GODS LIKE MEN

In ancient Greece, the earliest notion of a law or rule of conduct was the *Themis* of the Homeric poems.[1] As Maine suggested, Law had in those days hardly reached the footing of a settled practice or custom: it was rather "in the air". Recurrent action in the moral no less than in the physical world was most satisfactorily explained to the undeveloped intelligence by presupposing some divine agent as the active cause. The determination of right and wrong was not to be sought from any ascertainable body of precepts but consisted of a judicial sentence pronounced by divine authority after the dispute or problem had arisen. Such a decree did not presume the violation of a pre-existing law but was regarded as an inspired ordinance breathed into the mind of the adjudicator at the required moment.[2]

A *Themis* formulated a normal code of conduct

[1] H. S. Maine, *Ancient Law* (1861), pp. 4-8.

[2] Maine's theory of the divinely inspired decision has been criticised on the ground that the evidence which he adduced is not conclusive. An alternative suggestion made by more than one contemporary scholar is that the decisions of the ancient Greek kings were really based, consciously or unconsciously, on customary practices; and that among the early Greeks, as among other peoples, Law developed on the basis of custom. This conception, though more pedestrian, does not appear to be supported by a more impressive body of evidence than Maine's view. It is possible that the judges, although believed by themselves and others to be divinely inspired, gave decisions which in fact were in accord with established customs. In that case both Maine and his critics are right.

and indicated the way in which a contravention of normal behaviour should be remedied. Although elicited to deal with a particular situation, a *Themis* enunciated a general rule rather than a mere dispensation to fit a single occasion. It constituted the authentic vehicle by which the will of the gods was transmitted to human beings through the medium of individuals specially qualified to elicit the divine wisdom and counsel. The Homeric *themistes* relate essentially to the affairs of mankind, but even among the gods themselves there existed a personified Themis to assist them in the ordering of their lives.[1]

In early Hebrew times, the *tôrôth*, or decisions, were rendered by the priest, the representative of Jahweh, by means of the sacred lot. The other Hebrew word for law, *misphāt*, originally meant a specific judgment.[2] It was only on the basis of these isolated decisions that customs and oral laws subsequently grew up.

Tacitus observed that in Germany the priests sat in judgment upon all offences and had the exclusive power of punishment. When this power is exercised by the priests, he wrote, "it has neither the air of vindictive justice, nor of military execution; it is rather a religious sentence inflicted with the sanction of the god".[3]

The ancient Accadian laws contain few general rules, but consist for the most part of a series of stark and disjointed judgments obviously designed

---

[1] J. L. Myres, *The Political Ideas of the Greeks*, p. 138.
[2] C. F. Kent, "Law (Biblical, Old Testament)" in *Encyclopaedia of Religion and Ethics*, vol. vii, p. 823.
[3] *Germania*, sec. vii, tr. Arthur Murphy (Philadelphia, 1836), p. 536.

to settle particular issues.[1] The following are examples :

> A decision. A husband says to his wife: Thou art not my wife; half a maneh of silver he weighs out (in payment).
>
> A decision. A master kills (his) slaves, cuts them to pieces, injures their offspring, drives them from the land and makes them small; his hand every day a half measure of corn measures out (in requital).

In early Greek times and among these other peoples laws were thus not more than adjudications or decrees to deal with a single situation. There was as yet no conception of customary law, nor, indeed, a word to describe it.[2] *Themis* appears to us as an abstraction, as Law, Justice, Right, something different from a law or a body of laws. The Greek word *Themis* is related to the English word Doom, and Miss Jane Harrison remarked that their development had followed exactly similar lines. "Doom is the thing set, fixed, settled; it begins in convention, the stress of public opinion; it ends in statutory judgment. It is the collective doom, public opinion, that, for man's common convenience, crystallises into law. *Themis*, like Doom, begins on earth and ends in heaven. On earth we have our Doomsday, which, projected into high heaven, becomes the crack of doom, the last judgment."[3]

---

[1] A. H. Sayce, *Records of the Past*, iii, pp. 21-24 (London). The Accadians were the earliest people of Babylon. The name *Accada* signifies highlander and the name of Accad occurs in Genesis. The laws go back to a very remote period.

[2] A. H. J. Greenidge, *Handbook of Greek Constitutional History*, p. 17. Cf. Maine, *Ancient Law*, p. 5 (1st ed.).

[3] *Themis: A Study of the Social Origins of Greek Religion* (2nd ed., 1927), p. 485.

At Trozen, Themis was worshipped in the plural.
There was an altar to the Themides. Out of many
dooms, many judgments, there arose the figure of
one goddess. Out of many *themistes* arose Themis.
Themis was herself a divinity in the full and complete sense; yet she was also something more. She
was above and below every god—the substratum of
all the gods. She was to divinities what matter is to
materials.

The gods in ancient Greek mythology were constantly shown to bear a strong likeness to men. Their
general character was that of conquering chieftains
or buccaneers. They fight and feast and make merry
in a rollicking manner. They drink deeply and make
music and laugh at the lame smith who attends them.
They are afraid of no one save their own king.[1]

The gods of ancient Greece were often arbitrary
in the extreme in their behaviour towards mortals.
They force men again and again to commit sins for
which they afterwards punish them with ruthless
severity. Nor do they refrain from bringing down
evil on the heads of utterly innocent individuals. No
human happiness is safe from their whims and
caprice.[2]

The resemblance of the Greek gods to men was
specially marked in regard to matters of law and
justice. At the time of the *Iliad* human beings did
not feel impelled to punish wrong-doing unless they
were themselves the victims of it. Similarly the gods
of the *Iliad* do not display any disinterested concern
for the maintenance of impersonal justice, except in

[1] Gilbert Murray, *Four Stages of Greek Religion*, p. 65.
[2] Svend Ranulf, *The Jealousy of the Gods and Criminal Law at
Athens* (1934), i, pp. 30 *et seq.*, 59; ii, p. 38.

a few rare instances. Apollo protects Chryseis because her father is his priest, but no man and no god in the *Iliad* feels it his duty to protect Briseis or even to become indignant at her fate.[1] There are many other ways in which the deities of ancient Greece reflect the social state of their worshippers. In the Court of Areopagus, for instance, the gods deigned both to demand and to render justice for murder; and they sat in judgment upon one another there. The legend ran that Neptune demanded justice of Mars on behalf of his son Halirrhothius; and the twelve gods were reputed to have sat in judgment between the Furies and Orestes.[2] The gods in the Homeric poems are dominated by tradition and prescribed modes of conduct almost as much as the host of the Achaians before Troy.

The gods on Olympus are not only capable of communion and kinship with mortal beings, but they also share in man's law and custom. "Men say that the Gods have a King", said Aristotle, "because they themselves either are or were in ancient times under the rule of a King. For they imagine, not only the forms of the Gods, but their ways of life to be like their own."[3] They are the protectors of human justice. But they are not the authors of justice and law. To a Greek mind in the Homeric age, and probably much later, the reign of law was the same, or nearly the same, in nature and in man. The course of nature was transformed by anthropomorphic imagination; while at the same time the freedom of human action itself seemed but slight in comparison with the

---

[1] *Ibid.* i, p. 9.

[2] *The Orations of Demosthenes*, tr. by C. R. Kennedy. The Oration against Aristocrates.　　　　　　　　　[3] *Politics*, i, 2. 7.

bond of custom and the universal constraint of fate, beyond the gods themselves, which formed the mysterious background of the universe.[1]

What was more important, however, than the resemblance which the gods of Greek mythology bore to human beings, or their participation with men in a common system of law and justice, was the fact that the *Themistes*, the single decrees, became to the Greek citizen fixed conventions, the foundations of his government, the ordinances of what must be done, the prophecies of what shall come to pass. Themis represented the order of the world as the gods desired it to be and thus developed into a binding social force. She personified the collective conscience, the social sanction, the social imperative which was at first diffuse, vague, inchoate, which later crystallised into fixed conventions and customs, and finally emerged in the *polis* as law and justice.[2] If Themis was before the particular shapes of gods, not a religion but the stuff of which religion is made, she was also before the particular shapes of laws, not Law but the stuff of which Law is made.[3]

---

[1] F. Pollock, "The Laws of Nature and the Laws of Man" in *Essays in Jurisprudence and Ethics*, pp. 58-9.

[2] Jane Harrison, *op. cit.* p. 485.

[3] As to the relation between *Themis* and *Dike* see J. L. Myres, *op. cit.* pp. 124-5, 170-75, 180; Jane Harrison, *op. cit.* pp. 483-4, 533-4.

V

THE DIVINE LAW-GIVER

Since law in its most embryonic form appears as a series of isolated decrees received from a divine agent for the settlement of particular issues, it might be supposed that when law develops into more mature stages and becomes a body of rules of general import, governing various aspects of life, the idea of its association with the high heavens would somehow be preserved. This in fact we find to be the case. All over the world men have shown themselves eager to believe that rules for the guidance of their conduct have been specially laid down or revealed to them by some superhuman power.

The laws of ancient Egypt have never been discovered, but it is known that they were attributed to the gods.[1] In ancient Babylon the law had a similar divine origin. On the great block of black diorite, nearly 8 feet high, on which the code of Hammurabi was inscribed, there is a representation of the king receiving his laws from the seated figure of Shamas, the sun-god, "the judge of heaven and earth". Manu, whose book, the *Mânava Dharmasâstra*, is the authoritative source of law for all Hindoos, is declared to be an emanation from the supreme God. The Mosaic law is ascribed to Jahweh, who is depicted in Exodus as dictating the primitive decalogue

[1] J. H. Breasted, *History of Egypt*, p. 242; Adolf Erman, *Life in Ancient Egypt* (tr. H. M. Tirard), p. 141.

to Moses, who acts as amanuensis.[1] King Alfred the Great, when he collected the laws of his predecessors, placed at the head of the compilation the divinely inspired decalogue and other Mosaic precepts. The Lacedaemonians regarded Apollo, rather than Lycurgus, as their real law-giver; the Cretans attributed their laws to Jupiter, who instructed Minos; the Etruscans considered their legislation to be derived from Tages; the Romans believed that Numa had written at the dictation of the nymph Egeria.[2]

The opening passage of Plato's *Laws* is as follows:

The Athenian stranger: "Tell me, gentlemen, is a god or a man supposed to be the author of your laws?"
Clinicus, the Cretan: "A god, Sir, most decidedly. In our case it is Zeus; in that of Lacedaemon, as our Lacedaemonian friend will tell you, I think they say that Apollo is their law giver."
Megellus, the Lacedaemonian: "Just so."

The digest of Justinian contains the following passage which was taken over by the Romans in the original Greek from the speech of Demosthenes against Aristogeiton: "A law is . . . something which all men ought to obey for many reasons, and chiefly because every law is devised and given by God, but resolved on by wise men, a means of correcting offences both intentional and unintentional, a general agreement on the part of the community by which

[1] Exodus xxxiv, 1-28. Deuteronomy implies that all the commands contained therein were given directly to Moses by Jahweh. Cf. C. F. Kent, "Law (Biblical, O.T.)" in *Encyclopaedia of Religion and Ethics*, vol. vii, p. 823, and E. Sidney Hartland, *ibid.* p. 812-13.

[2] Coleman Phillipson, *The International Law and Custom of Ancient Greece and Rome*, i, p. 43.

all those living therein ought to order their lives".[1]
In this passage we see a double motive put forward to
secure obedience to the laws: on the one hand, respect
for their sacred origin; on the other, recognition of
their social value arising from their inherently rational
character. The distinction is completely slurred in
the Epistle to the Romans, in which Paul the Apostle
enjoined, "Let every soul be subject unto the higher
powers. For their is no power but of God: the powers
that be are ordained of God." And again, "For this
cause pay ye tribute also; for they are God's ministers
attending continually upon this very thing".[2] Here
the laws are not themselves alleged to be directly
sacred or God-given. But they come from human
beings upon whom God has conferred secular
authority and the power to levy taxes, and obedience
is enjoined on that account.

The advance made by the Romans in the direction
of separating law from religious rites and moral
injunctions is universally recognised as one of the
great landmarks in human history. It is, however,
easy to exaggerate the extent to which the jural order
of the Romans was established on a purely secular
basis.[3] At all stages of Roman history there is abun-
dant evidence to show that Cicero's conviction that
justice and the whole system of social life depend on
the gods and man's belief in them,[4] was a deeply held
belief of the whole people which found expression in

---

[1] *Digest of Justinian*, i, 3. 2, tr. Munro; Dem. xxv, 16, p. 774.
Original text slightly remodelled by Tribonian's Commission. Cf.
P. Vinogradoff, *Historical Jurisprudence*, ii, p. 18.

[2] xiii, 1 and 6.

[3] Cf. William A. Hunter, *Introduction to Roman Law* (1921),
pp. 2-3.

[4] *De Officiis*, 111. 28; *De Natura Deorum*, 1. 116; W. Warde Fowler,
Social Life at Rome, p. 341.

their legal and political institutions. In unambiguous terms Cicero designated religion as the fixed basis of the Roman state and declared that the state was governed by the power and help of the gods to a far greater extent than by human insight. "Indeed", he wrote, "when piety towards the gods is removed, I am not so sure that good faith, and human fraternity, and justice, the chief of all the virtues, are not also removed."[1]

Law, according to Roman ideas, appears to have rested on a double foundation of Divine revelation and human ordinance.[2] The influence of religion on the law of the Romans, as on that of all other ancient peoples, was very great, especially during the earlier part of their history. Originally, indeed, religion and law were not differentiated at all, and even when a distinction was eventually made, there still continued an intimate connection between the two, for the strictly religious law, the *ius sacrum*, impinged upon the ordinary civil law at many vital points. Almost the whole body of rules attributed to the monarchial period belong to the borderland between law and religion.[3] The sacred formula was the governing element and the indispensable condition in the adjustment of all kinds of legal relationships. Sincerity and good faith were the bases of all legal transactions; and *bona fides* was closely associated with religion.[4] For respect for the gods was the underlying foundation of the coercive force of *bona fides*. The gods

[1] *De Natura Deorum*, I. 2.
[2] G. Wissowa, "Law (Roman)" in *Encyclopaedia of Religion and Ethics*, vol. vii, p. 883.
[3] H. F. Jolowicz, *Historical Introduction to the Study of Roman Law*, p. 84 n. and p. 86.
[4] Coleman Phillipson, *op. cit.* i. p. 68.

know whether truth is in the hearts of men; they protect the faithful and punish those who commit a breach of *fides*. The pontiffs, who were priestly officers, acted not only as guardians of the religious tradition but also as watchdogs of the law. They were consulted in purely legal matters and exercised a considerable influence on the development of the law.[1]

Under the early republic the college of pontiffs, recruited exclusively from the ranks of patricians, enjoyed something approaching a monopoly of legal authority. The political reforms introduced about 300 B.C., whereby plebeians were admitted for the first time to the pontifical stronghold, were significant precisely because the pontiffs played so large a part in affairs of state through their power of interpreting the oracles.[2]

The Decemviral Code, drawn up and inscribed on the Twelve Tables in the middle of the 5th century B.C., was on the whole secular in character, but it nevertheless embodied some of the provisions of the religious law. The Twelve Tables were regarded as "a sacred text . . . taught, like a revelation, to children".[3] The laws long remained sacred; and even when in the course of time it came to be admitted that human will or the votes of the people might make or change the law, it was still necessary for the voice of religion to be consulted, in order that the

[1] H. F. Jolowicz, *op. cit.* p. 86 *et seq.*; W. W. Buckland, *A Text-Book of Roman Law* (2nd ed.), p. 2. The pontiffs were not a religious caste but rather members of an aristocracy who had been elected to occupy a position of ecclesiastical authority. Other careers were open to them.

[2] Jolowicz, *op. cit.* pp. 14, 86.

[3] W. W. Buckland, *The Main Institutions of Roman Private Law* (1931), p. 3.

consent of the gods should be obtained. No mere
vote, however unanimous, was sufficient to enact a
binding law at Rome. Before a legislative measure
could even be submitted to the people, the auspices
had to be taken to ascertain from the omens if the
gods were favourably disposed towards the proposal.[1]

The legislative process is worthy of special notice.
A statute (*lex*) consisted of a written enactment, put
forward by a magistrate after it had received favourable auspices. This proposal was submitted for
previous approval to the Senate; it was then voted
on by an assembly of the people, and was finally
subjected to the *patrum auctoritas*, which is generally
understood to have consisted of ratification by the
patrician members of the Senate.[2] The functions
of the Senate were, however, in no sense those of
a second chamber, for they had not to consider
the expediency of the course proposed, but rather
whether it was in accordance with the fundamental
religious basis of the state.[3] Legislation was thus to
a considerable extent "a religious act inspired or at
least permitted by the gods".[4]

The Senate occupied a position of supreme
authority over the entire realm of constitutional
government; and here again its powers must be seen
in the religious context in which they were set. The
framework of the Roman constitution was not regarded as a mere secular structure. It was believed
to enjoy the approval and blessing of the gods, and
any alteration in its principles might incur divine

[1] F. de Coulanges, *La Cité antique*, pp. 221-2; Jolowicz, *op. cit.*
p. 31 n.
[2] W. W. Buckland, *A Text-Book of Roman Law* (2nd ed.), p. 3.
Cf. J. Declareuil, *Rome the Law-Giver*, p. 18.
[3] Jolowicz, *op. cit.* p. 30.   [4] Declareuil, *op. cit.* p. 19.

wrath. Upon the Senate was placed the responsibility of avoiding the fearful dangers which might
thus descend upon the community; and with it lay
the final decision in any matter involving religion.
The senatorial functions in consequence came to have
a strongly marked religious tinge. At every meeting
precedence was given to religious matters over all
other business; and when a newly appointed consul
assumed office the first report which he submitted to
the senate was devoted to sacred matters. Money
could not be spent on religious rites or festivals, save
in the customary manner, without senatorial approval. It was the Senate which could order purification ceremonies to be carried out if the pontiffs discovered an omen indicating divine displeasure; it
was they who would decree the admission of a new
god into the public worship of the community; it was
on their initiative that the Sibylline books were consulted, sometimes with far-reaching political consequences.[1] At every point in the public life of Rome,
religion, law, and politics were closely intermingled.

[1] Jolowicz, *op. cit.* pp. 32-3 n., 40-41.

THE LAW AND THE CREED

SINCE law in early society is generally believed to have come directly from God, it would seem likely that we should find no clear dividing line between law and religion. This indeed is the case in almost all the great systems of law that are known to us. In the early ages of mankind, law and religion were often so closely interwoven that it is scarcely possible to say where one begins and the other leaves off. It might be said in some cases that law *is* religion applied to domestic, social, and political life. To infringe the law is to commit an offence against the gods. To-day, we judge the law by its results. In ancient times the results were judged by the law.[1] The justification of a law lay for the most part in its divine origin.

In the old Jewish law the distinction between civil law, criminal law, and ecclesiastical law did not exist. There was no essential difference between the obligation to do right towards man by respecting his person and property and the obligation to do right towards God by offering the customary devotion and the prescribed sacrifice. These obligations were alike regulated by a body of legal doctrine.[2] They were equally sacred for they had the same sanction, namely, the

[1] Coleman Phillipson, *op. cit.* i, pp. 43-6.
[2] "Law, Civil" in the *Jewish Encyclopaedia*, new Edition, New York, vol. vii, p. 633. For the history and growth of Hebrew law see G. C. Lee, *Historical Jurisprudence*, pp. 95-9; Sir J. G. Frazer, *Folklore in the Old Testament*, iii, p. 109.

command of the almighty. In Exodus (xxi-xxii) there is a considerable body of purely secular law, followed by such purely moral injunctions as:

> 21. Thou shalt neither vex a stranger, nor oppress him: for ye were strangers in the land of Egypt.

Here there is no sanction whatever. In the next paragraph it is laid down:

> 22. Ye shall not afflict any widow, or fatherless child.
> 23. If thou afflict them in any wise, and they cry at all unto me, I will surely hear their cry;
> 24. And my wrath shall wax hot, and I will kill you with the sword; and your wives shall be widows, and your children fatherless.

Here there is the penalty of the *lex talionis*, the eye for the eye and the tooth for the tooth; but it is to be carried out by the divine vengeance, not by the hand of man.

The next paragraph in Exodus deals with conduct in the economic sphere: "If thou lend money to any of my people that is poor by thee, thou shalt not be to him as an usurer, neither shalt thou lay upon him usury". If this were transgressed, there would be presumably a mere inability to enforce the claim. A few lines later there is the religious command: "Thou shalt not revile the gods, nor curse the ruler of thy people". Among the Israelites the right of property was first established by religion. In the Old Testament the Lord said to Abraham, "I am the Lord that brought thee out of Ur of the Chaldees, to give thee this land, to inherit it"; and to Moses, "Go up hence . . . into the land which I sware unto Abraham, to Isaac and to Jacob, saying Unto thee will I give it". Such passages as these may be regarded as conferring the right of collective occupation on the whole community. There are others which relate to specific individual ownership, an example of which is to be found in Ecclesiastes v, 19: "Every man also to whom God hath given riches and wealth, and hath given him power to eat thereof, and to take his portion, and to rejoice in his labour; this is the gift of God".

The Hindu law is no less confused. The code of Manu,[1] which has been regarded by Hindu sages from the earliest times as possessing supreme authority, contains far more about the observances of caste, domestic ceremonies, funeral rites, rules of diet, oblations to the gods, and similar matters than about questions of secular law. The other source-books of Indian law do not differ from Manu in this respect.[2] The strictly legal portion of the work occupies about a quarter of the whole. Some idea of the heterogeneous character of the code may be gleaned from an extract from the summary of contents which forms a prefix to the book. This announces that it deals, among other things, with:

"The creation of the universe, the rule of the sacraments, the ordinances of studentship, and the respectful behaviour, the most excellent rule of bathing (on return from the teacher's house).

---

[1] The age of the work is not known. Sir W. Jones gave the date as 1280 B.C., Max Müller suggested 200 B.C. Other authorities have given dates between these extremes. John D. Mayne, *Treatise on Hindu Law and Usage* (Madras, 1922), pp. 18-20.

[2] See on the main sources of law in India, G. C. Lee, *Historical Jurisprudence*, pp. 123-6.

"(The law of) marriage and the description of the marriage rites, the regulations for the great sacrifices and the eternal rule of the funeral sacrifices.

"The description of the modes of (gaining) subsistence . . . (the rules regarding) lawful and forbidden food, the purification of men and of things.

"The laws concerning women, (the law) of hermits, (the manner of gaining) final emancipation and (of) renouncing the world, the whole duty of a king and the manner of deciding law suits.

"The rules for the examination of witnesses, the laws concerning husband and wife, the law of (inheritance and) division, (the law concerning) gambling and the removal of (men noxious like) thorns.

"The threefold course of transmigrations, the result of (good or bad) actions (the manner of attaining) supreme bliss. . . ."[1]

Some of the injunctions are true rules of law, with a definite legal sanction. For example, "He who damages the goods of another, be it intentionally or unintentionally, shall give satisfaction to the (owner) and pay to the king a fine equal to the (damage)".[2] But a conspicuous feature of the code of Manu is the absence of a conscious distinction between what is law and what ought to be law. This characteristic is found in all the legal collections of India. After a time, however, statements of what the law ought to be came to be accepted as authoritative declarations of what the law actually was.[3]

A similar situation confronts us in Muhammadan

[1] F. Max Müller, *The Sacred Books of the East*, vol. xxv; *The Laws of Manu*, tr. by G. Bühler (Oxford, 1886), p. 27, paras. 111-17.
[2] *Ibid.* Book VIII, 288, p. 305.
[3] G. C. Lee, *Historical Jurisprudence*, pp. 123-6.

law. Law and religion are united, for the Qoran is the source-book of both the law and the religion of Islam. Every word of it is regarded as being the direct utterance of the Almighty, communicated word for word by the angel Gabriel, the Holy Spirit, to the Prophet Mahomet. The civil and criminal provisions of the Qoran are based either on old Arabian customs or on foreign practices; but this does not detract from the belief that the work is throughout of an inspired character.[1] The correct method of introducing a quotation from the Qoran is not, "It is written", but "God saith".[2] Only 27 out of the 114 chapters of the work were delivered at Medina, after Mahomet had acquired political power; and even these are chiefly filled with non-legal matter of a religious, hortatory, or personal nature. Less than a hundred verses, scarcely more than a fiftieth part of the whole, can be said to lay down general rules of conduct in matters which might come before an ordinary court of law,[3] and even in those verses emphasis is usually laid on the religious sanction.

Every rule of the Muhammadan system is supposed to partake of the sacred character of the whole, and even where its relation to the Qoran or the traditions associated with it are by no means clear, it is felt to be part of the logical consequences of divine revelation.[4] A Muslim is thus bound by

[1] A. A. Bevan, *Mahomet and Islam* in *Cambridge Medieval History*, ii, p. 315; E. Westermarck, *Origin and Development of the Moral Ideas* (2nd ed.), i, p. 164; W. Sumner, *Folkways*, p. 386.

[2] Seymour Vesey-Fitzgerald, *Muhammadan Law: An Abridgment according to its Various Schools* (Oxford, 1931), p. 3.

[3] Sir Roland Knyvet Wilson, *Introduction to the Study of Anglo-Muhammadan Law* (London, 1894), pp. 15-16.

[4] Seymour Vesey-Fitzgerald, *op. cit.* pp. 7-8.

religious ordinance not only in the performance of his daily prayers, on the occasion of the fast, the pilgrimage to Mecca, and during the observance of other pious acts, but also in the contraction or dissolution of his marriage, in commercial transactions and indeed in all events of any importance relating to his domestic or social life. All these religious decrees form a code of law, the way of life that faithful Muslims must follow in obedience to the will of Allah. A single illustration may be given in the rule against usury contained in the Qoran, which begins, "Those who devour usury shall not rise again, save as he riseth whom Satan hath paralysed with a touch".[1] After declaring that "God shall blot out usury, but shall make almsgiving profitable", the law is then laid down as follows: "O ye who believe, fear God, and remit the balance of usury, if ye be believers; and if ye will not do it, then hearken to the proclamation of war from God and His Apostle; but if ye repent, your capital is yours".[2]

The impact of Western civilisation, in the shape of the officials of the East India Company, on these ancient and divinely inspired systems of Hindu and Muhammadan law, formed one of the most dramatic juridical conflicts ever witnessed by the modern world.

In 1771 the Court of Directors of the East India Company announced their intention of "standing forth as Diwan". In the following year the Company took over the active administration of Bengal and appointed Warren Hastings as Governor of the province. This involved maintaining courts of law; and

[1] Qoran, tr. by E. H. Palmer (Oxford, 1880), ch. ii, § 275.
[2] Wilson, *op. cit.* p. 16; Qoran, ch. ii.

the question of the law to be applied to Indian subjects became of immediate importance.[1]

Warren Hastings found that in criminal matters
the Muhammadan Government had established its
own system, to the exclusion of Hindu law: while in
civil matters, the Hindus and Muhammadans had
each their separate systems of law. The main object
of the East India Company in its new role was to
make as little change as possible. The country courts
were therefore instructed that they should be guided
by Muhammadan law in administering criminal
justice. It soon appeared, however, that some of the
provisions of the Muhammadan penal code were
such that the civilised and civilising Englishmen
who composed the Government felt themselves unable to administer them. Distaste for such provisions
as the stoning of persons found guilty of sexual
immorality, mutilation for theft, the enforcement
of retaliation for murder, and the incapacity of un-
believers to give evidence in cases affecting Muhammadans, was no doubt nourished by the remoteness
from home of the outraged conquerors and their
ignorance of the barbarous system of criminal law
which still prevailed in England. The most glaring
defects in the Muhammadan system were thereupon
removed by regulation and a patched up and modified criminal law was put in its place. The process of
repealing and amending the system on English lines
was continued until 1860, when the entire fabric of
Muhammadan law was swept away and replaced by
the Indian Penal Code.[2]

With regard to civil matters, Hastings directed

[1] Sir Courtney Ilbert, *The Government of India* (1915), p. 354.
[2] Ilbert, *op. cit.* p. 355.

that in all questions concerning marriage, inheritance, caste, and other religious usages and institutions— succession was added shortly afterwards—the laws of the Qoran should apply to Muhammadans and those of the Shaster to Hindus. This was enacted at first by regulation, later by the Government of Bengal under the regulating Act of 1773, and finally by English statute in 1781.

It has thus come about that in British India there are in force such small fragments of the Hindu law and Muhammadan law as an alien Government "making no pretence with the general spirit of the whole"[1] has thought suitable for enforcement by its own tribunals. The British, Sir Roland Wilson pointed out with more than a touch of condescension, determine from time to time how much shall be left to the conscience of those who acknowledge it as religiously binding, how much forcibly suppressed as noxious and immoral, and how much treated as law in the English sense.

At almost precisely the time when Warren Hastings was introducing in India the changes which have been described, Blackstone was explaining to his fellow-countrymen at home exactly what was meant by law in the English sense. The creator, declared Sir William, laid down certain "eternal immutable laws of good and evil" which are founded in those relations of justice that existed "in the nature of things antecedent to any positive precept".[2] These include the Roman law maxims that we should live honestly, hurt nobody, and render to every-one his due. Any difficulty which might have been

---

[1] Sir Roland Wilson, *op. cit.* (1894), pp. 1-2.
[2] Blackstone, *Commentaries*, Introduction, § 2 (1st ed.), pp. 40-41.

experienced in discovering the exact character of the eternal, immutable laws of good and evil was fortunately avoided by the creator having "graciously reduced the rule of obedience" to all the various precepts of the law of nature to one simple precept, namely, that man should pursue his own happiness. "This law of nature," observed the author of the *Commentaries*, "being co-eval with mankind and dictated by God Himself, is of course superior in obligation to any other." It is binding in all countries at all times. No human laws contrary to it can be of any validity.

Despite the gracious act of the Almighty in providing mankind with a single axiom as a universal guide to conduct, it is still necessary, Blackstone admitted, in applying this precept, to discover exactly what the law of nature dictates in any particular situation. Our reason has become much corrupted since the Fall, he continued, and might conceivably fail in this task. But once again there has been "the benign interposition of divine providence" which in compassion to the frailty, imperfection, and blindness of human reason, has been pleased to discover and enforce its laws by direct revelation. The doctrine thus delivered are the revealed or divine law found in the holy scriptures.[1]

On these two foundations of the law of nature and the law of revelation, concluded Blackstone, depend all human laws. Thus murder is expressly forbidden by divine law and it is demonstrably forbidden by natural law. From these prohibitions arise its true unlawfulness. Human law must not be allowed to contradict natural law or divine law; and if human law

[1] Blackstone, *Commentaries*, Introduction, § 2 (1st ed.), pp. 40-41.

should permit or require us to commit murder, we are bound to transgress it. These gratifying sentiments were for the most part borrowed by Blackstone, without acknowledgment, from Burlamaqui (1694–1748), whose well-known treatise *The Principles of Natural Law* was translated into English in 1748.[1]

Unfortunately, these grand and simple harmonies between the decrees of nature and the dictates of society did not appear to hold good all along the line. Even Blackstone's complacent and not very acute intellect was compelled to admit that the export of wool to foreign countries, forbidden by English law, was not clearly against either divine or natural law.[2] There was a certain lameness in his explanation that "here the inferior legislature has scope and opportunity to interpose".

The attitude of mind disclosed by Blackstone in the introduction to his work in the latter part of the 18th century bears at least a discernible resemblance to the attitude of mind which many centuries earlier had produced the Qoran and Manu and the other sacred law books. He, like the authors of those books and the multitudes who attempted to live by their precepts, regarded divine law as the corner-stone of the whole edifice. He, like them, declared that divine law had been specifically revealed to men through inspired writings. He, like them, was convinced that the revealed law of God was in accordance with the workings of nature and the entire system of the universe. He, like them, sought to make secular law

---

[1] Compare, for example, Burlamaqui's treatise (tr. by Nugent), p. 77, with Blackstone (*Commentaries*, 1765), i, p. 39. See also the remarks on Blackstone in the *Dictionary of National Biography*.

[2] *Ibid.* p. 42.

approximate to the dictates of God and of nature. It is true that Blackstone was only expounding a body of law which already existed, and did not profess to be laying down new law. But his treatise came to be regarded as a source-book possessing high authority in the courts of law.

It is obvious, of course, that the differences between the works we are considering are so great as to make serious comparison out of the question; but there is sufficient resemblance to warrant a plea for more modesty and less arrogance in our outlook towards systems of law in which the secular and religious elements have not yet become differentiated.

If we go back ten centuries in English history, the resemblance becomes irresistibly strong. The dooms or laws of King Alfred (871–901) opens with the Ten Commandments, prefaced by the statement: "The Lord spake these words to Moses".[1] The laws themselves are as much a hotch-potch of commands and moral exhortations as the book of Exodus, from which several of the dooms were taken.[2] The following are a few examples:

> 29. If any one deceive an unbetrothed woman, and sleep with her; let him pay for her, and have her afterwards to wife. But if the father of the woman will not give her, let him render money according to her dowry.

---

[1] B. Thorpe, *Ancient Laws and Institutes of England*, printed under the direction of the Commissioners on the Public Records (1840), i, pp. 20-25. The religious element appears more strongly in the Laws of Alfred than in those of some of the earlier Anglo-Saxon kings.

[2] The desire to regard Law as springing from a canonised law-giver is illustrated by the fact that so late as the 14th century King Alfred was held to be the fount of everything specially excellent. Pollock and Maitland, *History of English Law* (2nd ed.), i, p. xxviii.

32. And let him who sacrificeth to gods, save unto God alone, perish by death.

33. Vex thou not comers from afar, and strangers; for ye were formerly strangers in the land of the Egyptians.

37. Revile thou not thy Lord God: nor curse thou the Lord of the people.

39. All the flesh that wild beasts leave, eat ye not that, but give it to the dogs.

48. Swear ye never by heathen gods, nor cry ye unto them for any cause.[1]

The laws of King Ethelred, who succeeded to the throne in 978, follow the same model. The ordinances of the Witan laid down at the Council of Ensham, embody the decrees of the bishops "that we all diligently turn from sins, as far as we can do so, and diligently confess our misdeeds, and strictly make *bōt* (*i.e.* compensation) and rightly love and worship one God, and unanimously hold one Christianity, and diligently promote prayer among us, and diligently love peace and concord, and faithfully obey one royal lord, and diligently support him with right fidelity".[2] The enactments of Ethelred at Ensham include provisions to comfort and feed the poor, to love one God, to refrain from oppressing widows and stepchildren "too often", and to avoid vexing foreigners or visitors.[3]

In 1017, on the decease of Edmund Ironside, King Cnut of Denmark became monarch of all England until his death in 1035. His laws show a slight advance in juristic development in that they are divided into Ecclesiastical and Secular. But the actual ordin-

---

[1] *Ibid.* p. 25.   [2] *Ibid.* p. 315.   [3] *Ibid.* pp. 317, 327.

ances themselves remain extraordinarily confused. Thus, the ecclesiastical laws require everybody above all other things not only to worship one God and unanimously observe Christianity, but also to "love King Cnut with strict fidelity". Furthermore, the ecclesiastical 'laws' instruct every man that he "constantly have the dread of God in his mind, and, by day and by night, that he fear for sins, dread dooms-day, and shudder for hell, and ever suppose the end of his day near to him".[1]

The so-called secular laws, on the other hand, are riddled with vague moral exhortations and spiritual injunctions. Thus, King Cnut commands that before all else "just laws be established, and every unjust law carefully suppressed, and that every injustice be weeded out. . . . And let God's justice be exalted; and henceforth let every man, both rich and poor, be esteemed worthy of folk-right, and let just dooms be doomed to him."[2] The secular laws then proceed earnestly to forbid heathenism, which is defined as the worship of idols, heathen gods, the sun or the moon, fire or rivers, water-wells, stones or trees, or the love of witchcraft and similar practices.[3] Then come provisions to rectify weights and measures and to "let cheats and liars, robbers and reivers, have God's anger, unless they desist, and the more thoroughly amend; and whoever will lawfully cleanse the country, and suppress injustice, and love righteousness, then must he diligently correct such things, and shun the like".[4]

It is worth remembering that throughout Europe in the Middle Ages the Church exercised jurisdiction

---

[1] Pollock and Maitland, *History of English Law* (2nd ed.), i, pp. 359, 373.   [2] *Ibid.* p. 377.   [3] *Ibid.* p. 379.   [4] *Ibid.* p. 381.

not only over its own clergy, over *miserabiles personae*, widows, orphans, and crusaders, but over the entire community. The range of matters in which the decision lay with the priestly authorities was large. It comprehended actions affecting adultery, matrimony, betrothal, legitimacy, wills, the right of asylum, contracts made under oath, as well as questions touching such ecclesiastical matters as heresy, sacrilege, sorcery, benefices, titles and patronage.[1] The attribution of one-third of a man's fortune for the benefit of his soul, which was customary throughout the Middle Ages,[2] is connected with the belief that the dead man would require part of his property for use in after-life, a notion as primitive as anything to be found in the sacred law-books of the East. With such analogies in our own recent past it it absurd for us to condescend or adopt an attitude of superiority towards those who happen to be a few paces behind us on the same path that we have ourselves trodden. Even to-day *Actus Dei nemini facit injuriam*[3] is a valid maxim of English law; and although the "act of God" for which the law will not hold any man responsible is now interpreted as meaning no more than an inevitable accident directly due to natural causes, the origin of the phrase clearly goes back to the time, not so long ago, when lawyers no less than laymen believed in the special intervention of supernatural powers in the ordinary affairs of life, and moulded the law to accommodate that belief.

---

[1] Raoul de la Grasserie, *Les Principes sociologiques du droit civil* (1906), Part II, ch. xx, pp. 285-411.
[2] P. Vinogradoff, "Customary Law" in *The Legacy of the Middle Ages*, p. 292.
[3] *Broom's Legal Maxims* (9th ed., 1924), ed. by W. J. Byrne, pp. 161-2.

The great code of fundamental Chinese law, known as the Ta Tsing Leu Lee, was first put into operation in an embryonic form in 249 B.C., assumed mature shape shortly after the accession of the Tsing dynasty in the middle of the 17th century, and remained in force until the 20th century throughout the entire Chinese Empire.[1] This vast code is remarkable in many ways; and considering its antiquity it is singularly free from religious influence. But it nevertheless contains numerous provisions which indicate the indispensable connection between law and religion which in early times existed all over the world. Thus section CLIX enacts that within the limits of the jurisdiction of each city of the first, second, and third order, the local genii, the genii of the hills, the rivers, the winds, the clouds, and the lightnings, also the ancient holy emperors, enlightened kings, faithful ministers, and illustrious sages, shall be severally honoured and commemorated by the oblations and other holy rites which the ritual code prescribes.[2] The officers responsible for the sacred rites shall incur a punishment of a hundred blows if they neglect to carry them out. Section CLXI deals with the dishonouring of celestial spirits by unlicensed forms of worship, and prescribes eighty blows with the bamboo if any private family "performs the ceremony of the adoration of Heaven and of the North Star", by burning incense for that purpose during the night or

---

[1] The administrative part of the code was repealed in consequence of the establishment of the Republic. The criminal part was repealed when the temporary criminal code of 1912 was promulgated. The civil part continued in force until 1929-30, when the new Civil Code was put into operation. Cf. V. A. Riasanovsky, *The Modern Civil Law of China* (Harbin, 1927).

[2] Sir George Staunton, *Ta Tsing Leu Lee, being the Fundamental Laws of China* (London, 1810), pp. 172-3.

lighting the lamps of Heaven and the North Star. To do so is declared to be a profanation of the sacred rites derogatory to the Celestial Spirits.[1] Another provision clearly possessing religious significance is section CLXXVII, which imposes sixty blows on astronomers attached to the astronomical board in Pekin if they neglect to observe the celestial appearances of the sun, the moon, the five planets, and other constellations.[2]

Among the Greeks and Romans, as among the Hindus and Muhammadans, law was at first merged with religion, and was indeed a part of it. The ancient codes of the cities were a collection of prayers and religious rites mixed with legislative regulations. The laws respecting property and succession were scattered about among rules for making sacrifices, for burial, and for the worship of the dead. The relics of the oldest laws of Rome, the royal laws, relate to religious worship as often as to secular affairs. They contain provisions forbidding the mistress of a married man from approaching the altars, prohibiting certain dishes to be served in the sacred repasts, prescribing the religious ceremony to be performed by a victorious general on re-entering the city. The Twelve Tables, later in date, contain provisions prohibiting the "charming away" of a neighbour's standing corn and others regulating the funeral rites.[3]

It is sometimes said that the Romans never allowed their religious concepts to interfere with the funda-

[1] *Ibid.* p. 174.   [2] *Ibid.* p. 187.
[3] Fustel de Coulanges, *La Cité antique* (17th ed.), p. 218; H. Stuart Jones and Hugh Last, *The Early Republic* in *Cambridge Ancient History*, vii, p. 462. The enactments relating to sepulchre were of a sumptuary character. Theodor Mommsen, *History of Rome*, vol. i, Book II, ch. viii.

mental features of their private law. The Sibylline
books were in constant use among them, but only for
political purposes. The Roman Senate frequently
instructed certain officers to consult these sacred
works, but never on questions of private law. Hence
the private law of the Romans is claimed to be un-
touched by the mystical influence which impeded
the scientific development of the private law of the
Hindus, Jews, and Muhammadans.

This view overlooks the fact that many significant
features of the private law of Rome owed their origin
to the dictates of religion. Thus, the domestic hearth
of the Roman was sacred because it was the scene of
the household worship. The sacred hearth, by virtue
of the religious law, passed from father to son; and
from this it followed that the house was hereditary
property. The man who had buried his father in his
field believed that the spirit of the dead took possession of the place for ever, and required a perpetual
worship of his posterity. It was therefore made legally
impossible to buy or sell the burial-ground. The soil
where the dead rested was inalienable and imprescriptible. Like other sacred things, it was outside
the sphere of commercial negotiation, so that if a
family sold the field in which the tomb was situated
the law of Rome required that the grave should be
excluded from the transaction. The family retained
the right to cross the field in order to perform the
ceremonies of worship. The right of property was
thus regulated, or at least modified, by religious ideas.[1]

Succession and inheritance also show signs of

---

[1] Fustel de Coulanges, *La Cité antique*, p. 221. Coulanges was wrong
in stating that the family retained the permanent ownership of the
burial-place. It was *res nullius*, and could be owned by nobody.

having been powerfully influenced by religious motives. We do not know the precise nature of the earliest laws on this subject, but from the time of the Twelve Tables onwards the agnatic principle of succession through the male line is of dominating importance. There can be little doubt that the original reason for this was to assimilate the law regulating the devolution of property with the religious rule for the transmission of the family worship. The rule for the worship was that it should be transmitted through the men of the family, for when a woman married she sacrificed to the gods of her husband's household. The principle of agnation proceeded upon the same basis by distributing the property of a dead man only to those who could claim through the male line.

Agnation was thus the tie connecting those who were related to one another, either by kinship or adoption, by legitimate descent from a male through male ancestors. Brothers and sisters of a civil marriage were agnates, and so, too, were a man and his brother's son or daughter. Again, a sister and her brother's child were agnates. But the sister's children were not in agnatic relation either with her brother's child, with the brother himself, or with any of her paternal relatives.[1] The tie existed only between persons who would sacrifice to the same set of ancestors or who would be in the power (*potestas*) of the same common ancestor, were he alive. It thus served to eliminate married women.[2]

We can see from these few illustrations that however secular in form the laws of ancient Rome may have become, however strictly disciplined in a

---

[1] W. W. Buckland, *A Textbook of Roman Law* (2nd ed.), pp. 105, 366.   [2] *Ibid.* p. 105 n. 3.

juristic sense, however detached from exhortation, prayer, superstition, ritual, and the whole paraphernalia of pious observance, they were nevertheless in substance largely derived from religious belief.[1] The provisions of much of the private law, no less than those of the public law, followed as direct and necessary consequences of the creed. They were the dictates of religion applied to the relations of human beings. Law, indeed, was one aspect of religion. Where men had no common religion, there was no common law between them.[2] The immense achievement involved in the secularisation of the form of the law, of its development as a separate science amenable to rational disputation, has made the name and fame of Rome ring down the ages. Its importance cannot be exaggerated. But the mystic origins which lay secreted in the substance of the law have also a significance which must not be overlooked.

[1] Cf. J. Bryce, "The Relations of Law and Religion" in *Studies in History and Jurisprudence*, p. 640.

[2] Fustel de Coulanges, *La Cité antique* (17th ed.), p. 226.

VII

THE LIVING WORD AND THE LETTER OF THE LAW

FOR long ages in the history of society the laws were not expressed in writing. They were committed to memory and handed down in that form from generation to generation. This may be termed the traditional method of transmitting customary rules of conduct. It has been of immense importance not only in connection with law but in many other departments of life. As I shall attempt to show, however, the medium of expression is of peculiar significance in the realm of legal institutions, and the transition from one medium to another has often produced far-reaching effects.

We must at the outset distinguish true customary law, that is, when it is unwritten, from the much later and more sophisticated phase when, as in the case of the modern English common law, it exists in written form, although the writing is based on custom.[1] There was a time when the law of most European communities could properly be said to reside in the customs of the people. Bracton claimed that this state of affairs existed in England when he asserted that she was governed by unwritten law and custom.[2] That time has long since passed away. Yet

[1] Cf. H. S. Maine, *Ancient Law*, p. 13.
[2] Cf. R. W. and A. J. Carlyle, *A History of Mediaeval Political Theory in the West*, vol. v, ch. v.

there is still plenty of true customary law remaining in the world. Among the Bedouin Arabs, for instance, the law is to this day entirely unwritten and depends for its existence upon verbal instruction handed down from father to son.[1] The

Every great system of law has at some time passed through the traditional stage. In the earliest days of Hindu law the art of writing was unknown, and exclusive reliance had to be placed on memory. The original sources of the law were *Scruti* (things heard) and *Smriti* (things remembered). The former were alleged to be the actual utterances of the creator, while the latter are the principal source of "lawyer's law".[2] Both the *Scruti* and the *Smriti* later became the bases for authoritative written records.

The ancient Jewish law originally consisted of immemorial customs which were recognised by the nomadic tribes long before a well-defined code had come into existence. In Genesis and Judges it is related that "every man did that which was right in his own eyes".[3] These customs referred to family relations, slavery, property, the rights of pasture and simple forms of trade. Some of them were embodied in the Pentateuch and thus came to acquire the sanctity of recorded law; some of them were abolished, and others modified. Many customary rules of conduct which are not alluded to in the Torah were carried on to the Talmudic period by means of oral tradition.[4] Among the Romans, again, the laws must have remained for long generations in an unwritten

---

[1] Austin Kennett, *Bedouin Justice*, p. 8.
[2] Sir Ernest John Trevelyan, *Hindu Law* (2nd imp., 1913), p. 7.
[3] Judges xvii, 6.
[4] "Law (Civil)" in the *Jewish Encyclopaedia*, vol. vii, p. 633.

form. They were transmitted from father to son together with the creed and the prayer.[1] Mahomet did not attempt to commit his laws to writing, being apparently unable either to read or to write.[2] The few literate disciples around him would occasionally note down a few scraps of his teaching.

The business of maintaining a body of law in existence before the widespread use of reading and writing constituted a huge problem, the dimensions of which it is not easy for us to appreciate. Human memory is a frail and imperfect thing, and all sorts of devices were employed to strengthen and assist it. "Keep my commandments, and live" runs the injunction in Proverbs vii, 2-3, "and my law as the apple of thine eye. Bind them upon thy fingers, write them upon the table of thine heart." The "binding" of the law on the fingers is an act of symbolism still required of orthodox Jews.

The early forms of traditional law were at first probably metrical. Each member of the decalogue in the Old Testament deals with a separate topic and is divided into two pentads. This suggests that they were intended to be memorised, each law being associated with a finger and thumb of the two hands.[3] Aristotle tells us that the Agathyrsians, a Transylvanian people, expressed their laws in song before they had a knowledge of writing, in order that they might not forget them.

[1] Fustel de Coulanges, *La Cité antique*, p. 223.
[2] Sir Roland Knyvet Wilson, *op. cit.* pp. 20-21; W. Muir, *Life of Mahomet* (3rd ed., 1894), p. xiv; Muhammad Ali, *The Holy Quran* (1917), pp. vii, xxxi.
[3] C. F. Kent, *Historical Bible* (*Founders and Rulers of United Israel*), pp. 210-19; also "Law (Biblical) (O.T.)" in the *Encyclopaedia of Religion and Ethics*, vol. vii, pp. 823-4; O. Schrader, "Law (Teutonic and Slavic)", *ibid.* vol. vii, p. 888.

There was a marked tendency before the spread of reading and writing, to convert rules of conduct, information, or conclusions into slogans, axioms, or doggerel verse in order that they might be more easily memorised. This occurred in many branches of learning, notably in law, in science, and in history. The practical wisdom of our popular proverbs is for the most part the quintessence in easily remembered form of the accumulated experience of everyday life. In this way knowledge and rules of conduct were passed on from one generation to another.

An interesting by-product of this aspect of human development is the emergence of the brocard, a generic term which includes proverbs, adages, maxims, aphorisms, legal rules, precepts, and so forth. The brocard is much more than a succinct statement of fact or résumé of practical wisdom, although conciseness is of its essence. It is a formula which by its terseness, alliterative form, symmetry, or other verbal quality carries authority where a merely logical or accurate pronouncement might fail to convince. Its persuasive character is, indeed, often in inverse proportion to its logical or scientific perfection, just as the attractive power of a modern advertisement is usually unrelated to the intellectual merit of its contents.[1]

The range of subjects covered by the brocard is as wide as human life itself. They include the relations of men and women, of parents and children, of masters and servants, of landlord and tenant, of buyer and seller. They relate to the weather, the rotation of crops, the proper hour of retiring to bed

[1] P. de Tourtoulon, *Philosophy in the Development of Law*, tr. M. McC. Read (New York, 1922), p. 310.

and rising, the management of money. They are to
be found in all languages and among all peoples.
Many of them are framed in the imperative mood,
such as: "Leave land and leet, to save thy life"; others
are attempts to embody in simple form the supposed
wisdom of the ages, such as "A friend when you lend
is your foe when you demand" (*Au preter ami, au
rendre ennemi*) or "To go surety is to go broke"
(*Bürgen soll man würgen*). Many of them utter
warning or advice: "Community breeds disputes"
(*Communio parit rixas*). It is common to find in them
an apt analogy likely to raise a vivid mental image,
such as "Oxen are bound by their horns and men by
their words" (*On lie les bœufs par les cornes et les
hommes par les paroles*).[1]

In the field of law these concise maxims have been
extensively employed, not merely as vehicles for the
transmission of rules but also as instruments for
asserting authority and securing obedience or compliance. No learned treatise or legal proclamation
could convey information to the multitude so easily
or so forcibly as the typical jural brocard, of which
the following are examples:

> The greater the right, the greater the wrong (*Sum-
> mum ius, summa iniuria*).
> No free man without a freeholding (*Nemo liber-
> alis, nisi liberatus*).
> Settling the title of the donor settles the title of
> the donee (*Resoluto iure dantis, resolvitur ius
> accipientis*).

The legal brocard seeks to be convincing rather

---

[1] All these examples are taken from P. de Tourtoulon, *op cit*. pp.
311-13, 319-20.

than imposing; it is designed to impress the mind by means of a verbal harmony which is easily mistaken for learning or reason.[1] Even to-day, despite the spread of education, the general public in the Western countries is profoundly ignorant of the law, and relies to no small extent in its daily life on a few inadequate or incorrect brocards. Their importance in the past may therefore be easily imagined.[2]

There are certain obvious disadvantages which result from the use of the brocard in connection with human laws. First, precision or accuracy is usually sacrificed to a deceptive simplicity. Second, the authority is derived from its form rather than from the soundness of the reason on which it is based. Third, it is impossible to control the currency of such statements, which are easier to put into circulation than to withdraw.

Occasionally, however, a juridical brocard has been instrumental in extending the influence of a rational principle of law in a highly effective manner. Thus, the Rhodian sea law laid down that the loss involved by jettisoning part of a cargo in order to preserve the safety of the remainder shall be distributed among all the owners of cargo on the ship. This principle became embalmed in the maxim *Omnium contributione sarcietur quod pro omnibus expensum est* (The contributions of all shall make good that which was expended for the good of all). In that form it passed far beyond the bounds of maritime law and became a juridical maxim of wide application.[3]

So long as the verses or the maxims were aids to lawyers or physicians who understood the principles

---

[1] P. de Tourtoulon, *op. cit.* p. 311.   [2] *Ibid.* p. 310.
[3] *Ibid.* p. 317.

underlying the formulae, they served a useful purpose in preserving experience or conveying information. But when the verses endured after the knowledge or reasoning which created them had decayed, they degenerated, in the case of law, into meaningless wooden rules, and, in the case of medicine, into mere incantations. Such incantations were sometimes based on former knowledge or beliefs as to the properties of herbs and drugs. Sometimes they were no more than attempts at verbal imitation designed to terrify and appal.[1] The one uttered by the witch in *Macbeth* (Act IV, Sc. I) is of the latter type :

> Fillet of a fenny snake
> In the cauldron boil and bake;
> Eye of newt, and toe of frog,
> Wool of bat, and tongue of dog,
> Adder's fork, and blind-worm's sting,
> Lizard's leg, and howlet's wing,
> For a charm of powerful trouble,
> Like a hell-broth boil and bubble.

A modern edition of *Broom's Legal Maxims*[2] contains numerous outworn maxims which, although not of great antiquity, have long ceased to have any real application in English law, such as *Acta exteriora indicant interiora secreta* (acts indicate the intention). Sir Frederick Pollock[3] has parodied in an amusing fashion the mnemonic doggerel once employed as an *aide-memoire* of legal dogma :

> The birds on the bough sing loud and sing low
> What trespass shall be *ab initio*.

The difficulty of maintaining a body of purely

[1] W. Sanderson and E. B. A. Rayner, *An Introduction to the Law and Tradition of Medical Practice* (London, 1926), p. 8.
[2] 9th ed., 1924, p. 210.
[3] *Leading Cases Done into English and other Diversions* (London, 1892), p. 2, verse 1.

traditional law in oral form led, perhaps inevitably, to the establishment of a series of juristic oligarchies equipped with trained memories who claimed to monopolise all knowledge of the law, to be in exclusive possession of all principles by which disputes must be decided. This was regarded by Maine as the stage of true customary law.[1]

In some communities the authority recognised as knowing the law was a secular official. Thus, among the early Scandinavians the highest civic position was that of the "man of law". He was the living custodian of the law for the province. He was the director of the Thing, he announced its decisions to the populace and expounded the law in cases of doubt or difficulty. It was his duty to keep a knowledge of law alive among the people. Every third year he was required to stand on the "cliff of the law" and recite in a manner intelligible to all the whole body of civil law; and every year to declaim the procedure of the law courts.[2]

More frequently, however, the claim to possess an authoritative knowledge of the law was made not by a single individual but by a small group or caste. During the lifetime of Mahomet, and for a year or two after his death, reliance was placed for a knowledge of the divinely inspired law on a class of Qoran reciters who "strained naturally retentive memories to the utmost while vying with each other who should repeat the longest portions by heart".[3] The dangers inherent in this method were brought home to the Caliph and his advisers in a vivid manner by the

---

[1] H. S. Maine, *Ancient Law* (1861), p. 12.
[2] K. Weinhold, *Altnordisches Leben* (Berlin, 1856), p. 400.
[3] Sir Roland Knyvet Wilson, *op. cit.* pp. 20-21.

battle of Yemána in A.D. 633 in which a large number
of these reciters were slain.[1] In early Greek times
the king was the judge, as the keeper of the ordinances of Zeus and interpreter of the unwritten law
of the community. But he did not act alone, and in
the trial scene on the shield of Achilles there is no
mention of a king at all. Even in the oldest parts of
the Homeric poems reference is made to more than
one judge. Some of the other nobles also received
themistes from Zeus, and assisted the king with their
knowledge of the customary law.[2]

It is obvious that the authority of the group would
at all times have been greatly strengthened by the
association of its members with religious offices; and
it is not surprising therefore to find that knowledge of
the law was most usually claimed by the priesthood.
The maintenance of the priesthood was, indeed, immensely assisted in some cases by the absence of a
body of written law. Among the ancient Israelites,
the priests at the local sanctuaries were the reposi-
tories of the law, and they handed down the ordinances from one generation to another. The priests
gave their decisions on doubtful points of usage and
in all legal disputes. These decisions were oral; and
they comprised the original law of the land, the
Torah, long before that word came to be narrowed
down to mean the written law based on the Pentateuch. This early Torah included also the divinely
inspired instructions of the prophets. There was thus
a prophetic as well as a priestly Torah, all of which
was oral and unwritten.[3] At Rome, again, in early

[1] *Ibid.*
[2] A. H. J. Greenidge, *Handbook of Greek Constitutional History*, p. 17.
[3] Sir J. G. Frazer, *Folklore in the Old Testament*, iii, pp. 99-100.

times it was the pontiffs who were the authoritative exponents of the law. They were for long the only jurisconsults and the only competent judges in innumerable matters.

The most ancient body of written law that has come down to us is the code of Hammurabi. Unfortunately we have no knowledge of the circumstances in which the law of Babylon came to be inscribed nor of the results which followed that event. But there are several systems of law of which something is known concerning the transition from oral tradition to the written word.

The early Hebrew law which had once been customary in the true sense was transmitted to writing at various times. The Book of the Covenant,[1] which constituted the first legislation, is generally believed to have been written in or about the 9th century B.C. The Deuteronomic code probably dates from the 7th century B.C. The Priestly Code was issued at Jerusalem by Ezra in 444 B.C. The publication of Deuteronomy constituted a landmark. The change from oral tradition to a written code stereotyped religion and, as Sir James Frazer remarks, "laid thought under shackles from which in the western world it has never since succeeded in wholly emancipating itself. The spoken word before was free, and therefore thought was free. . . . The prophets enjoyed full freedom both of thought and of speech, because their thoughts and words were believed to have been inspired by the deity. . . . But when once the oracles were committed to writing they were stereotyped and

---

[1] This comprises Exodus xx–xxii. Exodus xxxiv, 11-27, is closely related. Sir J. G. Frazer, *Folklore in the Old Testament*, iii, pp. 99-100.

immovable; from the fluid they had solidified into the crystalline form with all its hardness and durability; a living growth had been replaced by a dead letter; the scribe had ousted the prophet and even the priest. . . . Henceforth Israel became the 'people of the Book'; the highest wisdom and knowledge were to be obtained not by independent observation, not by the free investigation of man and of nature, but by the servile interpretation of a written record . . . the genius, which had created the Bible, accommodated itself to the task of writing the Talmud." [1]

A huge body of jurisprudence developed among the Jews. The attempt to trace it all back to the Torah and its few simple laws laid down for a community living under utterly different conditions produced what has been euphemistically described as "a peculiar Talmudic system of reasoning".[2] By means of this the legal principles contained in the Bible were examined and re-examined, traditions reviewed, analogies discovered, differences glossed over, difficulties overlooked, and an elaborate course of mental gymnastics undertaken in order to reconcile the irreconcilable and prove that all possible extensions or modifications of the law had been foreseen from the outset and secreted in the womb of the written code.

The stifling effect of superimposing a written record upon a sacred origin is illustrated no less vividly by the law of Islam. After Mahomet's death the need was felt for some kind of Book to serve as an authoritative record of the faith and law which had been transmitted to the Prophet. The slaughter

---

[1] Sir J. G. Frazer, *op. cit.* iii, pp. 102-3.
[2] Cf. *Jewish Encyclopaedia*, vol. vii, p. 635.

of the Qoran reciters at the battle of Yemána made this need doubly urgent. Accordingly Zeíd, a former amanuensis to Mahomet, was commissioned to "search out the Qoran and bring it together". The result of his labours, as gathered from "palm leaves, skins, blade-bones, and the hearts of men", is recognised to have been very nearly identical with the present text.[1]

Once the work of collection and compilation had been completed all possibility of organic growth was at an end. It merely remained to apply and refine the principles of action which had been laid down for all time by a voice which was now for ever silent. Herein lies the explanation both of the rapidity with which Muhammadan law reached its full maturity and of the rigidity which has always been one of its leading characteristics. Within 350 years of the Flight to Medina a complete body of law was evolved. From that day to this it has neither changed nor been added to in any essential matter,[2] despite the fact that the small, homogeneous, and primitive community for which it was originally laid down has grown into a vast cosmopolitan aggregate living under different and far more complicated conditions.

The late Lord Bryce described in one of his essays a visit which he paid in 1888 to El Azhar in Cairo, an Islamic "university" as it is often called, where law and religion are studied as a single subject. Muhammadan law, he wrote, "has become petrified and casuistical. Religion has become definite, positive, frigid, ceremonial. Theology, in swallowing up law, has itself absorbed the qualities of law. Each

---

[1] Sir Roland Knyvet Wilson, op. cit. pp. 20-21.
[2] Seymour Vesey-Fitzgerald, Muhammadan Law, pp. 7-8.

has infected the other. In El Azhar theology is taught as if it were law, a narrow sort of law, all authority and no principle. Law is taught as if it was theology, an infallible, unerring, and therefore un-progressive theology. . . . Since the revealed law is unerring it cannot be questioned, or improved, or in any wise varied. Hence it becomes to those who live under it what a coat of mail would be to a growing youth. It checks all freedom of development and ultimately arrests growth, the growth both of law and of religion." [1] Such, he reflected, was the result of regarding the law as a divine revelation dictated by God or his mouthpiece and fixed for all time, rather than as a body of principles containing the power of growth and variation. [2]

In ancient Greece the law passed from the stage of traditional custom to a body of written enactment without apparently suffering restrictive effects of the kind noticed above. The prophets who uttered the pronouncements at Delphi, like the Hebrew prophets of old, preceded and assisted the appearance of the written law. [3] The art of writing spread through the Greek states in the 7th century B.C., and thus the ground was prepared for the conversion of the legal order to a written form. Lycurgus is said by Plutarch to have refused to allow his laws to be committed to writing, though doubt is cast by modern scholars on the accuracy of this statement. [4] But we know that Solon, who was elected archon at the beginning of

[1] J. Bryce, "The Relations of Law and Religion" in *Studies in History and Jurisprudence*, p. 660.
[2] *Ibid*. p. 662.
[3] Alfred Zimmern, *The Greek Commonwealth*, pp. 122-6.
[4] Plutarch's *Lives*: Lycurgus. Cf. C. W. C. Oman, *A History of Greece* (7th ed.), p. 65.

the 6th century B.C., inscribed his laws on wooden pyramids or rollers about the height of a man. These rollers had three or four sides and could be turned round. They stood on the Acropolis until the Persian wars, when they were removed to Salamis for safety.[1] The more usual practice in Greece was for the laws to be inscribed in or near the judgment-seat of the magistrates who were charged with administering them. The law of Athens in the 5th and 4th centuries B.C. has been described by Dean Pound as a codified tradition eked out by legislation and individualised in its application through the administration of justice by large popular assemblies. Thus, in spite of being formally reduced to writing it preserved the flexibility of the more primitive stage of law and was able to provide a philosophy for Roman law in its later period.[2]

Roman law was itself, however, at certain times extremely rigid. The earliest written laws were recorded in the sacred books and consigned to the care of the priests, together with the rituals, among prayers and ceremonies. Later, the laws were removed from the rituals and were inscribed separately. But the practice of depositing them in the temple with the priests continued.[3] When the desire arose for a codification of customary law, a body of ten commissioners were appointed in 451 B.C. to write the law. The new code was then carved on ten tables of wood and brass which were set up for public observation in the forum. Another two were added soon afterwards. These twelve tables were regarded

---

[1] Plutarch's *Lives*: Solon; Oman, *op. cit.* p. 112.
[2] Roscoe Pound, *Introduction to the Philosophy of Law*, p. 21.
[3] Fustel de Coulanges, *La Cité antique*, p. 223.

with reverence and retained their authority for something like a thousand years. For 250 years there was no legislation which modified any matter that was dealt with in them; and it is probable that for a long time it was considered actually beyond the competence of the Assembly to alter any rule laid down by the Decemvirs.[1] Such alterations as occurred were for the most part brought about through the power of interpretation possessed by the pontiffs.

An illustration of the precise literal adherence to the Twelve Tables which was insisted upon is given by Gaius. If, he said, you sued by *Legis Actio* for injury to your vines, and called them vines, you would fail in your claim, because the text of the Twelve Tables spoke only of trees. A similar rigidity descended upon the old Teutonic law. According to the Malberg Gloss, which contains a collection of ancient legal formulas, if a man sued for a bull, his action would fail if he described him as a bull. The animal had to be designated by the ancient juridical name of "leader of the herd", just as a goat had to be called the "browser upon leeks" and the forefinger of the hand the "arrow-finger".[2]

In Rome, again, even apart from the Twelve Tables, strict verbal conformity to the letter of the law was required. In making a contract, for instance, one party was required to say, *"dari spondes"*, and the other had to reply, *"spondeo"*. If these words were not pronounced, no contract was formed.[3] The formula of the law was in early times like the formula

[1] W. W. Buckland, *The Main Institutions of Roman Private Law* (1931), p. 3; *A Text-book of Roman Law* (2nd ed.), p. 3.

[2] H. S. Maine, "Primitive Forms of Legal Remedies" in *Early History of Institutions*.

[3] Cf. Fustel de Coulanges, *op. cit.* p. 224.

of the prayer or of the charm; it had to be recited correctly, and a single mistake deprived it of its entire force. The form was everything, the spirit nothing.

We must not overlook the fact that one immense advantage which flowed from the reduction of the law to writing was that henceforth it became possible for everyone to ascertain with some precision the code of conduct to which he was expected to conform. The judicial order became for the first time a public document, available indirectly even to those who had not themselves acquired the art of reading. It is difficult to realise how novel and attractive a development this must have appeared to our remote ancestors. In ancient Rome, prior to the compilation of the Twelve Tables, the law had not only been administered by patrician magistrates but it was unknown to the general public.[1] In such circumstances the benefits of a written code must indeed have seemed great. Euripides makes Theseus declare:

> With written laws, the humblest in the state
> Is sure of equal justice with the great.

To recapitulate: In this short survey I have attempted to show the immense influence exerted on the development of law by the invention of writing. The sacred inspiration to which most systems of law are believed to owe their origin produced an inevitable element of irrationality in their substance. But so long as law remained in the traditional stage it was always capable of growth, modification, and development in the very process of being handed down from one generation to another. Despite the tyranny which

[1] H. F. Jolowicz, *Historical Introduction to the Study of Roman Law*, pp. 4, 12.

often resulted from the claims of small oligarchies to possess exclusive knowledge of the law, there was no automatic check to the conscious or unconscious modification of the law so long as its authoritative exposition lay in the mouths of the living generation. The various devices by which men sought to aid their memories sometimes led them to adhere to empty rules from which all significance had departed; but stagnation in its most acute form did not come until the conversion of the law to written form. It was when the divinely inspired law appeared as a permanent inscription that it tended to lose all capacity for growth. The letter of the law came to be supreme. and men were called upon to obey a body of decrees every syllable of which was regarded as inexorably and unalterably fixed for all time.

One clear gain to be set against all these disadvantages which attended the advent of the written law was the fact that the juridical order became for the first time definite, public, and ascertainable. The rules of law emerged from the aura of vagueness, mystery, uncertainty, and liability to change which had enveloped them for so long, and stood forth stark and bare to the public scrutiny. The spoken law had sometimes been all things to all men. The written law was one and the same to all men.

VIII

CRIMINAL LAW IN PRIMITIVE SOCIETY

THE study of rudimentary forms of criminal law is highly significant as an illustration of the connection between men's ideas about the universe and the institutions of human law and government.

In view of the magical origin of kingship and the fact that the earliest lawyers were medicine-men or priests, it is not surprising to find that in primitive communities criminal law, or what most nearly resembles it, is closely associated with supernatural beliefs.

Among the Melanesians, for instance, there is nothing equivalent to an administration of justice in the modern sense. The principles according to which crime is punished are very vague, and retribution is carried out in a fitful manner. The most important methods of law-enforcement, Professor Malinowski tells us, are through such institutions as sorcery, suicide, the supernatural consequences of taboo, and the power of the chief.[1] The main instrument for enforcing the chief's power is black magic, a private instrument wielded by professional sorcerers. It operates as a support for the vested interests of wealth, power and influence, and in the long run helps to maintain law and order. It is a conservative force and provides the main source of the fear of punishment and retribution which all societies have

[1] *Crime and Custom in Savage Society*, pp. 98-9.

74

so far found to be necessary for the preservation of order.[1] Among the Kaffirs, again, witchcraft has been employed as "the state engine for the removal of the obnoxious".[2] A similar condition of affairs has been observed among many primitive communities.[3]

The other great instrument for enforcing the pattern of conduct accepted by the Melanesians is suicide. Suicide, like sorcery, is used as a method of securing obedience to the law, of preventing and punishing extreme or unusual types of behaviour. It has, we are assured, a distinct legal aspect; it is self-enforced criminal law. In order to bring it into operation there must be, in the first place, a sin, a crime, or some passionate outburst which requires expiation; and secondly, an accusation against the miscreant followed by a protest by him against those who have brought the trespass to light. The culprit is thus forced into an unbearable position from which he escapes by taking his own life.[4]

---

[1] *Ibid.* pp. 92-3.

[2] Rev. A. H. Dugmore, *A Compendium of Kaffir Laws and Customs* (1858), p. 27.

[3] H. Ian Hogbin, *Law and Order in Polynesia* (1934), pp. 216, 223.

[4] Malinowski, *op. cit.* p. 98. Suicide has been employed as an instrument to secure obedience to law or political authority among several civilised peoples. In ancient Egypt persons condemned to death were allowed to commit suicide, especially when the Pharaoh did not consider it expedient to impose a penalty, as in the case of high treason or conspiracy (cf. W. M. Flinders Petrie, *Social Life in Ancient Egypt*, p. 83; Adolf Erman, *Life in Ancient Egypt*, p. 144). In ancient Greece the Athenian practice in favoured cases is illustrated by the death of Socrates. In Japan the method of suicide by disembowelment known as Harakiri has been practised by the Samurai, or warrior class, for many centuries. Harakiri was formerly either obligatory or voluntary. The compulsory kind was a privilege granted to criminals of the Samurai class, who were permitted to destroy themselves rather than suffer the degradation of being handed over to the public executioner. This custom is now extinct. Voluntary harakiri may be undertaken

Sympathetic magic, which plays so large a part in the criminal law of savage society, is the outcome of erroneous ideas of the relation of cause and effect. Sir James Frazer explains that it is based on two principles of thought. First, that like produces like, or that an effect resembles its cause: this he calls the law of similarity. Second, that things which have once been in contact continue to act on each other even after the contact has ceased: this is the law of contact or contagion. From the first of these principles the magician infers that he can produce any effect he desires by imitating it. From the second, that whatever he does to a material object will affect in a similar manner the person with whom the object was once in contact, whether it formed part of his body or not.[1] The law of similarity, it may be remarked, appears to have an important bearing on the idea underlying the *lex talionis*. Even highly civilised persons often feel a strong and perhaps instinctive

from various motives, and is still of common occurrence in Japan. It may be practised out of loyalty to a dead superior, as, for example, when General Nogi and his wife committed suicide on the eve of the funeral of their Emperor. It may be performed to avoid capture or execution by the enemy, and was resorted to during the Russo-Japanese war. It may be used as a form of protest against an official abuse to remonstrate with a superior who is pursuing an erroneous or dishonourable course. In all circumstances harakiri removes every stain and assures those who commit it of an honourable burial and a revered memory (E. Westermark, *Origin and Development of the Moral Ideas* (2nd ed., 1917), ii, p. 243; B. H. Chamberlain, *Things Japanese* (1927 ed.), p. 219. A recent revival of the old Egyptian practice occurred in Germany during the massacre of political malcontents on 30th June 1934. It was announced by the Hitler government that some of the captured members of the Brown Army had committed suicide on realising the awful nature of the wrong they were alleged to have contemplated. Others who were invited to take their own lives refused on the ground that to do so would be to admit a guilt of which they declared themselves to be innocent.

[1] *The Magical Origin of Kings*, pp. 37-8.

desire to apply the principle by "making the punishment fit the crime".

On the basis of sympathetic magic primitive societies have formulated an elaborate system of negative prohibitions and positive prescriptions. The former are implemented by taboos, the latter by charms. Negative magic or taboo says, "Do not do this, lest so and so should happen". Positive magic or sorcery says, "Do this, in order that so and so may happen".[1] Thus the false science of the savage provides him with something not unlike the injunction and mandamus of English law. Much magic is of a private character, consisting of incantations or rites performed for the benefit or injury of individuals. But there is also in savage society what may be called public magic, that is, sorcery practised for the benefit of the whole community. Whenever ceremonies of this sort are observed the magician ceases to be merely a private practitioner and becomes in some sense a public functionary.[2]

The institution of suicide, when used to secure compliance with the law, may be regarded as an extreme form of penance. Penance precedes punishment in many systems of law, especially those closely connected with religion. The Book of Manu, for in-

---

[1] J. G. Frazer, *op. cit.* p. 52.

[2] *Op. cit.* p. 82. Sometimes a belief in supernatural powers leads not to the prevention or punishment of crime but to the committing of it. In modern India, for example, we are told that crude superstition as to persons being possessed or infected with evil spirits, witchcraft, and so forth, leads to many serious crimes such as murder and wounding. The individuals who commit these offences are entirely devoid of anything which could be called "criminal intent" in the Western sense. The less men know of the laws of nature the more prone they are to attribute to supernatural agency all disturbances in the normal course of events. Cf. R. T. F. Kirk, "Crime and Superstition in India", *Edinburgh Review*, vol. 24, no. 504 (April 1928).

stance, contains hardly any punishments to be inflicted by human agency on an offender against the
law. The main sanctions consist of penances, precise
and inexorable, which he who breaks the code is
required to impose upon himself. Thus, in one place
the offender is directed to mutilate himself and then
to walk on until he drops down dead; in another he
is ordered to cast himself three times into the fire, or
to go into battle and expose himself to the enemy. A
Brahman who drinks a particular kind of forbidden
liquor is enjoined to drink that liquor boiling hot until
his throat is scalded.[1]

Among Christian peoples penance has been imposed since the earliest days of the Church.[2] It has
at all times been associated with confession, and, like
the latter, was for long a public rite. The penitential
discipline was prescribed for a variety of trans-
gressions which became greatly extended with the
approach of the Middle Ages. Penance was required
for homicide, wounding, waylaying, and treason
against a lord, for perjury, incest, sodomy, and
bestiality.[3] In some countries misdeeds in general
were to have penance done for them. In the 4th and
5th centuries A.D. the penitent was required to shave
his head, wear mourning, abstain from the management of his business, mortify the flesh with a hair-

[1] *Laws of Manu*, tr. by Max Müller (Sacred Books of the East),
xi, p. 91. Cf. Sir Henry Maine, *Early Law and Custom*, pp. 10, 37-8.

[2] It is derived from the power of forgiving or remitting sins conferred on the priests by Matthew xvi, 18-19; xviii, 15-18; and John xx,
21-23. Oscar D. Watkins, "Penance" in Hasting's *Encyclopaedia of
Religion and Ethics*, ix, pp. 711-13.

[3] Thomas P. Oakley, *The Co-operation of Medieval Penance and
Secular Law*, vii, "Speculum", pp. 517-18. For some offences the penance formed the only penalty, in others it was reinforced by secular
punishment.

shirt, and practise continence. By the end of the 11th century the penitential discipline had become less severe in many instances, but in serious cases the sinner was ordered to undergo prolonged fasts, to make distant pilgrimages, and to scourge himself. Those who refused were liable to be sentenced by the secular authority to fine or imprisonment, or be outlawed.

In the course of time penance ceased to be performed in public. Public penance almost disappeared in the 14th century. At the same time the practice grew up of redeeming the obligation to fulfil the prescribed penance by making a material compensation such as building a road or a bridge, or equipping a soldier for the Crusades.[1] These were symptoms of decline; and the whole practice gradually ceased to be an important factor in the administration of the law.

While it flourished, however, the Christian penitential was an interesting and significant institution. I shall show later how it came to be used as an instrument for securing obedience to the secular law by punishing those who transgressed. Here we may note that both the spiritual and the temporal power in the Middle Ages regarded every crime as a sin. There could scarcely be a criminal act which was not sinful in greater or less degree.

The Christian penances contained a specifically medicinal element. They were not merely punitive but were designed to wash away the sin of which the transgressor was guilty, to cleanse him of his defilement. This brings us to the subject of purification, an immensely important conception in the development of criminal law.

[1] Watkins, *op. cit.*

Among the ancient Greeks there was a belief that if a man was murdered his soul became angry and tormented the slayer. So even an involuntary murderer had perforce to go away until the wrath of the dead person had cooled down; and he might not return until after sacrifice and purification had purged the offence. In the drama of Aeschylus, Orestes roamed about pursued and maddened by the ghost of his mother, whom he had killed, and the people of Troezen refused to receive him until he had been purified of his guilt and thereby freed from his mother's ghost. The Greek method of purification was to kill a sucking pig and to wash the hands of the guilty person in its blood.[1] The literature of all countries includes numerous stories, from *Macbeth* downwards, on the theme of the ghost of a murdered person revisiting the earth to torment the guilty slayer.

The social and legal significance of this superstitious fear lay in the fact that it led people to imagine that the whole community would suffer from the anger of the dead person's ghost unless the ghostly infection were washed away, literally, either by water, by the blood of an animal, or by some other prescribed means. When purification took the form of restraining the murderer, or killing him in order to appease the ghost, it became indistinguishable from punishment. Its deterrent effect, moreover, would no doubt be as great as though it had been designed as a punishment.[2]

In Rome a person who committed an offence of a

---

[1] Sir James Frazer, *Psyche's Task*, pp. 113-15. This work has now been issued under the title of *The Devil's Advocate*.
[2] *Ibid.* pp. 151-2.

religious character became *"sacer"*: separated from other men, made over to the offended gods. His goods were set apart and consecrated, for they were contaminated by his impurity. He was banished in order that no one should come into contact with his accursed person. He was cut off from fire and water, not because it was desired to deprive him of things necessary to his existence but for fear that his touch should pollute the sacred elements and cause injury to others.[1] It may have been a satisfactory concomitant that the wrongdoer also suffered; but the main object was to protect the fire and water from pollution. Among the ancient Jews even an animal which killed a human being was regarded as contaminated. Exodus xxi, 28 declares that if an ox gore a man or a woman to death, the ox shall be stoned, but his flesh shall not be eaten.

It was obviously a matter of great importance when the community felt itself to be concerned in cases of homicide. It is true that the treatment of the homicide by the tribe or state was conceived as a measure of self-defence, a moral quarantine, a process of spiritual disinfection, rather than as a punishment. But the two conceptions merged easily. What was at first a religious rite later became a civil function, the sacrifice developed into execution, the priest steps back and the hangman appears.[2] Dread of the ghost, says Frazer, has operated in a twofold way to protect human life. On the one hand it made every individual more reluctant for his own sake to slay his fellow. On the other hand it roused the whole community to punish the slayer. "It placed every man's life within

---

[1] L. T. Hobhouse, *Morals in Evolution* (1906), i, p. 83.
[2] Sir J. G. Frazer, *Psyche's Task*, p. 152.

a double ring-fence of morality and law. The hot-headed and the cold-hearted have been furnished with a double motive for abstaining from the last fatal step: they have had to fear the spirit of their victim on the one side and the lash of the law on the other." [1] Criminal justice was based on superstition long before it was deduced from a theory of retribution, a desire to deter the wrongdoer or reform his soul in another world by hanging or burning his body here. "And when with the progress of thought the shadow of the ghost passes away, the grim shadow of the gallows remains to protect society without the aid of superstitious terrors. It is thus that custom often outlives the motives which originated it." [2]

Far less primitive but no less potent than the superstitious beliefs of which mention has here been made were the Hebrew notions that it is man's duty to avenge offences against God; that every crime involves a breach of God's law, punishable as such; and that scarcely any measure is too severe to be inflicted on the ungodly. These ideas were taken over by the Christian Church and by governments which were officially Christian; they were acted upon until quite modern times and contributed to the increased severity of the criminal codes of Western States. This view is well illustrated by the laws of Cnut, which declare that "it belongs very rightly to a Christian king that he avenges God's anger very deeply, according as the deed may be". [3]

The criminal law of a society tends to reflect in a

---

[1] Sir J. G. Frazer, *Psyche's Task*, p. 152.
[2] *Loc. cit.*
[3] E. Westermarck, *Origin and Development of the Moral Ideas*, i, p. 198; B. Thorpe, *Ancient Laws and Institutes of England*, i, p. 377 *et seq.*

remarkable way the degree of understanding of the laws of nature achieved by that society and its atti-tude towards the universe in general. In the *Lex Salica*, the old Germanic code, there is a provision that "If any person have bewitched another, and he who was thus treated shall escape, the author of the crime who is proved to have committed it shall be sentenced to 2500 denars" (*i.e.* 63 shillings).[1] The *Ta Tsing Leu Lee*, which contained the fundamental laws of China, confers special privileges upon astronomers and then declares that these privileges shall not apply to such offences as killing by magic, clearly showing that the so-called astronomers were mere superstitious star-gazers.[2] When we find the Parliament of James I solemnly passing "An Act against Conjuration Witchcraft and dealinge with Evill and wicked Spirits" for "the better restrayninge of the saide offences", a statute which imposed fearful penalties on anyone who should "consult covenant with enter-taine employ feede or reward any evill and wicked spirit", or who should "use practise or exercise any Invocation or Conjuration of any Evill and wicked spirit", it is evident that the English people of the early 17th century—including the educated political classes—believed in the efficacy of these practices.[3]

---

[1] Ernest F. Henderson, *Select Historical Documents of the Middle Ages* (London, 1892), pp. 180-81, translated from Gengler's *Germanische Rechtsdenkmäler*, p. 267. The date of the *Lex Salica* is not defin-itely known. It is the oldest surviving Germanic code, except possibly fragments of the Visigothic code. It was recorded in writing probably towards the end of the 5th century A.D. The extract given above is Title xix (2).

[2] Sir G. Staunton, *Ta Tsing Leu Lee, being the Fundamental Laws of China* (London, 1810).

[3] James I, c. 12, s. 2. The Act remained on the Statute Book until 1736. It repeated 5 Eliz. c. 16.

We have seen that Hebrew law drew little distinction between an ox which killed a man and a human murderer.[1] In Athens, during the most highly civilised period of Greek history, animals which caused the death of a man were condemned and their bodies thrown across the border in order to rid the land of pollution.

The most extensive application of the criminal law to the animal world occurred, however, during the Middle Ages. It was a common thing in medieval Europe for animals to be subjected to judicial process either as sole offenders or as the accomplices of human beings in the commission of crime. An animal which killed a child, for example, might be arrested and imprisoned. The forms of a judicial trial would then be gone through and sentence of death solemnly pronounced. This would be attended with the customary ceremony at the usual place of execution. Judgments have been found pronounced against bulls, cows, pigs, mules, asses, goats, horses, sheep, dogs, cocks, tortoises, rats, mice, and even worms, grasshoppers, and caterpillars. These trials of animals took place in France, Switzerland, Spain, and Germany. They were particularly frequent from the 12th to the 15th centuries, and they continued even into the 16th, 17th, and 18th centuries.[2]

In ancient Greece not only animals but also inanimate objects were held responsible for wrongdoing

---

[1] Exodus xxi. 28 ; see p. 81 *ante.*

[2] Jean Boca, *La Justice criminelle de l'échevinage d'Abbeville au moyen âge* (Lille, 1930), p. 264; Glasson, *Histoire du droit et des instituts*, vi, pp. 649-50. Louandre, "L'Épopée des animaux" in *Revue des Deux-Mondes* (1854); Berryat-Saint Prix, *Rapport et recherches sur les procès et jugements relatifs aux animaux*: Mem. Soc. Antiq. de France (1829), pp. 403-50.

in appropriate circumstances. Thus the Court of
Prytaneum had jurisdiction to try senseless material
objects which had in some manner caused injury to
a human being. If, said Demosthenes, a stone or a
piece of wood or iron or anything of the kind falls
and strikes a man, and we are ignorant who threw it,
but know and have in our possession the instrument
of death, proceedings are taken against such instruments in this Court.[1] A similar type of belief underlies the English law of deodands, and clearly shows
that the sacral element in criminal law did not dis-
appear with the advent of Christianity.[2]

The deodand was that unhappy instrument[3]
which occasioned the death of a man. The law required that it should be forfeited to the king to be
disposed of in pious uses by the King's Almoner "for
the appeasing of God's wrath", as Coke put it. An
animal such as a horse or ox, and inanimate objects
such as carts, boats, mill-wheels, weapons, and caul-
drons were the commonest type of deodand.[4] The
law was precise and elaborate. Where a cart met a
loaded wagon and was overturned in attempting to
pass it, the occupant of the cart being thrown under
the wagon wheels and killed, it was held that the cart,
wagon, loading, and all the horses were deodands.[5]
But where a man riding on the shafts of a wagon fell
to the ground and broke his neck, only the horses and
wagon were forfeited. The loading was spared be-

---

[1] *Oration against Aristocrates*, tr. C. R. Kennedy (London, 1877),
p. 192.
[2] Pollock and Maitland, *History of English Law*, ii, p. 474.
[3] Hawkins, *Pleas of the Crown*, c. 27.
[4] Pollock and Maitland, *op. cit.* ii, p. 473.
[5] Lord of the Manor of Hampstead's case. Salk 320; 3 Inst. 58;
5 P.C. 20; Hawkins P.C. c. 27.

cause it did not in any way contribute to the killing. Forfeiture did not extend to a ship in the open sea or in salt water; but the principle applied elsewhere, and if a man fell from a boat in fresh water and was drowned the craft would be forfeited. Death had to occur within a year and a day; and a formal finding that the deodand was the responsible instrument had to be made at a coroner's inquest.

Formerly, according to Blackstone,[1] the chattel which became forfeited as an expiation of the soul of the dead person ought properly to have been given to the Church. In course of time it became the practice to pay the value of the deodand rather than to yield up the actual object. With this development the justices would sometimes name the charitable purposes to which the money was to be applied. Thus they ordered the price of a boat to be devoted "for God's sake" to the repair of Tewkesbury bridge. The sister of a man who was run over receives the value of the condemned cart because she is poor and sick.[2] It was not until 1846 that the English law of deodands was abolished by statute as "unreasonable and inconvenient".[3]

The law of deodands contains one element which is highly characteristic of early criminal law, namely, that all harm must be requited, whether it were intended or not. The notion that accidental injury should not be punished at all, or should be punished less severely; the idea that an unsuccessful attempt to commit a crime is itself a crime; the distinction

---

[1] *Commentaries* (23rd ed.), i, pp. 348-9. Cf. Matthew Bacon, *A New Abridgment of the Law* (7th ed., 1832), 9. v. Deodands.

[2] Pollock and Maitland, *loc. cit.*

[3] 9 and 10 Vict. c. 62.

between murder and manslaughter and justifiable homicide; the division of murder into different grades or categories: these are mature refinements of which but few traces, if any, are to be found in early criminal law.[1]

[1] Examples of the distinction which was occasionally made in early law between intentional and unintentional homicide are to be found in Exodus xxi, 12-14; Deuteronomy xix, 4-13. See also Frederic Hrozny, *Code Hittite* (Paris, 1922), par. 1 (2) of which possibly suggests intention. In the Twelve Tables there was apparently a provision which declared that "if the weapon sped from his hand rather than been aimed" a ram was to be tendered to the kinsmen of the slain man in place of the usual penalty. But these must all be regarded as exceptions to the general rule. Cf. Percy H. Winfield, "The Myth of Absolute Liability", xlii, *Law Quarterly Review*, p. 42. For medieval illustrations see Jean Le Foyer, *Exposé du droit pénal Normand au XIII siècle* (Paris, 1931), pp. 50-56; Jean Boca, *La Justice criminelle de l'échevinage d'Abbeville au moyen âge* (Lille, 1930), pp. 263-73.

RETRIBUTION AND RESTITUTION

In all modern societies a clear distinction is drawn between criminal law, by means of which the State inflicts punishment on persons guilty of prescribed offences, and the law of civil wrongs, or torts, whereby individuals or corporate bodies are given the right of claiming money damages from anyone who has injured them in a manner recognised by the law. A great deal has been made of the fact that there is no separation between tort and crime in ancient or primitive communities. It is often suggested that early law is mostly penal, but that it is neither true criminal law, because not enforced by the community, nor true civil law, for the reason that it aims at punishing the wrongdoer rather than compensating the person injured. The doctrines of Sir Henry Maine in particular have given rise to much confusion and misunderstanding on this subject.[1]

We may take as a starting-point the well-established fact that in early society self-redress, in the form of private vengeance, everywhere preceded the establishment of a system of regular adjudication. The injured person, with his kinsmen or dependents, would make a foray against the wrongdoer, and might sweep away his family, cattle, and other belong-

---

[1] *Ancient Law*, ch. x. The various stages in the development of criminal law postulated by Maine are quite incorrect and misleading. See my essay on Maine in *Modern Theories of Law* (1933).

ings, or the sufferer might endeavour to cast a spell upon the wrongdoer or call in the aid of supernatural powers by fasting upon him, a custom which still prevails in the East. Another form of vengeance practised in ancient Rome was for an injured man to take the life of his adversary, or to make him his slave. There are only slight traces of self-redress remaining in the Roman law of the time of Gaius and Justinian,[1] but they are sufficient to show that in this respect the evolution of law followed the same lines in Rome as elsewhere.[2]

Early law continued to rely on the emotional and instinctive bases of private vengeance by recognising the individual sufferer as the aggrieved party, and permitting, or rather expecting, that he and his kin would requite the wrong. To avenge the death of a kinsman was for long more than a right. It was a religious duty.[3]

The kinsmen played an essential part in the proceedings. Without them the whole system would have broken down, for where death occurred to the injured man there would have been no one left to redress the wrong. I shall have occasion to refer later to the fact that the original basis of society lay in the family and that formerly the only link which was recognised between human beings was the tie of blood relationship. Here we need only note the supreme importance of the principle of group solidarity in the machinery of law enforcement.

By this principle a wrong is not confined to the

[1] *Justinian Institutes*, ed. Moyle, i, p. 614.
[2] Richard R. Cherry, *The Growth of Criminal Law in Ancient Communities* (Lecture on Primitive Criminal Law) (1890), p. 8.
[3] James Muirhead, *Historical Introduction to the Private Law of Rome* (2nd ed.), p. 53.

actual offender but extends to all his fellow-members. It is common to find slaves and animals treated as part of the group to which they are attached.[1] The group to which the sufferer belongs will support the injured man's claim and participate actively in whatever steps may be necessary to obtain requital or revenge. If the victim has been killed, hordes of avengers pursue the murderer and his kinsmen seeking redress. Conversely, the members of the wrongdoer's own group will endeavour to protect him against the opposing group with life and limb. They will unite with him for the purpose of giving satisfaction or resisting retribution no less than for that of demanding it. Group solidarity in its purest form does not admit the idea of guilt. Collective liability belongs to the political rather than to the jural order.

This system of collective responsibility for wrongdoing has existed all over the world and is still to be found in various communities, such as, for example, the Bedouin Arabs.[2] It has led to the blood feud and to civil war; it is the direct ancestor of war between nations. There is little difference in principle between the rule which permits any member of a murderer's family to be killed among the Hupa[3] and the practice which allows the soldier of a civilised country to kill any soldier in the service of another nation with which his country is at war.

It must have called for an immense effort and taken a long period of time to emancipate mankind

[1] Gustave Glotz, *La Solidarité de la famille dans le droit criminel en Grèce* (Paris, 1904), pp. 175-8.
[2] A. Kennett, *Bedouin Justice*, p. 30.
[3] Robert H. Lowie, *Primitive Society* (1921), p. 385.

from the purely tribal conception of group solidarity and to inculcate a sense of individual responsibility for wrongdoing. In this evolution the institution of noxal surrender doubtless played a part of some importance. It must not be assumed, however, that the trend of legal development invariably goes from group solidarity direct to individual responsibility. There are many intermediate or alternative forms, such as the payment of compensation by the group, the rendering of talion, and so forth.[1]

Noxal surrender was a device employed in ancient Greece and Rome whereby a group could disengage itself from the tie of collective solidarity by which it was normally bound to defend one of its members who had committed wrongdoing. In Greece, a father could liberate himself from liability for the offences of his children by disavowing and banishing a son or daughter who injured a stranger.[2] The laws of Gortyn provide that if a slave kill a freeman (other than his master) the master's family will deliver him to the parents of the victim, who will kill him in whatever manner they please. Similarly, if a slave wounded a freeman, the master, in order to avoid liability, must hand him over to the injured man to do with him as he please.[3]

The essence of noxal surrender was a rupture in the collective solidarity of the family or group. The yielding-up, banishment, or disavowal of the culprit by his kinsmen corresponded to the right of venge-

---

[1] I am indebted in connection with this topic to an excellent lecture on "Individual Responsibility in Primitive Law", given in the University of London on 15th February 1933, by Professor C. de Visscher.

[2] Gustave Glotz, *La Solidarité de la famille dans le droit criminel en Grèce*, p. 174.

[3] *Ibid.* pp. 177-8. Noxal surrender was applied even to animals.

ance on the part of the victim or his associates. The act of delivering up the miscreant served the purpose of ensuring the safety of the group to which he belonged by appeasing the kinsmen of the victim. The refusal of assistance, not to a stranger, but to a member of one's own community, may be regarded as an early form of extradition. He who kills goes abroad, says the *Iliad*; and voluntary flight was, indeed, the last service a murderer could render his family.[1]

Here, then, in the institution of noxal surrender, we have the beginning of the idea of individual responsibility, though it is still closely embedded in the older notion of group solidarity.

A further step was taken with the recognition of a general interest in the enforcement of personal responsibility. Plutarch relates that Solon, in order to promote the security of the common people in Athens, conferred a general right to prosecute for an injury; so that if someone suffered from an act of violence anybody who wished could, save in the case of exceptional crimes such as parricide, indict the wrongdoer. By this means Solon intended to make the citizens conscious that they were members of the same body, and to resent and be sensible of one another's injuries. He believed, says Plutarch, that the best city was that in which those who have not suffered injury are as anxious to punish the wrongdoer as those who have.[2]

In the Old Testament there is a strong contrast between the insistence on the responsibility of the continuous family group, expressed in the words of

---

[1] Gustave Glotz, *La Solidarité de la famille dans le droit criminel en Grèce*, p. 171.

[2] Plutarch's *Lives*: Solon, 18.

the Second Commandment, "I the Lord thy God am a jealous God, visiting the iniquity of the fathers upon the children", and the emphatic repudiation of this conception in Ezekiel xviii, 20, written about 440 B.C., in the passage which declares "The soul that sinneth, it shall die. The son shall not bear the iniquity of the father, neither shall the father bear the iniquity of the son."

The Christian religion has at all times laid the utmost emphasis on personal salvation. Hence the canon law endeavoured in general to uphold the principle of individual responsibility for fault, although the Church did not altogether escape from the tendency, common to all medieval systems of law, of taking the group into account when determining the penalty, and in demanding reparation from the innocent if it could not be paid by the guilty.[1]

The practice of penance, imposed by the priests from the earliest days of the Christian Church, was based essentially on the doctrine of individual responsibility for sin. It was thus directly opposed to the conception of group solidarity, and played a part of great importance in fixing the liability for criminal offences on the shoulders of the wrongdoer himself rather than on those of his kinsmen.

The power of the clergy to impose penance is derived from certain passages in the Gospels.[2] But this purely Scriptural authority was reinforced by

[1] Gabriel le Bras, "Canon Law" in *The Legacy of the Middle Ages*, p. 357.

[2] Matthew xvi, 18-19, xviii, 15-18; John xx, 21-23; Oscar D. Watkins, "Penance" in Hastings' *Encyclopaedia of Religion and Ethics*, ix, pp. 711-13. For the ecclesiastical history see Oscar D. Watkins, *A History of Penance* (1920), *passim*.

continuous and consistent support from the temporal power. Thus we find the capitularies of Charlemagne frequently ordaining penitentials and assisting the Church in various ways to maintain its disciplinary jurisdiction. In A.D. 779 the bishops were empowered to deal with cases of incest; in 802 a capitulary instructs certain highly placed officers to coerce everyone refusing to submit to the sentences of the bishops. Another capitulary of the same year passed at Aix calls for penance in cases of homicide, parricide, infanticide, and illicit conduct. The Frankish kings who succeeded Charlemagne continued to pass laws enforcing penance. Louis le Debonnaire (814–40) revised public penance by this means. Charles the Bald required the bishops to impose penance on those who retained his lawless nobles for the purpose of committing rapine, and to excommunicate anyone who failed to desist and repent.[1]

The old Welsh laws of Hoel the Good ordered penances for homicide, waylaying, and treason against a lord. The Brehon laws of ancient Ireland required penance to be exacted of criminals in addition to other penalties; and the culprit was partially outlawed until he had fulfilled the penitential discipline. The laws of Alfred the Great remitted half the secular composition in the case of criminals who confessed to a priest and submitted to the penitential. The laws of other Anglo-Saxon kings ordered penance to be imposed under penalty of a fine for failure to obey.[2]

---

[1] Thomas P. Oakley, *Medieval Penance and Secular Law*, vii, "Speculum" (October, 1932), pp. 518-19. There were many earlier decrees of a similar kind passed by Merovingian kings.

[2] *Ibid.* p. 517. *E.g.* Ancient Laws of Ireland, i, 57; iv, 229, 369; v, 449, 121; Ancient Laws of Wales, i, 135, 551; ii, xxxv, 409, 411, 769, 857.

The co-operation of Church and State in com-
bating wrongdoing was to the mutual advantage of
both. On the one hand, the penitential discipline
helped to strengthen the authority of the secular
government by calling in the aid of the Church to
punish transgressors. On the other hand, the ecclesiastical power was itself greatly reinforced by the
recognition given to the priestly jurisdiction by the
secular laws. It was the practice of the Church to
insist that the penitent should obey the sentence of
the temporal power under pain of being required to
perform additional penance.[1] Thus tribute was rendered for tribute received. Political interest was in
perfect accord with the generally accepted doctrine
which identified crime with sin and held that the
secular law had a religious purpose as well as a
punitive function to perform.

From the standpoint from which we are now considering the matter the significant result of this inter-
action between Church and State was the emphasis
which was laid by the penitential discipline on
individual responsibility for wrongdoing, as contrasted with the more primitive notion of group
solidarity.[2] The ecclesiastical authorities were resol-

[1] Oakley, *op. cit.* p. 522.

[2] In our own day the question of group responsibility is presenting
many new and difficult problems to the modern world. On the one
hand, we have the establishment of group liability among, for instance,
the shareholders of a joint stock company for the acts of their agent
or among the inhabitants of a city for the wrongdoing of a municipal
official, while, on the other hand, such statutes as the Workmen's Compensation Act, 1925, recognise the solidarity of the family by conferring on the dependent relatives of an employee accidentally killed
certain rights to recover compensation of a monetary kind from the
employer. (See also the Fatal Accidents Act, 1842, for another illustration.) The question of corporate responsibility becomes more complicated, Professor Morris Cohen points out, when we approach nations

utely opposed to the spilling of blood through the blood feud, even where retribution was permitted by the strict letter of the law. Hence there were penances for homicide committed in revenge. An Irish penitential, which was subsequently adopted all over Christendom, required that he who wounds another must pay for medical treatment, do the work of the injured man, and perform penance, in addition to paying the composition demanded by the secular law.[1]

In primitive communities the function of the adjudicating authority was for long no more than to declare the law.[2] The Court did not attempt to enforce its decision, and self-help or private redress was recognised as a proper and lawful proceeding. The early Courts were merely an alternative to savagery: they did not suppress it entirely.[3]

In Wessex, in King Alfred's time, the pursuer of a lawful feud might besiege his opponent and overwhelm him by force if he did not surrender on being called upon to do so. "Law is not yet the active

and states: Who, he asks, is rightly responsible for the damage done to Belgium by Germany in the war of 1914–18? "Not the Kaiser alone, nor his immediate advisers, nor the members of the Reichstag who voted supplies, nor even all the citizens who supported the war. Germany as a whole is held responsible, and that means that those who opposed the war as well as generations of Germans yet unborn must be made to pay. This certainly does not agree with the prevailing theory that no one should be punished except for some fault of his own. But most people believe both in individual and in collective responsibility" (*Reason and Nature*, p. 393).

[1] *Ibid.* p. 523.

[2] Of course in a very strict sense even a modern Court does no more than to declare the law, leaving it to the executive arm of the Government to carry out the decision. But for broad purposes we may overlook such fine distinctions and assert that modern Courts enforce their decisions because there is an official apparatus to secure compliance.

[3] H. S. Maine, *Early Law and Custom*, p. 387.

minister of justice, but rather a formalised voice of
the popular conscience declaring to each man the
point at which he may without blame use whatever
power he has to do himself right." [1] The Courts of
law at this stage of evolution make up for their lack
of executive power by an excessively elaborate and
rigidly formal procedure. Yet the very imperfection
of their powers and the irregularity of their operation
made their value all the more conspicuous—a reflec-
tion which may bring a ray of comfort to the minds of
those who are discouraged by the weakness of public
international law in the modern world and the
inadequacy of the machinery for enforcing it. It is
only by slow degrees that revenge has yielded to
punishment even within each community and the
private avenger been succeeded by the judge and the
public executioner or the prison.

In the inevitable reliance of undeveloped systems
of law upon self-help as the normal method of redress,
and the absence of any official or governmental
organs capable of enforcing the decisions of the
Court, lies the key to understanding why it is that
primitive communities do not distinguish between
what later comes to be called crime and tort. The
Hebraic society for whom the Mosaic law was intended would have been utterly unable to differenti-
ate between penal offences committed against the
community and civil wrongs done to individuals.
The book of Exodus (xxi and xxii) deals in a hotch-
potch way with a wide variety of delicts, such as
manslaughter, the stealing of men, hurting by chance,
goring by oxen, the cursing of parents, theft,

[1] Sir Frederick Pollock, "Archaism in Modern Law" in *Essays
in the Law*, p. 203.

damage, trespass, borrowing, fornication, witchcraft, bestiality, idolatry, and usury. Among the
Bedouin Arabs at the present day the law consists
entirely of retribution and restitution. It knows no
punishments as such, but is concerned solely with
the requital of wrong by an injured person and his
kinsmen.[1]

The early Saxon tribes reached a stage of development midway between the primitive condition just
described and the modern conception to which we
are ourselves accustomed. A distinction was drawn
between the public and private aspects of injurious
acts: *Wer* was the value set on a man's life, varying
according to his rank, while *Wite* was a penal fine
payable to the king or to some other public authority.
The word *Bōt* stood for compensation of any kind in
a more general sense, and some of the most serious
offences were *bótleás* (bootless), which meant that a
person who committed them could not redeem himself and was at the king's mercy.[2]

A wonderful picture of the way in which early
courts of justice worked is to be found in the Ice-
landic saga *The Story of Burnt Njal*. The Njals saga
is believed to have been written about A.D. 1100,
although the exact date is not known.[3]

In the Njals saga we see law depicted at a stage
where it has thrown off the trammels of superstition
but has not yet arrived at a point where it receives

---

[1] A. Kennett, *Bedouin Justice*, p. 30.

[2] Pollock and Maitland, *The History of English Law before the
Time of Edward I* (2nd ed.), i, p. 48.

[3] Sir F. Pollock suggests that the elaborate pleadings were introduced much later than the Norman Conquest: *First Book of Jurisprudence*, p. 9. But the tendency to-day is to attribute the saga to an
earlier period.

unquestioned recognition. The decisions of the Court are generally regarded as alternatives to the settlement of the issue by private violence. Outlawry is of great importance: the man who has broken the law or who disobeys the order of the Court goes out of the law and carries his life in his hand.[1] The law is in the truly traditional stage: it is imperfectly known and, moreover, cannot be easily ascertained. Symbolic forms and customary phrases are to be found at every turn. The procedure is formal and the pleading intricate.

The Story of Burnt Njal[2] opens with the statement that "there was a man named Mord, whose surname was Fiddle; he was the son of Sigrat the Red, and he dwelt at the Vale in the Rangrivervales. He was a mighty chief, and a great taker-up of suits, and so great a lawyer that no judgments were thought lawful unless he had a hand in them." Mord's daughter, Unna, married one Hrut, who received her dowry. The marriage proved unsatisfactory, and Unna therefore followed a line of conduct planned by her father in order to enable her to procure "such a lawful separation as may hold good according to the judgment of the Great Thing and the laws of the land".[3]

Hrut was angry at this treatment but kept his feelings well in hand for some months. When summer came he rode to the Thing with his brother Hanskuld and a great following.[4] "But when he came to the Thing, he asked whether Fiddle Mord,

---

[1] Cf. H. S. Maine, *Early Law and Custom*, p. 387.
[2] The extracts are taken from the translation by Sir George Webbe Dasent.
[3] Ch. vii: "Unna separates from Hrut".
[4] Ch. viii: "Mord claims his Goods from Hrut".

his wife's father, were at the Thing, and they told him he was; and all thought they would come to words at once about their matter, but it was not so. At last one day when the brothers and others who were at the Thing went to the Hill of Laws, Mord took witness and declared that he had a money suit against Hrut for his daughter's dower, and reckoned the amount at 90 hundreds in goods, calling Hrut at the same time to pay and hand it over to him and asking for a fine of three marks. He laid the suit in the Quarter Court, into which it would come by law, and gave lawful notice, so that all who stood on the Hill of Laws might hear.

"And when he had thus spoken, Hrut said 'Thou hast undertaken this suit, which belongs to thy daughter, rather for the greed of gain and love of strife than in kindliness and manliness. But I shall have something to say against it; for the goods which belong to me are not yet in thy hands. Now, what I have to say is this. . . . I challenge thee to fight on the island; there on one side shall be laid all thy daughter's dower, and on the other I will lay down goods worth so much, and whoever wins the day shall have both dower and goods; but if thou wilt not fight with me, then thou shalt give up all claim to these goods.'

"Then Mord took counsel with his friends about going to fight on the island, and Jorund the priest gave him an answer:

" 'There is no need for thee to come to ask us for counsel in this matter, for thou knowest if thou fightest with Hrut thou wilt lose both life and goods. He has a good cause, and is besides mighty in himself and one of the boldest of men.'

"Then Mord spoke out that he would not fight with Hrut, and there arose a great shouting and hooting on the hill, and Mord got the greatest shame by his suit."

Mord dies shortly afterwards, and Unna is left without means. She asks her kinsman Gunnar to try to recover her dowry from Hrut, and Gunnar thereupon seeks the advice of the great lawyer Njal. The latter tells Gunnar to get into conversation with Hrut, to discuss the manner in which Mord has brought his suit and to state the reasons for Mord's defeat. Njal outlines the conversation which will take place:[1]

" 'I can answer thee that well enough', thou must say. 'Thou challengedst him (Mord) to single combat; but he was old, and so his friends advised him not to fight with thee, and then they let the suit fall to the ground.'

" 'True enough', Hrut will say. 'I said so, and that passed for law among foolish men; but the suit might have been taken up again at another Thing if he had had the heart.' "

Later on Gunnar himself gets into trouble by killing Otkell. Geir, the priest, was to take up the suit against him for this, and Geir gave notice on the Hill of Laws that he had a suit of manslaughter against Gunnar for the slaying of Otkell, Andulf, and others. The neighbours who were summoned to the inquest found Gunnar guilty of killing Otkell. Gunnar in his turn calls upon Geir to listen to his oath and the defence he is about to bring forward. He takes the oath and says: [2]

---

[1] Ch. xxii: "Njal's Advice".
[2] Ch. lvi: "Gunnar and Geir the Priest strive at the Thing".

" 'This defence I make to this suit, that I took witness and outlawed Otkell before my neighbours for that bloody wound which I got when Otkell gave me a hurt with his spur; but thee, Geir the Priest, I forbid by a lawful protest made before a priest, to pursue this suit, and so, too, I forbid the judges to hear it . . . I forbid thee by a lawful protest, a full, fair and binding protest, as I have a right to forbid thee by the common custom of the Thing and by the law of the land. Besides, I will tell thee something else which I mean to do', says Gunnar.

" 'What', says Geir, 'wilt thou challenge me to the island as thou art wont, and not bear the law?'

" 'Not that', says Gunnar. 'I shall summon thee to the Hill of Laws for that thou calledst those men on the inquest who had no right to deal with Andulf's slaying, and I will declare thee for that guilty of outlawry.' "

We cannot follow the complicated convolutions of the narrative, but there are two later chapters in the saga which are of special interest from the standpoint of primitive legal institutions. One of these chapters (cxl.) is entitled "Of the Declaration of Suits"; the other bears the title "Now Men go to the Courts" (cxli.). In the former we are told of the occasion when Mord Valgard's son made the following declaration at the Hill of Laws: "I take witness to this that I give notice of an assault laid down by law against Flosi Thord's son, for that he rushed at Helgi Njal's son and dealt him a brain, or a body, or a marrow wound, which proved a death wound and from which Helgi got his death. I say that in this suit he ought to be made a guilty man, an outlaw, not to be fed, not to be forwarded, not to be helped or harboured in any need. I say that all his goods are forfeited, half to me, and half to the men of the Quarter, who have a right by law to take his forfeited goods. I give notice of this suit for manslaughter in the Quarter Court into which this suit ought by law to come. I give notice of this lawful notice. . . ." At the conclusion of this declaration "a great shout was uttered at the Hill of Laws, that Mord spoke well and boldly".

In the next chapter the parties to the conflict go to the Courts for the great trial. Both sides arm themselves and put war-tokens on their helmets. One Eyjolf took witness that he challenged two men out of the inquest on the ground that they were related to Mord and therefore legally incapable of uttering a finding. A highly technical argument then takes place on this point, at the conclusion of which Flosi enquires somewhat naïvely of Eyjolf, "Can this be law?" Eyjolf answers that he had not wisdom enough to know for certain, so they send someone to enquire from Skapti, the Speaker of the Law. Skapti sent back word that "it was surely good law, though few knew it".

One of the most significant characteristics of early systems of law is that they are concerned less with giving reparation for the loss or damage incurred than with visiting the wrongdoer with injuries similar to those he has himself inflicted. Professor Jolowicz, in an illuminating essay on the subject, emphasises the contrast between the modern notion of the assessment of damages quantitatively in terms of money and the ancient idea of requital in qualitative terms. Under the latter method the penalty is made to fit the nature of the offence rather than the damage resulting

from it.[1] The governing principle is that of appropriateness. This comes out most clearly in the *lex
talionis*, an eye for an eye and a tooth for a tooth,
which in one form or another has been found all over
the world.[2] According to Diodorus, in ancient Egypt
treachery was punished by cutting out the tongue,
forgery by cutting off the hand, and infanticide by
compelling the culprit to hold the corpse of the infant
in her arms for three whole days.[3] Again, in medieval
German law arson was punished by burning, coining
by boiling, the removal of a boundary stone by
ploughing off the offender's head.[4] Similarly there is
the practice of inflicting injury on the particular part
of the body which was instrumental in breaking the
law, as where the hand of the son who strikes his
father is cut off, or castration inflicted for sexual
offences.[5] In early law this is what is meant by making
the punishment fit the crime.

In this principle of appropriateness we have a clear
explanation of the absence in early law of the distinction between crime and tort. Let us look, with
this in mind, at the portion of the code of Hammurabi relating to medical attendance. First comes a
series of provisions laying down the scale of remuner-
ation for successful operations performed on gentle-

----

[1] H. F. Jolowicz, *The Assessment of Penalties in Primitive Law*
in *Cambridge Legal Essays*, pp. 204-5.

[2] The most perfect expression of the law of talion is to be found in
Exodus xxi, 23 *et seq*.: "And if any mischief follow, then thou shalt
give life for life, eye for eye, tooth for tooth, hand for hand, foot for
foot, burning for burning, wound for wound, stripe for stripe".

[3] Adolf Erman, *Life in Ancient Egypt*, p. 141; Diodorus, i, pp.
77-8.

[4] Rudolf His, *Das Strafrecht des deutschen Mittelalters* (Leipzig,
1920).

[5] Jolowicz, *op. cit.*

men, plebians, and servants. Then section 218 states that "If a doctor has treated a gentleman for a severe wound with a lancet of bronze and has caused the gentleman to die or has opened an abscess of the eye for a gentleman with a bronze lancet and has caused the loss of the gentleman's eye, one shall cut off his hands". The next section enacts that "If a doctor has treated the severe wound of a slave of a poor man with a bronze lancet and has caused his death, he shall render slave for slave".

In the law of ancient Rome, where redress of a physical character was laid down no right of compensation was given to the person wronged. Thus, the free man caught in the act of thieving (*furtum manifestum*) became bondsman to the owner of the stolen property; a slave guilty of the same offence was hurled to death from the Tarpeian rock. The freeman no doubt had some value as a slave, but there was no relation between the potential loss and the economic advantage.[1] Where a slave was convicted, no provision was made to enable the property-owner to claim compensation in lieu of the death penalty. On the other hand, where the "appropriate" requital was purely economic, no punishment is called for. Thus Exodus xxii, 5 enacts that "If a man shall cause a field or vineyard to be eaten, and shall put in his beast, and shall feed in another man's field; of the best of his own field, and of the best of his own vineyard, shall he make restitution".

The idea of requital in kind gradually yielded to the notion of compensating the injury in terms of money. In the Hittite code, a fine is fixed in two

---

[1] H. S. Jolowicz, *op. cit.* p. 230, Twelve Tables, viii, 14. Cf. H. S. Maine, *Ancient Law*, ch. vii.

cases, but the code states that this is an innovation. Formerly, certain forms of stealing were redressed by means of torture: the code introduced a penalty of six shekels of silver. The theft of beehives appears at one time to have been requited by suffering the guilty person to be stung to death by bees; here again the code substitutes a penalty of three shekels of silver.[1]

In old German law, the *weregild* laid down a scale of money payments to be paid by or on behalf of anyone who caused the death of another person, according to his rank. In one form or another the system of composition prevails or has prevailed almost to the present day over a great part of the barbaric world.[2] It has been found among the North American Indians, in the Malay Archipelago, in New Guinea, among the Indian hill tribes, among the rude tribes of the Caucasus, the Somali of East Africa, the negroes of the west coast, the Congo folk of the interior, the Kaffirs and Bantus of the south, and among many other peoples.

Among the Bedouin Arabs it was ordained in more primitive times that a life must be given for a life. But as the tribes became more civilised, opinion began to react against the crudity and cruelty of this custom, and a system of blood-money payments came to be substituted. But we are told by a careful observer that in cases of obviously intentional murder the blood-money system loses much of its

---

[1] H. F. Jolowicz, *op. cit.* p. 221; Frederic Hrozny, *Code Hittite* (Paris, 1922). D. G. Hogarth suggests that the translation of the Hittite code must be regarded as somewhat conjectural at present: *The Hittites of Asia Minor* in *Cambridge Ancient History*, ii, p. 269.

[2] L. T. Hobhouse, *Morals in Evolution* (1906), i, p. 88.

force, and the individual will sometimes take matters into his own hands regardless of the rest of the tribe and the elaborate codes and schedules by means of which the "wound-assessors" regulate the scheme of monetary compensation.[1]

We have already noticed the idea that like produces like, the belief that an effect resembles its cause, to be one of the main foundations supporting the whole superstructure of sympathetic magic. This law of similarity is in large measure responsible for the false science and the elaborate body of superstitious practices which play so important a part in the life of primitive communities. I suggest that the almost universal adoption of "appropriate" forms of penalty or retribution, whereby the requital of an offence is made to reflect the apparent nature of the wrongdoing, springs from exactly the same root idea. Man's idea of justice and his conception of the nature of the universe are related at innumerable points, and this one is not the least interesting. It will be found, I think, that the replacement of retribution by reparation in legal institutions, the substitution of compensation for an "appropriate" requital or revenge, did not take place on any large scale until false notions of the law of similarity in nature had given way to truer ideas concerning the physical world.

[1] A. Kennett, *Bedouin Justice*, p. 49, 56. The wound-assessors are hereditary experts in assessing wounds. A knowledge of bones and muscles, and the schedule of damage appropriate to various wounds provided by Arab law, are handed down from father to son: *ibid.* p. 107.

X

THE JUDGMENT OF GOD

PERHAPS the most impressive manifestation of the connection between human laws and the institutions of government on the one hand, and men's conceptions of the universe on the other, is to be found in the complete reliance which has everywhere been placed in various forms of divine intervention as a sure and certain method of solving the most difficult problems of legal right, and of indicating the true requirements of practical justice or political expediency.

The most generalised form of the divine judgment is where the whole community is supposed to be afflicted with a disaster as a punishment for failing to obey the will of God, which is, of course, believed o be identical with perfect justice.[1] An example of this is given in Plutarch's *Lives*,[2] where it is related that in the reign of Tatius some of his friends and kinsmen, meeting ambassadors coming from Laurentium to Rome, attempted to rob them, and when they resisted, killed them. Tatius was himself killed in revenge by relatives of the slain. Soon afterwards, the narrative continues, a plague broke out, causing sudden death without any previous sickness; it infected also the corn with unfruitfulness, and the cattle with barrenness; there rained blood in the city, so that fear of the wrath of the gods was added to the

---

[1] *E.g.* numbering the people, II Samuel xxv, I Chronicles xxi.
[2] *Romulus.*

actual sufferings of the people. But when the same evils fell upon Laurentium, then "everybody judged it was divine vengeance that fell upon both cities, for the neglect of executing justice upon the murderers of Tatius and the ambassadors. When the murderers on both sides were delivered up and punished, the pestilence visibly abated; and Romulus purified the cities with lustrations. . . ."

Out of this type of divine judgment arose the augury, whereby the will of the gods was anticipated and the divine displeasure avoided by foretelling the events which would arouse it. This was a prominent feature of Graeco-Roman society in the classic age. When Xenophon wished to increase the taxes and to change the laws, he sent to Dodona and to Delphi to enquire of the gods if they approved the measures he proposed to introduce.[1] Similarly, Plato assumed that whenever it appeared desirable to change the laws, the oracles must be consulted.[2] In Sparta, the gods were consulted every nine years as to their will concerning the kings. The Ephors chose for the purpose a clear moonless night and sat in silence with their eyes fixed upon the heavens. If they saw a shooting star cross the dome of the sky, this indicated that their kings were guilty of some neglect of the gods. The kings were then suspended from their duties till an oracle came from Delphi to permit their reinstatement.[3]

In Rome no international agreement and no alliance was made without invoking the gods, for under the ancient public law an important governmental act could be carried through only if it had first been

---

[1] *De Vectigal.*, vi.   [2] *Laws*, vi, p. 772.
[3] Plutarch, *Agis*, ii; Fustel De Coulanges, *La Cité antique*, p. 205.

sanctioned by divine approval.[1] The king-priests of Rome were inaugurated with a religious ceremony expressly designed to evoke the divine will. The new king was conducted to the summit of the Capitoline Hill and seated there facing southward. On his left sat an augur, who marked off certain lines in the heavens, uttered a prayer and supplicated the gods to show by a visible sign that the new ruler was acceptable to them. Then, when a flash of lightning occurred or a flight of birds had revealed the will of the gods, the king-designate would enter upon his office.[2] In view of the close connection between sacred rites and secular authority it was, indeed, essential for the people to know that their magistrates were loved by the gods, or at the very least not offensive to them. The Athenian senate commonly enquired of a magistrate-elect if he suffered from any bodily defect, if he possessed a domestic god, if his family had always been faithful to his worship, if he had himself constantly fulfilled his duties towards the dead. All these questions were designed to discover if the intended magistrate would be agreeable to the gods.[3]

The Augury had its foundation in religious belief. But it was not based on religion alone. It represented, in Kohler's expressive phrase, the totality of means used to discover the mystery of the future.[4] If it was

[1] Ludwig Felix, *Der Einfluss der Religion auf die Entwicklung des Eigenthums*, tr. by A. Kocourek in *Evolution of Law*, vol. iii; *Formative Influences of Legal Institutions* (ed. Wigmore and Kocourek), p. 379; Livy, i, 24; iii, 25; ix, 5; xxx, 42.

[2] Fustel de Coulanges, *loc. cit.* Livy describes this ceremony for the installation of Numa; Dionysius assumes it took place for all the kings, and after the kings for the consuls. Livy, i, 18. Dionysius, ii, 6; iv, 80.

[3] Fustel de Coulanges, *op. cit.* p. 217.

[4] Joseph Kohler, *Philosophy of Law* (tr. Albrecht, 1921), Philosophy of Law Series, p. 251.

the mother of law, it was also the parent of science. It did not appear to the same extent among all nations but reached its highest development, significantly enough, among the star-interpreting peoples—the Babylonians, the Etruscans, the Romans, and the Chinese.

The divine judgment has taken many forms. At its lowest stage it is scarcely more than a magical process of divination applied to the determination of legal questions. The Burmese practice of requiring the parties to a suit to light candles, the victory being accorded to him whose candle remains alight the longer, belongs to this order. So, too, does the custom prevailing in Borneo in which the plaintiff and the defendant are represented by two shell-fish on a plate: the shell-fish are irritated by lime-juice and the one which moves first determines which of the parties is in the right.[1]

The divine judgment appears in its most universal form in the shape of the ordeal. There is scarcely a country in the world which has not at some time resorted to a test whereby someone whose innocence is in doubt, or who seeks to enforce a claim, is placed

---

[1] "Ordeal" in *Encyclopaedia Britannica* (14th ed.), vol. xvi, pp. 850-51. Among the early Frisians, if a man were killed in a crowd and the kinsman entitled to sue for his weregild was unable to charge any particular person, the liability was determined by a process of divination. The claimant could select any seven persons from among those who had been in the crowd. Two twigs were then wrapped up in white wool, one of them having been marked with a cross and placed on the altar. A priest or a child then drew one of the twigs. If the plain one were drawn it indicated that the guilty person was among the seven. Thereupon seven other pieces of twig were drawn and the "owner" of the last-drawn twig was declared to be guilty. *Leg. Fris. Al.* 14. 1; Tacitus, *Germania*, c. 10; George Spence, *An Enquiry into the Origin of the Laws and Political Institutions of Modern Europe* (1826), pp. 224, 462.

in mortal peril from which he can emerge safely only with the aid of omnipotent Providence.[1] There are endless variations on this theme. Underlying them all is the belief that if the suspected person or the disputants are exposed to serious danger the divine powers will be compelled to take sides and the truth will thereby be revealed or the matter determined.

Before we examine some of the ordeals which have actually been practised it is worth while to look for a moment at the vast number of legends in ancient Greek mythology which contain an ordeal.[2]

A favourite story was the case of the woman whose delivery or pregnancy indicated misconduct. If she introduced into the group of relatives a child of alien blood, then she was guilty. But if she had had intercourse with a scion of the gods she would be excused, for the blood of the child would be that of the gods who protect the family group, the ever-ready champions of all who share their blood and race. Again and again in the legends the woman excuses herself by alleging that she had been visited by a divinity. But this she had to prove; and the usual mode of eliciting the proof was to subject her to mortal danger from which, if her story were true, she would be rescued by the god.

A typical instance was the case of Danaë. In the legend this maiden was immured in a cave by her father Acrisius in order that she might never become a mother. Some years afterwards he heard the cry of a child in the hollow of the earth and found his

---

[1] A possible exception is China. There appears to be no trace of the judgment of God among the Chinese.

[2] I owe most of the ideas here put forward in connection with Greek mythology to Gustave Glotz.

daughter with a boy. When he required her to name
the father, she replied that it was Zeus. Acrisius was
not convinced and, to obtain proof, set her afloat on
the sea.

This same test recurs in a whole series of Greek
and Latin legends. Rhea Silvia, the vestal virgin,
when she gave birth to Romulus and Remus, declared that Mars was their father; and the children
were set afloat in a cradle. It was, indeed, common
to subject the child to the same treatment as the
woman herself. Thus Perseus accompanied his
mother on the waters, Telephus went with Auge,
Dionysus with Semele. Sometimes only the child
was exposed to the ordeal, the erring mother being
reserved for dishonour and a harsher fate.

Gustave Glotz points out in his remarkable *Études
sociales et juridiques sur l'antiquité Grecque* that
there are innumerable heroes who entered upon life
through the test of exposure to death. "The legends
abound in them. This exposure takes place nearly
always under conditions which clearly indicate an
ordeal. In most of the instances the test was that of
cold water. The story of Romulus and Remus is well
known; it is the same as the story of the twins Neleus
and Peleus in Greece, of Moses among the Hebrews,
of Sargon of Agade, King of Chaldea. Was all this
nothing more than an imaginative fable, transmitted
from country to country? Surely not. It was a primitive custom reappearing everywhere from age to age.
Proof enough of this is found in the fact that it was
practised with its original signification by the primitive Celtic and Germanic peoples at the fall of the
Roman Empire. The Emperor Julian, and many
others, report that the married women of those tribes,

when they bore a child of suspected birth, were made to set it afloat on the waters of the Rhine; if the child drowned, the woman was deemed guilty of adultery; if it survived, it was deemed legitimate and the mother innocent." [1] Thus the ordeal served to decide questions of personal status as well as the determination of innocence or guilt.

The Greeks were a maritime people, susceptible alike to the fascination and the terror of the sea. They believed the country of the dead lay far away on the other side of the ocean, where the sun sank from sight beneath the waves. And so, in order to place a human being in the presence of death, it was sufficient to set him afloat on that sea which led to the ocean. Such a being would either be carried off to the country of the dead, never to return, or he would be saved by miraculous intervention, and thereby be vindicated. This, suggests Glotz, is the explanation, in terms of the ordeal, of the legends in which the hero is subjected to the judgment of the waves. [2] Among other peoples the use of fire has been the predominating element in proving feminine virtue by means of the ordeal. In the Râmâyana code of the Hindus the virtuous Sitâ vindicates her honour to her jealous husband by passing through the flames unharmed; and Richardis, wife of Charles the Fat, similarly proves her innocence by going unhurt through a fire clothed in a waxed shift. [3]

Another variant of the same theme was the leap from a cliff. The kingdom of the dead, according to

---

[1] G. Glotz, *op. cit.* p. 79.

[2] *Ibid.* pp. 84-5.

[3] "Ordeal" in *Encyclopaedia Britannica* (14th ed.), vol. xvi, p. 851; Pictet, *Origines Indo-Européenes*, Part II, p. 457.

Greek notions, was bounded by a vast cliff, the white or Leucadian rock bathed in the ghostly light that envelops the souls of the dead. Rocks of this kind abound on the Greek coast. Wherever some unfortunate mortal had challenged death by leaping from the cliff into the vortex, this was enough to make one more Leucadian rock. The leap might have been taken in expiation or it might have been done as an ordeal.[1] All along the Mediterranean there are traces of the cult of Ino-Lucothea, the erring wife who leaped into the sea in order to become the White Goddess.[2]

The Leucadian leap to death, to punishment or glorification, had at one time both a legal and a religious significance. The ordeals of the sea produced a deep and lasting impression on the Hellenic mind.[3] The false science which made the Greeks imagine that beyond the ocean there lay the land of the dead led them to the false notion of law which was embodied in the belief that there is a Justice of the Sea.

This explanation of the ordeal and proof themes in ancient Greek mythology put forward by Gustave Glotz with so much learning and eloquence appears to me remarkably convincing, and I find it difficult to resist his suggestion that the legends are in truth an idealised form of history—the history, as he says, "of real men, who loved and hated, triumphed and suffered, lived and died. These fantastic shadows of divine puppets, viewed more closely, become

---

[1] Glotz, *op. cit.* pp. 88-9.

[2] *Ibid.* Glotz also refers to the cult of Britomartis-Dictynna, "the virtuous maiden who cast herself into the sea to save her innocence and became the 'virgin of the net', the virgin of safety".

[3] Glotz, *loc. cit.*

beings of flesh and blood, who breathe and move."[1] The myths are on this interpretation the ingenuous memorials of early beliefs and primitive customs through which was transmitted the law and the religion of a rudimentary social condition.

If we turn from the legends of ancient Greece to the practical tests of a supernatural character, we find that in their most primitive form there is no separation between proof, verdict, and penalty. The divine judgment is executed at the moment of its pronouncement. The judgment is, indeed, revealed by the act which enforces the sentence. The guilty man is condemned by the very fact of his death; the innocent acquitted by his survival. The underlying idea is that God will pronounce the truth either by letting the individual perish or by deliberately saving him from destruction.[2]

At the other end of the scale is the revelation which serves only as proof of guilt. Thus, a murdered man was supposed to indicate in some way the person who had murdered him: the wounds would bleed at the latter's approach, or the bearers of the body would become paralysed at sight of him.[3]

A large number of ordeals come midway between these extremes. The guilty person may suffer some physical penalty as a result of the divine revelation, but the main purpose of the test is to indicate guilt, and the full punishment remains to be carried out by human agency. It is obvious that the function of the ordeal would to some extent vary according to the

---

[1] Gustave Glotz, *Études sociales et juridiques sur l'antiquité grécque*, p. 74.
[2] *Ibid.* pp. 70-72.
[3] Joseph Kohler, *Philosophy of Law* (tr. Albrecht, 1921), p. 252.

authority possessed by the courts of law. When they had become strong enough to formulate and enforce judgment the ordeal would tend to develop on the side of proof and to decay on the side of penalty.

A test of this intermediate character is contained in the Old Testament, where the book of Numbers [1] prescribes an ordeal for married women suspected of infidelity. The husband is to bring his wife to the priest with "an offering of jealousy, an offering of memorial". The priest is to take holy water and put dust from the tabernacle floor into it. He is to put the offering of memorial which is the jealousy offering into her hands and have in his own hands the bitter water that causes a curse. He then charges her as follows: "If no man have lain with thee, and if thou hast not gone aside to uncleanness with another instead of thy husband, be thou free from this bitter water that causeth the curse:

"But if thou hast gone aside to another instead of thy husband, and if thou be defiled, and some man have lain with thee beside thine husband:

"Then . . . the Lord make thee a curse and an oath among thy people, when the Lord doth make thy thigh to rot, and thy belly to swell;

"And this water that causeth the curse shall go into thy bowels, to make thy belly to swell, and thy thigh to rot: And the woman shall say, Amen, amen."

She then has to drink the jealousy offering and her innocence or guilt will be proved by the result. This may be contrasted with the ordeal intended for a similar purpose in Hammurabi: If the finger have been pointed against a man's wife (*i.e.* if she has been suspected) but she have not been caught lying with

---

[1] Numbers v, 15-22.

another man, she shall plunge into the river for her husband's satisfaction.

The ordeal found a place in almost all religious systems, among the Hindus no less than among the Graeco-Roman peoples of antiquity. But it flourished to a remarkable extent in the Christian countries of Europe during the Middle Ages, when it came to be a recognised method of determining guilt. The ordeals were no doubt of pagan origin but they were adopted by the Christian communities and adapted to the rites of the Christian faith. The Church itself accepted and encouraged the use of the ordeal from the 8th century onwards, and it was not until the Lateran Council definitely forbade the practice in the 13th century that it quickly died out.[1] The intense seriousness with which divine intervention was regarded in Christendom is shown by the fact that from early times games of chance were prohibited, not so much because various secular evils might result from them, but because they constituted a species of blasphemy in that they invoked the judgment of God in matters of trivial import.[2]

[1] I am concerned here with practice of the Church, not with its precepts. There were papal utterances from the time of Gregory I disapproving of the ordeals, but these had no effect, and many local ecclesiastical councils expressly authorised them. For a learned discussion of the attitude of the Church see A. Michel, "Ordalies" in *Dictionnaire de théologie catholique* (Vacant), Paris, 1930–32. Cf. A. Esmein, *Les Ordalies dans l'Église gallicane au IXe siècle* (Paris, 1898), p. 3.

[2] "We are not to tempt the Almightie by a vaine desire of manifestation of his power and speciall providence. But by using Lots in sport we tempt the Almightie, vainly desiring the manifestation of his speciall providence in his immediate disposing. Therefore the use of Lots is not to be in sport" (J. Balmford, *A Short and Plaine Dialogue concerning the unlawfulness of playing at Cards or Tables, or any other Game consisting of Chance*, London, 1593); Jean Barbeyrac, *Traité du Jeu* (Amsterdam, 1709), i, p. 22.

The liturgical formulae which have come down to us give an exact account of the manner in which the ceremony was carried out. The following directions prescribe the mode of obtaining the Judgment of the Glowing Iron:

> After the accusation has been lawfully made, and three days have been passed in fasting and prayer, the priest, clad in his sacred vestments . . . shall take with the tongs the iron placed before the altar; and, singing the hymn . . . "Bless him all his works" he shall bear it to the fire, and say this prayer over the place where fire is to carry out the judgment. "Bless, O Lord God, this place, that there may be for us in it sanctity, chastity, virtue and victory, and sanctimony, humility, goodness, gentleness and plentitude of law, and obedience to God the Father and the Son and the Holy Ghost."
> After this, the iron shall be placed in the fire and shall be sprinkled with holy water; and while it is heating he shall celebrate mass. But when the priest shall have taken the Eucharist, he shall adjure the man who is to be tried . . . and shall cause him to take the communion. Then the priest shall sprinkle holy water above the iron and shall say: "The blessing of God the Father, the Son and the Holy Ghost descend upon this iron for the discerning of the right judgment of God". And straightway the accused shall carry the iron to a distance of nine feet. Finally his hand shall be covered under seal for three days, and if festering blood be found in the track of the iron, he shall be judged guilty. But if, how-

ever, he shall go forth uninjured, praise shall be
rendered to God.[1]

A very similar ordeal by fire is resorted to to-day
by the Bedouin Arabs, except that the test consists of
licking a red-hot spoon instead of grasping a glowing
iron in the hand.[2]

In the Judgment of the Morsel, the preliminary
prayer asked the deity to arrange that whoever was
concerned in any way with the theft under investigation should not be able to swallow the bread and
cheese used in the ordeal. Then there was an exor-

---

[1] Ernest F. Henderson, *Select Documents of the Middle Ages* (1892),
pp. 314-15, tr. from Gengler's *Germanische Rechtsdenkmäler*, pp. 759-
65. The laws of King Aethelstan (A.D. 924) contain the following doom
concerning the ordeals of hot iron and water: "And concerning the
ordeal we enjoin by command of God and of the archbishop, and of all
bishops: that no man come within the church after the fire is borne
in with which the ordeal shall be heated, except the mass-priest and
him who shall go thereto: and let there be measured nine feet from
the stake to the mark, by the man's feet who goes thereto. But if it be
water let it be heated till it be boiling. And be the kettle of iron, or
brass, of lead or of clay. And if it be a single accusation, let the hand
dive after the stone up to the wrist; or if it be threefold, up to the
elbow. And when the ordeal is ready, then let two men go in of either
side; and be they agreed that it is so hot as we before have said. And
let go in an equal number of men of either side, and stand on both
sides of the ordeal, along the church; and let these be fasting, and
abstinent from their wives on that night; and let the mass-priest
sprinkle holy water over them all, and let each of them taste of the
holy water, and give them all the book of the image of Christ's rood to
kiss; and let no man mend the fire any longer when the hallowing is
begun; but let the iron lie upon the hot embers till the last collect;
after that, let it be laid upon the 'stapela'; and let there be no speaking
within, except that they earnestly pray to Almighty God that he make
manifest what is soothest. And let him go thereto; and let his hand be
enveloped, and be it postponed till after the third day, whether it be
foul or clean within the envelope. And he who shall break this law,
be the ordeal with respect to him void, and let him pay to the King
cxx shillings as 'wite' " (B. Thorpe, *Ancient Laws and Institutes of
England*, i, p. 227).

[2] A. Kennett, *Bedouin Justice*, pp. 110-11.

cism addressed to the "Most unclean dragon, ancient serpent, dark night" not to permit "that man to eat this bread and cheese who has committed this theft or consented to it or advised it. Adjured through Him who is to come to judge the quick and the dead do thou close his throat with a band, not, however, unto death." Finally there came a conjuration in which the suspected person was called upon not to pass the bread and cheese down his gullet and throat if he were in any way guilty, but to tremble like an aspen-leaf until he had vomited the morsel forth with blood.[1] In the Judgment of the Ploughshares the person undergoing trial had to walk over the ploughshares with bare feet. If his feet were unharmed, it was God's proof of his innocence; if a manifest burn appeared on his feet, that was a sign from heaven of his guilt.[2]

An immense number of ordeals were carried out by means of water. It may be said, indeed, that water appears to have been regarded as the most suitable vehicle for conveying the judgment of God to human beings. It has certainly been more widely used than any other medium of expression. The Judgment of Boiling Water involved the extraction of a stone from boiling water, the subsequent procedure closely resembling that employed in the Judgment of the Glowing Iron. The vast majority of ordeals connected with water consisted, however, of simply throwing the accused into the sea or a river or a tank and considering him to be adjudged guilty by divine providence according to whether he floated or sank to the bottom.

[1] Henderson, *op. cit.* pp. 317-18.
[2] *Ibid.* 315-16.

It is interesting to note that there has been a diversity of practice as to what result demonstrated guilt and what innocence in the water test. According to the code of Hammurabi[1] the Babylonians believed that the man was retained below by the river gods if he were guilty and restored to the surface if innocent. King Minos and the judge Thémisôn followed the same line of thought as Hammurabi's code. But the great majority of peoples have held precisely the opposite view: that is, they have regarded it as favourable to the accused if he sank to the bottom and unfavourable if he floated. It was so that the law book of Manu regards the matter.[2] Archbishop Hincmar of Rheims declared in the 9th century: "*Innoxii submerguntur et aqua culpabiles supernatant*".[3] And the liturgical formula used for the ordeal in medieval Christendom enjoined that if the person under trial were guilty, "may the water which received thee in baptism not receive thee now; if, however, thou art innocent, may the water which received thee in baptism receive thee now".[4]

It is possible that this divergence in the method of interpreting the ordeal is due to the fact that the two

[1] "If a man has accused another of laying a spell upon him, but has not proved it, the accused shall go to the sacred river, he shall plunge into the sacred river, and if the sacred river shall conquer him, he that accused him shall take possession of his house. If the sacred river shall show his innocence and he is saved, his accuser shall be put to death. He that plunged into the sacred river shall appropriate the house of him that accused him" (Johns, *Babylonian, etc., Laws, Contracts*, p. 44; R. Campbell Thompson; *The Golden Age of Hammurabi* in *Cambridge Ancient History*, i, p. 518).

[2] *Laws of Manu*, tr. G. Bühler (*The Sacred Books of the East*, edited by Max Müller), viii, 113, p. 274.

[3] Hincmar, *De Divortio Lotharii et Tetbergæ*; J. P. Migne, *Patrologiæ*, cxxv, col. 665.

[4] Henderson, *op. cit.* p. 317.

views of the test represent different stages of civilisation. In the earlier stage the disappearance of the accused beneath the waters is attributed to his death. Death and culpability, proof and punishment, are merged in a simple and realistic manner. But at a later stage the conception of the life hereafter becomes more beatific. It is now believed that those whom the gods love die young, and it follows that the gods desire to keep among themselves the worthiest men in order to bestow upon them a share in their own eternal happiness. Hence the Greeks may have imagined that the water gods retained in the depths those who were dear to them, and rejected to the surface the unworthy, who were guilty. The transference of this belief to the Christian faith, with its emphasis on the world hereafter, was an easy step, though certain alterations in the symbolism of the ordeal were necessary.

In all the ordeals of which we have any detailed knowledge there is always at the crucial moment a direct appeal to the supernatural powers to manifest the divine judgment in the case under trial by means of the particular test being applied. The Hindu priest invokes the fire; the Christian priest utters a supplication in the name of the Father, the Son, and the Holy Ghost; the Jewish priest calls upon the Lord God. The elaborate ritual which surrounded the ceremony no less than the inherently religious character of the test made it inevitable that its application should for the most part be entrusted to the clergy. Even among the Bedouin Arabs of the present day, where the ordeal by fire has become to a large extent secularised, the only persons qualified to carry out the test are the two or three sheikhs who occupy the position of "Hereditary Holder of the Red-hot Spoon".[1]

The mechanism of the tests tended to become more refined in the course of time. The directions for carrying out the Judgment of the Psalter, for instance, read like the instructions for conducting an early scientific experiment. A piece of wood made with a button on top is to be put in a Psalter above a specified verse, and the Psalter closed and strongly pressed with the button projecting. Another piece of wood is to be made with a hole in which the button can be placed so that the Psalter hangs from it and can be turned freely. Two persons hold the wood with the Psalter hanging in the middle. The suspected individual is placed between them. One of the holders says three times to the other, "He has this thing" (*i.e.* the stolen article). The other replies three times, "He has it not". The priest then calls on God to make the truth manifest in a prayer which concludes that if the accused is guiltless "that book which we hold in our hands shall (in revolving) follow the ordinary course of the sun; but if he be guilty that book shall move backwards".[2] It is curious that men who recognised that the sun had an "ordinary" course should have failed to realise that the motion of a suspended book had any relation to the laws of physical causation.

We must not forget that the question of proof presented perhaps the most difficult and perplexing of all juridical problems to our ancestors. Elaborate rules were prescribed which the party to a suit had to follow in order to prove his case or clear himself of

---

[1] A. Kennett, *Bedouin Justice*, p. 108.
[2] Henderson, *op. cit.* pp. 318-19.

the allegations made against him. The sages of the past were extremely reluctant to decide disputed questions of fact. The arbitrament of the ordeal was welcome not only because it appealed strongly to the prevalent belief in supernatural intervention, but also because it enabled the judge to dispense with the necessity of examining witnesses and sifting the evidence which responsibility for discovering the truth would have involved.[1] The oldest forms of trials were thus not trials in the modern sense of the word at all. They were methods of proof. Hence the question of proof dominated the scene, and was the crucial element in the judicial process. The vocabulary of the law possessed, indeed, no word for trial even so late as Bracton's day. Men spoke of proof; and by proof they meant the oath and the ordeal, each of which involved an appeal to the supernatural.[2]

It would be false to imagine, therefore, that the people of past ages were intentionally deceiving themselves by hypocritically pretending to submit disputed questions to tests alleged to elicit the divine judgment when they knew that the result would in fact be determined by physical causes or by pure chance. There must have come a time, of course,

[1] Pollock and Maitland, *A History of English Law* (2nd ed.), i, p. 603; Sir F. Pollock, *Archaism in Modern Law* in *Essays in the Law*, pp. 203-4.

[2] Pollock and Maitland, *op. cit.* ii, p. 598; W. S. Holdsworth, *A History of English Law*, ix, p. 130. A judgment of the Court, called by Bigelow the "medial judgment", awarded that one of the two litigants must prove his case, by his body in battle, or by a one-sided ordeal, or by an oath with oath-helpers, or by the oaths of witnesses. "The court had no desire to hear or weigh conflicting testimony. To do so would have been to exercise critical faculties, which the court did not possess, and the exercise of which would have been foreign to the whole spirit of the age" (Sir Courtney Ilbert, "Evidence" in *Encyclopaedia Britannica* (11th ed.), vol. x, p. 11).

when faith wavered, and conviction gave way to scepticism or disbelief. And no doubt a period of decadence set in during which the ordeals were carried out by priests who had ceased to believe in their efficacy, or who perhaps manipulated the implements employed, and when the results were accepted by a public which no longer put its trust in the divinely inspired judgment. Most institutions outlive the ideas on which they are based, and the ordeal was no exception to the rule. But we may certainly suppose that during the greater portion of its long life, the ordeal was regarded by all concerned as an infallible method of determining the truth.

It may be said that in some cases at least we can discern a certain empirical foundation for the ordeal in the psychological behaviour of the accused.[1] Such tests as the Judgment of the Morsel might be influenced by the consciousness of guilt or innocence of the accused. In a purely mechanical test like that of the revolving psalter, in which the only human actions likely to affect the results were those of the attendants holding the wood, this factor was entirely absent.

It was through the action of the Church in adopting the various ordeals and consecrating them with all the panoply of religious ritual, that the practice survived in full vigour in Western Europe after the barbarian invasion.[2] And it was when the Christian Church set her face against the system that it died out in a remarkably short space of time. From 1159 to 1227 the Popes were vigorously opposed to the

[1] Cf. Josef Kohler, *Philosophy of Law* (tr. Albrecht, 1921), pp. 252-3.
[2] Pollock and Maitland, *loc. cit.*

THE JUDGMENT OF GOD

ordeal and denounced it in unmeasured terms. Innocent III, who undermined the wager of law or
compurgation, made a still more deadly attack upon
the ordeal by forbidding it to be attended by the rites
of the Church. This was a fatal blow, and the judgment of God died out in the 13th century in every
form save one.[1] The one ordeal which persisted for
centuries longer was the wager of battle. To this we
may now turn our attention.

The ordeal by battle is an institution of very great
antiquity and widespread use. In ancient times it
was sometimes employed to decide the fate of whole
communities. In the warfare between the Greeks
and Trojans, between the Jews and the Philistines,
the Vandals and Alamans, we learn of heroes who
come out from both sides to do battle and the combat
of these warriors decides the victory of the entire
host.[2]

In its judicial form the wager of battle is said to
be of Teutonic origin, but it was employed also by
the Celts and the Slavonic tribes; it existed in Hun-
gary, Poland, Bohemia, Servia, Moravia, Pomer-
ania, Lithuania, and Russia.[3] It was introduced from
France into Anglo-Saxon England by the Normans[4]
and was not finally abolished until the 19th century.

The wager of battle took its place in the judicial
system as an ordeal of a bilateral character. It was,
in essence, an appeal to the god of battles to see that
justice was done among human beings. It was also

---

[1] Henry C. Lea, *Superstition and Force*, p. 274 *et seq.*
[2] E. B. Tylor, "Ordeal" in *Encyclopaedia Britannica* (14th ed.),
vol. xvi, p. 852. Cf. Marc Bloch, *Les Rois thaumaturges* (1924),
pp. 15-16.
[3] Henry C. Lea, *op. cit.* pp. 85-6.
[4] Pollock and Maitland, *op. cit.* ii, p. 600.

an assertion of the creed that might is right and right is might, and at the same time the sanction of that creed. Too much emphasis cannot be laid on the identification of might and right implied by the wager of battle, for it was this which enabled it to become firmly rooted in the morals and religion of the day and thereby to become an established feature of the legal order. The Church accepted the judicial combat as a sacral process because men believed that what triumphed was not force but truth.[1] The just man not only deserved to win, but would in fact vanquish his adversary.

The method by which the combat proceeded was for each party to assert the absolute justice of his cause, to which end a solemn oath on the Gospels, or on some relic of approved sanctity, was administered to the contestants before the conflict commenced. The result was that defeat involved not merely the loss of the suit, but also a conviction of perjury to be punished with brutal severity. In criminal cases defeat automatically convicted the loser of malicious prosecution.[2]

The wager of battle was applied to every type of legal dispute.[3] Civil litigation concerning the ownership of land or dower, the recovery of vineyards,

---

[1] It was on these grounds that Gundobad justified the edict of Lyons in A.D. 502 which established the wager of battle as a recognised form of trial. See "Laws of Gundobad", Tit. XLV, in *Monumenta Germaniae Historica*, Legum Sectio I, Tomi II, par. I, pp. 75-6.

[2] Henry C. Lea, *Superstition and Force*, p. 112. In A.D. 819 Louis-le-Debonnaire decreed that where testimony was evenly balanced, one of the witnesses from each side should be chosen to fight it out, the losing champion suffering the loss of a hand—the usual penalty for defeat of the accuser. Cf. Pollock and Maitland, *loc. cit.*

[3] For cases illustrating its use see *Bracton's Note Book*, edited by F. W. Maitland.

money, or other property; criminal appeals of treason, felonies such as murder, adultery, arson, witchcraft, or theft; and even international cases were decided by means of the judicial combat.[1] In criminal cases, if the prisoner demanded battle of those who accused him, the judge was bound to concede it unless the man's guilt was too notorious for question. Conversely, if the accuser offered combat, the defendant was compelled either to accept or to confess his guilt, unless he could prove an alibi or unless the prosecutor was himself notoriously guilty of the crime.

In England, where wager of battle alone survived the ban placed upon judicial ordeals by the Lateran Council in 1215,[2] the procedure in a criminal case was as follows. The appellant first formulated a charge at five successive County Courts. If the person accused failed to appear, he was thereupon outlawed. In the event of his desiring to answer the charge, he was obliged to offer battle by throwing down his glove as a gage. If he was defeated, he was liable to be hanged, while if the contest was undecided he might still be tried on indictment. The right to wager of battle was successfully claimed in the English Courts in the year 1818 by a man named Thornton, who had been acquitted at assizes of the charge of violating and murdering a Miss Ashford. Her brother thereupon brought an appeal of death against

---

[1] George Spence, *An Enquiry into the Origin of the Laws and Political Institutions of Modern Europe* (1826), pp. 479-81; Henry C. Lea, *op. cit.* pp. 89, 95, 101, 105; E. B. Tylor, "Ordeal" in *Encyclopaedia Britannica* (11th ed.), vol. xxviii, p. 229.

[2] In France, wager of battle declined after the 13th century but occasional instances of its use occurred in the 14th and 15th centuries. Jean Boca, *La Justice criminelle de l'échevinage d'Abbeville au moyen âge* (1184-1516) (Lille, 1930), p. 128.

Thornton, who then demanded the ancient ordeal, which was granted by the Court.[1]

The wager of battle was an ordeal from which no man could procure exemption, no matter how exalted in rank he might be, if his adversary was of equal station. The appearance of the Champion of England at the coronation of the English sovereign was a picturesque survival from the days when it was no empty ceremony for the armed and mounted knight to fling his gauntlet and proclaim his readiness to do battle with anyone who challenged the right of the new monarch to the crown.[2] Women and clergy were accorded exemption only at the price of being deemed incompetent to appear as witnesses, until at a later date they were represented by champions. Under the German laws there are instances where even a woman might go to the ordeal in person, and the amazing spectacle was presented of attempting to redress the physical inequalities of the opponents by burying the man to his waist, tying his left hand behind him and arming him only with a mace, while the woman was permitted the free use of her limbs and a heavy stone securely fastened in a piece of stuff.

In normal circumstances, at any rate in England, the judicial combat was fought on foot with staves and leather shields. Where the wager of battle was ordered by a court of chivalry, the opponents were mounted and armed with spear and sword. The institution was, indeed, well suited to the age of

[1] Ashford v. Thornton (1818), I. Barnewall and Alderson's Reports, p. 405.

[2] *Coutumes du Beauvoisis of Beaumanoir*, ch. lxi. The earliest record of the ceremony at the coronation of an English king was on the accession of Richard II. It was allowed to lapse after the coronation of George IV.

chivalry. It is significant that in the 14th century, when the wager of battle had been largely superseded as a legal institution, the duel of chivalry began to flourish. The duel of honour sprang from aristocratic and military impulses and had little in common with the legal combat.[1]

The object of the two types of physical encounter was, of course, entirely different. The purpose of the ordeal by battle was to evoke the judgment of God and thereby to reveal the truth and secure the impartial administration of justice. The purpose of the duel was to wreak vengeance, vindicate honour, and obtain reparation. The only common element was the appeal to force of arms; and it is this which persisted when the religious faith on which the judicial combat was founded had long since passed away. Thus did violence survive the decay of what men believed to be its moral justification.

As the wager of battle developed, it became customary, and in some cases compulsory, to employ champions to do the actual fighting. This practice probably arose from an abuse of the liberty whereby witnesses could be challenged personally in Court. This enabled parties who were "unwilling themselves to encounter the risks of a mortal struggle, to put forward some truculent bravo who swore point-blank, and whose evidence would require him to be forced out of court at the sword's point". Whatever the cause, "the use of a professional gladiator is so inconsistent with the pious reference to the judgment of God, which formed the only excuse for the whole system, that some external reason is required to

[1] G. Neilson, "Duelling" in *Encyclopaedia of Religion and Ethics*, v, p. 114.

account for its introduction".[1] Bracton states that in
criminal cases a witness suspected of being a hired
gladiator was not permitted to fight but was tried for
the attempt by a jury and was liable to lose a hand
and a foot.

It is scarcely surprising that the occupation of
hired champion became infamous. Those who professed it were classed with criminals and prostitutes,
and were incapable of appearing as witnesses. In
some countries, such as Germany in the 13th and
14th centuries, they were deprived of many legal
rights and privileges, and these disabilities extended
even to their children. Yet despite all this the fact
remains that "the extraordinary anomaly was ex-
hibited of seeking to learn the truth in affairs of the
highest moment by a solemn appeal to God, through
the instrumentality of those who were considered as
convicts of the worst kind, or who, by the very act,
were branded with infamy if successful in justifying
innocence, and if defeated mutilated and hanged".[2]

The avoidance of personal encounter through the
engagement of a hired champion was not the only
sign of a growing lack of confidence in the impartial
arbitrament of the judicial combat. There is evidence
of occasional attempts on the part of the combatants
to bribe heaven either to assist the right or to defend
the wrong. One Sir Miles the Stammerer, for instance,
apparently believing that even God had his price,
conveyed lands to the monastery of St. Peter at Bèze

---

[1] Henry C. Lea, *op. cit.* p. 120. See also pp. 89, 105.

[2] *Ibid.* pp. 124-5. In the graduated list of fines for insults offered
to nobles, merchants, peasants, and other classes in compensation for
their wounded honour the champion and his children came last of all,
below even the mountebank and juggler. The only redress he was entitled to was a glance of sunshine cast upon him by the offender from a
polished shield.

in order to purchase assistance in a combat about to take place.

The wager of battle and all the other ordeals which flourished so abundantly in medieval Christendom as long as the Church accepted or tolerated them, faded into insignificance once the spiritual power withdrew the mantle of its authority. Thus the Church played a dominant part in abolishing the judicial combat and in making people aware of the cruelty and injustice which it involved.[1] The simple faith which had reposed a childlike confidence in the miraculous outcome of the ordeal of the burning ploughshare was undermined by the rise of Aristotelian dialectic. The logic of the medieval schoolmen made it somehow harder for even the untutored serf to retain his unswerving conviction in the divine instrumentality of the hired champion.

Events in the temporal sphere conspired to assist in discrediting the judgment of God, whether manifested by the wager of battle or in its other forms. Chief among these was the revival of Roman law in the 13th century, which, by virtue of its doctrine of royal authority, had the effect of undermining all the institutions of the feudal system. The theory of regal supremacy introduced by the revived study of Roman law was welcome to princes whose authority over powerful vassals was often only nominal; and the conception of equity between man and man which it embodied offered an attractive alternative to the complicated and fantastic privileges of ecclesiastical, feudal, and customary law.[2]

---

[1] A. Esmein, *Les Ordalies dans l'Église gallicane au IXe siècle* (Paris, 1898), p. 2.
[2] Lea, *op. cit.* pp. 148-9.

The first definite blows struck at ordeal by battle were the enactments passed in the reign of Henry II to provide alternative methods of proof in certain specified cases.

The Constitutions of Clarendon (1164) declare that no one is to be compelled to defend his title to land by physical combat. The claimant who disputed the possessor's right had to offer battle, but the man in possession could, if he desired, decline the ordeal and have the question determined by the grand assize—that is, a body of twelve sworn recognitors selected by four knights specially summoned by the sheriff under the royal writ.[1] Two years later, the Assize of Clarendon introduced a similar system for criminal cases. Twelve lawful men from each hundred, with four lawful men from each township, were to be sworn to present persons suspected of crime in each county court.

Those who were presented in this way were required to submit to the ordeal, for the old modes of proof were not abolished.[2] But with the emergence of the Grand Jury they were pushed into the background. The superiority of the new method of determining guilt or innocence led to the rise of the petty jury and the complete effacement of the crude feudal methods[3] which had hitherto prevailed.

A similar trend took place on the continent, where we find the emperor Frederick II declaring in the earlier part of the 13th century that wager of battle

---

[1] W. Stubbs, *Select Charters* (9th ed. revised by A. W. C. Davis), p. 27; Pollock and Maitland, *History of English Law before the Time of Edward I*, i, p. 147-50.

[2] Proof by battle lingered on until 1819; proof by oath-keepers until 1833.

[3] W. S. Holdsworth, *A History of English Law*, i, p. 322-4.

is not in any sense a legal proof but a mere species of divination utterly incompatible with equity and justice. In his Neapolitan code he prohibited it for future use save in cases of murder or treason where no other proof was obtainable, and even then only if the accuser desired.

The Christian Church and the Roman law, it might appear at this point, had combined to accomplish a great civilising step in emancipating mankind from the superstitious practices in which society had been submerged. But such a statement can only be made by overlooking the hideous system which replaced the ordeal and which was a direct result of the very forces that destroyed the latter.

The introduction of torture in the Middle Ages may be traced to the decline of the ordeals and trial by battle; for so long as appeal can be made to the judgment of God, confession is unnecessary. It is highly significant that when in the 13th century the judicial use of torture was becoming systematised as a means of obtaining evidence and confession, the ordeal was falling out of use.[1]

The institution of torture in the modern world was clearly derived from the civil law of ancient Rome. Italy was the radiating centre for the revived study of the Roman law in Western Europe, and it is in Italy that we find the first example of torture being imported into modern criminal jurisprudence. This occurred in the first half of the 13th century. Later in the century the practice began to take root in France, where the classical Roman text-books had for many

---

[1] "Torture" in *Encyclopaedia Britannica*, vol. xxii, p. 311; Henry C. Lea, *op. cit.* pp. 258, 327. The Visigoths were the only primitive people who excluded the ordeal and yet permitted torture.

years formed an important subject of study. Torture gradually spread from one country to another like an evil weed, and all over the Continent it became a juristic maxim that confession is the best evidence, and that all the machinery of the law should be directed towards extorting it.

The Church had been active in suppressing the ordeal. It was no less active in promoting torture when it suited the purposes of those who were responsible for the Inquisition to use the basest of all methods to further its ends. In A.D. 1252 Pope Innocent IV issued detailed instructions for the operation of the Inquisition in Tuscany and Lombardy. These contained directions ordering the civil magistrate to wring from all heretics by torture not only a confession of their own guilt, but also an accusation of their accomplices. He indicates that this was the customary practice with thieves and robbers, which shows, observes Lea, "the progress made during the quarter of the century and the high appreciation entertained by the Church for the convenience of the new system".[1]

In ancient Rome torture had been sparingly applied in the case of a few specified offences, and was accompanied by a substantial safeguard in that an accuser who failed to prove his charge was liable to the *lex talionis*; and this meant that in crimes involving torture he was duly tortured. The deterrent effect of this must have been considerable. But the new dispensation introduced by the Church admitted of no such scruples. The theory of the Inquisition, upon which the practice of the criminal law proceeded, was that "the suspected man was to be hunted

[1] Lea, *op. cit.* p. 330.

down and entrapped like a wild beast, that his guilt was to be assumed, and that the efforts of his judges were to be directed solely to obtaining against him sufficient evidence to warrant the extortion of a confession without allowing him the means of defence".[1]

I shall exclude from this account any description of the hideous practices which were devised with loathsome ingenuity and carried out with almost incredible cruelty under the system of torture. The sickening details are available in books written in all languages for those who have a taste for them. It is difficult to contemplate the well-authenticated record of the past without feeling that the methods used to extort confession, not only by the Inquisition, but by the contemporary criminal codes of the temporal rulers, were such as to give an opportunity for the unbridled expression of sadistic impulses unequalled either in preceding or succeeding ages save in the case of a few Oriental despots with diseased minds. It is probable that the officials who operated the system in its day-to-day application were mostly abnormal men, for ordinary beings would scarcely have been willing to earn their livelihood by inflicting unbearable agonies on their fellow-creatures.

What I am concerned to emphasise is the social transformation brought about by the abandonment of the judgment of God as the principal means of determining legal issues and the substitution, in criminal cases, of torture as a method of producing evidence of guilt or innocence. "The purgatorial oath was administered at the altar of the parish church; the ordeal was a public spectacle; and the judicial duel drew thousands of witnesses as eager for the

[1] *Ibid.* p. 348.

sight of blood as the Roman plebs. These were all ancestral customs, inspiring implicit reverence, and forming part of the public life of the community. To substitute for them the gloomy dungeon through whose walls no echo of the victim's screams could filter, where impassible judges coldly compared the incoherent confession wrung by insufferable torment with the anonymous accusation or the deposition of unknown witnesses, required a total change in the constitution of society."[1] The ordeals were cruel and barbarous, always superstitious and often unfair. Yet, seen in the context of religious faith and primitive belief in which they were set, they did not disfigure the age that practised them because they were the genuine result of convictions widely held and deeply felt. Torture, on the other hand, was an institution which had no organic relation to medieval society or the needs of the time. It claimed to rise superior to superstitious belief and yet was utterly irrational in its essential character. It had no roots either in feeling or in faith. It is for these reasons, as much as for the horrible suffering which it inflicted, that torture appears as one of those practices which leave an indelible stain upon a whole epoch.

One feature of the judgment of God which may be noted in conclusion is the development of the idea of divine justice. In ancient Greek mythology the gods were not dispensers of justice.[2] They wielded the supreme forces of the world; but they were creatures of caprice and passion who possessed many of the

---

[1] Henry C. Lea, *Superstition and Force*, p. 321.
[2] Cf. E. Burle, *Essai historique sur la développement de la notion de droit naturel dans l'antiquité grecque* (Trevoux, 1908), p. 44, on the special position of Zeus.

passions and frailties of human beings. In the early legends the purpose of the ordeal is to reveal the will of the gods, the divine pleasure or displeasure, rather than to serve as a measuring rod of justice in any abstract sense. But with the progress of human thought the conception of Justice became of increased importance; and religious doctrine evolved the idea that the divine will is identical with perfect justice. God thus becomes the supreme Judge. "Thou art just, O Lord, and righteous are Thy judgments" runs the Psalm; "Thou who art just and a Judge, make a manifest burn to appear on his feet" echoes the ordeal of the Ploughshares. Which was cause and which effect it is impossible to say. It was probably an inter-action between religious creed and legal institution. But for whatever reason, the will of the gods gave way to the Justice of God and a new chapter in human history was begun. Once it was postulated that Justice was an attribute of the heavenly powers, the business of establishing it on earth became a task to which men could address themselves without constraint or misgiving.

XI

CURSES, BLESSINGS, OATHS

In view of the explicit faith evinced by nearly all communities in the past in the reality of divine intervention in worldly affairs, it is not surprising to find that the utterances by which the supernatural powers were invoked should come to be regarded as forces of the gravest import requiring recognition and regulation by law. Moreover, the law itself came to depend in large measure on the powerful influence which these utterances exerted on men's minds.

As we have already seen, sympathetic magic is used among primitive peoples for the purpose of bringing advantages to friends and disaster to enemies. In its earliest form the curse represents the essential mechanism for setting in motion the magical powers on which so much reliance is placed. In primitive codes of law almost every command is accompanied by a curse for those who obey it not. But before cursing had become articulate, the more rudimentary device was adopted of putting maimed and tortured effigies in the graves or other habitations of those whom it was desired to injure. Curse tablets deposited in tombs and sanctuaries have come to light in thousands.[1]

On its religious side the curse developed into the vow and the prayer, on its social side into the ordin-

[1] Jane Ellen Harrison, *Prolegomena to the Study of Greek Religion* (3rd ed., 1922), p. 138 *et seq.*

ance and ultimately into regular law. Early legal codes usually embody the curse as an indispensable sanction to enforce their commands. The law seldom calls upon the subject to do this or that; the formula more frequently declares "cursed be he who does this or does not do that".

An example is to be found in the inscription known as the Dirae of Teos, which runs as follows:[1]

> Whosoever maketh baneful drugs against the Teans, whether against individuals or the whole people:
> May he perish, both he and his offspring.
> Whosoever hinders corn from being brought into the land of the Teans . . . and whosoever drives out what has been brought in:
> May he perish, both he and his offspring.

And so on, clause after clause, comes the refrain of cursing. Finally there is the curse on the magistrate who fails to curse:

> Whosoever of them that hold office doth not make this cursing . . . let him be bound by an over-curse, and whoever either breaks the stelae on which the cursing is written, or cuts out the letters or makes them illegible:
> May he perish, both he and his offspring.

Many instances occur in Deuteronomy, two whole chapters of which (xxvii and xxviii) consist almost entirely of blessings for obedience to the law and

---

[1] *Ibid.* pp. 142-3.

curses for disobedience. Thus:

> Ch. xxvii. 17. Cursed be he that removeth his
> neighbour's landmark.[1]
> 20. Cursed be he that lieth with his father's wife.
> 24. Cursed be he that smiteth his neighbour
> secretly.

In some cases the curses are left in a generalised
form; in others the exact nature of the disaster is
specified in a more or less detailed manner. The
Twelve Tables also utilise the sanction of the curse
by enacting that if a patron defrauds a client, he
shall be accursed.[2]

The ancient Egyptians were throughout their
entire history addicted to the use of supernatural
formulae which they firmly believed could effect
results beyond the power of ordinary mortals. They
were convinced that every word spoken in specified
circumstances must produce some effect, either good
or bad. Thus curses were bound to bring harm.[3]

Amenhetep in the xviiith dynasty grandly curses
all those who transgress the laws. The curse appears
to be regarded as sufficient punishment in itself, for
no other penalty is actually mentioned. A similar
absence of any physical punishment is found in the
deposition of a nomarch, or head of a local government, dating from the time of the Middle Kingdom.

[1] In ancient Babylon boundary stones were secured by a curse
which would fall on those who removed them. L. T. Hobhouse, *Morals
in Evolution* (1906), i, p. 333.

[2] *Patronus si clienti fraudem faxit sacer esto.* Cf. J. Muirhead,
Historical Introduction to the Private Law of Rome (2nd ed.), p. 101.
Tab. VIII, 21, tr. by J. Wigmore from the restored text in C. G. Bruns,
Fons juris Romani Antiqui (7th ed., 1909); ed. Otto Gradennitz follow-
ing Mommsen. Cf. Tab. VIII, 1: "Whoever shall chant an evil spell . . ."
A. Kocourek and J. H. Wigmore: *Evolution of Law*, i. p. 467.

[3] E. A. Wallis Budge, *The Book of the Dead*, The Chapters of Coming Forth by Day (ed. 1898). Introd. pp. xclvii-iii.

The nomarch had harboured in the temple enemies of the king, probably agents of a rival dynasty. The punishment imposed upon him for this grave offence is that he is deposed and no longer permitted to share in the endowments; and his documents are to be destroyed in the temple and the government office. Curses are pronounced on any ruler who may forgive him, and no subordinate may plead for him under pain of confiscation. Yet no physical penalty is inflicted on his life or estate.[1]

A more elaborate example of the use of cursing as an instrument of law-enforcement in ancient Egypt is to be seen in the case of the founding of the little temple of Dêr-el-Medineh dedicated to Amon Ra in Thebes. When the king visited the new sanctuary a decree was issued by the governor, the superintendent of the house of silver, and certain other high state officials. It was couched in the following terms:

"Hear the decree, issued at the establishment of the temple of Kak, belonging to the hereditary prince . . . that his temple of Kak, with the slaves belonging thereto both male and female, should endure eternally from son to son, from heir to heir, and that no one should ever transgress this decree, for so long as this temple stands upon the earth, it is sacred to Amon Ra, king of the gods, who is king eternally and the protector of the dead.

"If . . . my successor shall find that the temple of Kak has fallen into decay, and that certain belongings thereto have been taken away from the slaves who raise the corn for my endowment—if he then uphold all the laws and ordinances of Pharaoh, then shall his bodily life be satisfied.

[1] W. M. Flinders Petrie, *Social Life in Ancient Egypt*, p. 83.

"But those who transgress them and render no account thereof, upon them shall fall the destruction of Amon, the Lord of Thebes. He will deliver them up to the wrath of the king on the day of his anger, his snake diadem shall spit fire on the crown of their head destroying their sons. It shall eat their body, and they shall become like the snake Apophis (the enemy of the Sun-god) on the New Year's Day. They shall be drowned in the ocean, which shall conceal their bodies; they shall not receive the funeral services of the just, they shall not eat the food of the God Querte, they shall not cool themselves on the water. . . . Their sons shall not succeed them, their wives shall be used shamefully even in their sight. Honourable men shall not enter their houses. . . . They shall not hear the voice of the king when he rejoices. They shall be slain on the day of destruction. . . ."

There is a good deal more in the same vein, followed by a mouth-watering account of the blessings which shall be bestowed upon those who take care to protect the temple of Kak in the prescribed manner.[1]

The immense importance attached to the imprecation as an instrument of evil is shown by the fact that early law not only uses the curse as its most potent sanction, but also makes unauthorised cursing itself a serious offence. The code of Hammurabi enacts that if a man weave a spell and put a ban upon a man, and has not justified himself, he that wove the spell upon him shall be put to death. Exodus xxi, 17 declares that he that curseth his father, or his mother, shall surely be put to death. The Fundamental Laws

[1] Adolf Erman, *Life in Ancient Egypt*, pp. 148-9. The decree has come down to us from an abstract of later date.

of China contained in the *Ta Tsing Leu Lee* imposed heavy penalties on "magicians, who raise evil spirits by means of magical books and dire imprecations"; and anyone who employs magical writings and imprecations to occasion the death of another is to be punished as for murder.[1] Many other instances could be given.

Closely related to the curse is the oath. For this too is an imprecation to heaven. But whereas the curse calls upon the supernatural powers to bring disaster to an enemy or wrongdoer, the oath brings down divine wrath on the speaker himself if he utter falsehood. The oath is also connected with the ordeal, which we have already seen to be a direct appeal to supernatural guidance in the affairs of men. Proof of innocence by oath, where the oath is conclusive, as in the case of the medieval compurgation, is the same thing in a milder form.[2]

The oath has served a double purpose in human society. It has been employed in the first place as a means of compelling people to tell the truth, and in the second place as a method of making them fulfil their solemn undertakings. The oath, the vow, the solemn promise have played a conspicuous part in instilling mankind with the qualities of truthfulness and reliability.

The practice of supporting a promise with an oath is probably as old as the existence of a belief in God or in many gods. It appears to have been utilised from the earliest times to ratify and ensure the fulfilment of any special undertaking, by importing into

---

[1] Sir G. Staunton, *Ta Tsing Leu Lee, being the Fundamental Laws of China* (London, 1810), sections clxii and cclxxix, pp. 175, 310.
[2] Sir F. Pollock, *First Book of Jurisprudence* (5th ed.), p. 44.

the transaction the fear of divine wrath for wilful failure to perform the obligation entered upon. The oath was used as a means of binding the conscience by the Medes and Persians, by the Egyptians and Assyrians, by the ancient Greeks and Romans.[1]

Both in Greece and in Rome the oath was regarded as an institution which upheld the civil law; it was also an indispensable feature of the religious (*fas*) law. The *Iliad* depicts the procedure for making a covenant. The pact was sealed with oaths and ended with the imprecation: "Whosoever shall violate this oath, may their brains and their children's brains be dispersed on the ground like this wine".[2]

In the *Oedipus* of Sophocles there is a passage in which Creon passionately denies participation in a plot to injure the king, of which he has been accused, in terms that must have seemed conclusive to a Greek audience:[3]

> *Creon:*
>> Ye Gods, if such a thing
>> Hath once been in my thoughts, may I no more
>> See any health on earth, but, festered o'er
>> With curses, die!—Have done. There is mine oath.
>
> *Leader of the Chorus:*
>> Reject not one who never failed his troth
>> Of old and now is strong in his great oath.

A violation of an oath was an offence against the gods, who would wreak their vengeance on the transgressor. The revenge of all the gods might be expected, even though the oath was addressed to but a single god.

---

[1] *Encyclopaedia of the Laws of England* (2nd ed.), vol. x, p. 102, art. "Oaths (Origin of)".

[2] *Iliad*, iii, 268.

[3] Sophocles, *Oedipus*, tr. Gilbert Murray (640-55).

In the Roman world, wrote Cicero, "there is nothing our ancestors took greater care of than that
the tie of an oath should always be held as most
sacred and inviolable. This appears plainly from the
Twelve Tables; it appears from those laws which are
called sacred (*sacratae*); it appears from the strict
observance of treaties, by which we are obliged to
keep faith even with enemies; and lastly, it appears
from the punishments and penalties which have been
inflicted by the Censors, who in nothing have been
more severe than in punishing those who had transgressed their oaths." [1]

The Old Testament contains numerous instances
of oaths being used to support covenants between
man and man or between man and God. One of the
most significant is that related in Genesis xv, for this
shows the elaborate sacrificial rites which usually
accompanied the oath in primitive times in order to
impart greater solemnity. Genesis relates that God
made certain promises to Abraham, who thereupon
asked for some assurance that these would come to
pass. God then commanded Abraham in the following terms:

9. Take me an heifer of three years old, and a
she-goat of three years old, and a ram of three
years old, and a turtle-dove, and a young pigeon.
10. And he took unto him all these, and divided
them in the midst, and laid each piece one
against another; but the birds divided he not. . . .
12. And when the sun was going down, a deep
sleep fell upon Abram; and, lo, an horror of
great darkness fell upon him. . . .

[1] *De Officiis*, vol. iii, ch. xxxi.

17. And it came to pass, that, when the sun went down, and it was dark, behold a smoking furnace, and a burning lamp that passed between those pieces.

18. In that same day the Lord made a covenant with Abram, saying. . . .

The horror of darkness is a premonition of God, who in the darkness is supposed to pass between the pieces of the slaughtered animals in the likeness of a smoking furnace and a flaming torch. In doing this, Sir James Frazer remarks, the deity was only complying with the legal formalities required by ancient Hebrew law at the ratification of a covenant. We know from Jeremiah that it was the custom of contracting parties to cut a calf in two and to pass between the pieces. That this was the regular form observed on such occasions is indicated by the fact that the Hebrew phrase for making a covenant is literally to "cut a covenant". The Greeks used similar phrases when they spoke of cutting oaths in the sense of swearing them, and of cutting a treaty instead of making one. These expressions derive from the custom of sacrificing victims and cutting them in pieces as a mode of adding solemnity to an oath or treaty.

A huge machinery of cruelty, blood-spilling, and superstition has thus everywhere been employed to impart seriousness to vows and promises on such occasions.[1] The Baralong of South Africa, when making a covenant, force themselves through a hole in the stomach of a slaughtered animal. The half skeletons of a boy and a girl found at Gezer in

[1] Sir J. G. Frazer, *Folklore in the Old Testament*, i, p. 392 *et seq.*

Palestine appear to be relics of the bodies of children sacrificed at the conclusion of a covenant. The Wachaga of East Africa indulged in a similar practice of cutting a boy and a girl in two in order to ratify an agreement.[1]

An example of the simple promissory oath between man and man is contained in Genesis xxi when Abimelech says to Abraham, "Now therefore swear unto me here by God that thou wilt not deal falsely with me, nor with my son, nor with my son's son: but according to the kindness that I have done unto thee, thou shalt do unto me, and to the land wherein thou hast sojourned. And Abraham said, I will swear it".[2]

Promissory oaths have survived up to the present time. The coronation oath taken by the King on his accession, the oath of allegiance taken by Privy Councillors, the judicial oath and many other vows of a promissory character are firmly established practices in modern English life which are by no means regarded as empty formalities or as mere relics of a bygone age. Most other Western countries have similar institutions. The first step in the critical conflict between the Irish Free State and Great Britain which arose in 1932 was the abrogation of the oath of allegiance required to be taken by members of the Free State legislature under the agreement made between the two countries in 1923 and regarded by at least one of them as an essential feature of the settlement.

During the 17th and 18th centuries the taking of solemn promissory oaths by persons holding minor offices was carried to absurd lengths in England.

[1] *Ibid.* pp. 409-25.   [2] Cf. Numbers xxx, 2.

An ale-taster, the forerunner of our present-day sanitary inspector, was called upon to swear "that you shall well and truly execute the office of ale-taster within this leet. You shall see that all victuals, bread and beer put to sale within this leet be sweet and wholesome." Even a worsted weaver and a Kidderminster weaver were required to swear they would discharge faithfully the duties of their offices.[1]

The second great function of the oath has been to force people to tell the truth by making them fearful of the consequences of speaking falsely. As far as we can go back in recorded history, the imprecation to supernatural powers to bring disaster on the head of him who invokes them if he bear false witness has been considered the most efficacious method of eliciting the truth. The code of Hammurabi manifests a remarkable degree of confidence in the power of the oath to secure truthful testimony.[2]

The business of making mankind even moderately truthful has been a matter of extreme difficulty. Once again we find a vast background of animal sacrifice and human slaughter, of cruelty and of superstition, behind the simple belief in truth-telling which seems so obvious to-day. The solemn oath, observes Frazer, has been supported by "purifications", bisections, and mutilations of every kind, and men have fortified their word by orgies of "solemnity".[3] We know from Demosthenes that in the Areopagus, where proceedings for murder were taken, the party who

---

[1] Cf. *The Book of Oaths Faithfully collected from Authentic Books of Record* (1689).
[2] Johns, *Relations between the Laws of Babylonia*, etc. (1914), p. 6.
[3] Sir J. G. Frazer, *op. cit.* i, pp. 392-409.

charged another with a capital offence had to make
the oath with imprecations upon himself, his family
and his house. While doing so he had to stand upon
the entrails of a boar and a ram and a bull, which
were required to have been immolated by prescribed
persons on appointed days.[1] Even then, declared
Demosthenes, "the party who has sworn such an
oath is not believed, but, in case he should be convicted of untruth, he will carry away the curse of
perjury upon his children and his family, and that is
all he will get by it".

The purgatorial oath of innocence, or compurgation, persisted throughout the Middle Ages, and
was embodied in the English criminal law until the
14th century.[2] A fatal blow was struck at its authority
by the Assize of Clarendon in 1166, which provided
that suspected persons who had proved their innocence by this method should objure the realm. The
regular use of the jury for the purpose of discovering
and presenting to the king's officers individuals suspected of serious crime dates from the same Assize.[3]

The canonical compurgation, or wager of law as
it was called, was the procedure whereby the defendant, when denying under oath the allegation made
against him, appeared in Court surrounded by a
number of companions who swore in a similar sense,

---

[1] *Oration against Aristocrates*, from *The Orations of Demosthenes*,
tr. C. R. Kennedy, pp. 189-90.

[2] A similar practice was observed by the ancient Israelites, who derived their doctrine from Exodus xxii, 11, wherein it is declared that
if a man deliver an animal to his neighbour to keep (presumably by
way of sale or exchange) and the beast die, or was injured or driven
away secretly, "Then shall an oath of the Lord be between them both,
that he hath not put his hand unto his neighbour's goods; and the
owner of it shall accept thereof, and he shall not make it good".

[3] W. S. Holdsworth, *A History of English Law*, i, pp. 322-4.

had to be undertaken before society arrived at the point where the secular power has the authority and the ability to legislate freely to meet the needs of the community—a position which has been reached, broadly speaking, in all civilised countries of the modern world.

I have already drawn attention to the tendency towards stagnation usually produced by the replacement of the spoken word and the oral tradition by the written code.[1] It is worth noticing in this connection that the early codes were recorded on material of the hardest and most durable character. Thus, Hammurabi inscribed his laws on diorite, the Ten Commandments and the Mosaic laws were written on tables [2] of stone, and the Decemviral code was engraved on tables of wood and brass. It is obvious that the use of materials of this unmalleable character made partial alteration impossible without rewriting the entire code, while the durability of the medium must have emphasised in people's minds the static nature of the law.

The Greeks appear to have been the first people to introduce flexibility into their legal order after it had been reduced to writing. At first the kings decided particular causes with the aid of divine inspiration. Then the customary course of decision became a tradition possessed by an oligarchy. The third stage was reached when popular demand for publication resulted in a body of recorded decisions. Early Greek society accepted the juridical and governmental order without question. "Men were born, and lived, and died, under old customary laws,

---

[1] *Ante*, pp. 57–73.
[2] Exodus xxiv, 12; xxxi, 18; xxxii, 15-16.

whose origin no man knew. It was dimly felt that they were divine: it was certainly recognised that they were rigid and fundamental. Custom was Lord of all things, as Pindar sang and Herodotus repeated after him." [1]

Gradually a change began to set in. At first the enactments were no more than declaratory of the existing law. But it was easy to slip from the promulgation of existing customs to the introduction of changes, which were announced as though they were established customs. This led in time to the conscious devising of new rules by legislative process. It is highly significant that the law-making element crept in by the device of announcing changes "as if" they were provisions of the existing law. In the 5th and 4th centuries B.C. the law of Athens had become a codified tradition eked out by legislation. [2]

Despite the fact that in this way the legislative element had definitely crept in as an operative process, the age-long feeling of the people that law was of divine origin and immutable character remained the dominant conviction of the time. When Creon asks Antigone in the drama of Sophocles why she dares to disobey what he calls "these laws"—actually his own decrees—she answers, "It was not Zeus who proclaimed these, nor Dikē, fellow-lodger with the gods below, who set these 'laws' among men, nor did I think thy proclamations have so much force that, being a man, thou couldst overrun the gods' unwritten and unshaken customs". [3] Medea, in the great

---

[1] Ernest Barker, *The Political Thought of Plato and Aristotle*, p. 28.
[2] Roscoe Pound, *An Introduction to the Philosophy of Law*, p. 21.
[3] *Antigone*, pp. 450-51.

tragedy of Euripides which goes by her name, demands of Jason in anger and despair:[1]

> Is sworn faith so low
> And weak a thing. I understand it not.
> Are the old gods dead? Are the old laws forgot,
> And new laws made?

In a passage which comes a little later [2] Jason tries to persuade her that far from being wronged she has on the contrary much to be grateful for by reason of the very immutability of the law:

> . . . A good Greek land hath been
> Thy lasting home, not barbary. Thou hast seen
> Our ordered life, and justice, and the long
> Still grasp of law not changing with the strong
> Man's pleasure.

The law of ancient Rome is, of course, distinguished from that of all preceding societies by reason of the very fact that it underwent a continuous process of improvement and expansion. But even among the Romans the law was for a long period highly immobile. It originated with them, as with other peoples, in customs which were either religious in character or sanctified ancestral tradition. The Twelve Tables held absolute sway in their original form for two hundred and fifty years, during which time there was no legislation on any matter that touched their provisions; and the Tables retained their authority for nearly a thousand years.[3] The Roman people showed, indeed, a tendency to ascribe

---

[1] *The Medea*, tr. by Gilbert Murray, p. 28 (American ed.).
[2] *Ibid*. p. 30.
[3] For nearly two centuries after the Twelve Tables there was no legislation at all in the field of private law. Most of the laws passed in that period were of a political or constitutional character. W. W. Buckland, *The Main Institutions of Roman Private Law* (1931), p. 3.

all ancient rules to the enactments of former kings, and the Twelve Tables was, of course, a statutory code. This did not affect for a long time the immobility of the legal system, but tended rather to emphasise its static nature. Apart from the Tables, statute was not a very fruitful source of law during the republic.[1] Legislation, although possible, was not a normal activity in republican times.

The later Roman jurisprudence evolved the clear and emphatic doctrine that law was that which was approved or ratified by the Roman people, or those upon whom they conferred the authority to make law[2] Universal consent is the voice of nature, declared Cicero,[3] in that famous phrase in which he was only voicing the tradition both of Rome and the barbarians that law issued from the people and not from the prince, although the latter could issue capitularies which might become law through the consent of the people[4] But whether the source of authority lay in prince or in people, the process of legislation became at any rate possible when once the power of deliberately making law had become recognised as a normal and necessary function of society. The great difference, said Maine, between the Roman Empire and all other sovereignties of the ancient world lay in its legislative activity, through the edicts of the Praetor and the constitutions of the Emperors. It repealed the customs of many races and replaced them with others. Among certain peoples the results

[1] H. F. Jolowicz, *Historical Introduction to the Study of Roman Law*, pp. 83-4, 99.
[2] R. W. and A. J. Carlyle, *A History of Medieval Political Theory in the West*, v, p. 82.
[3] *Omnium consensus naturae vox est*, Tusc. i, 13, § 35.
[4] Bede Jarrett, *Social Theories of the Middle Ages*, p. 19.

of the Roman legislation became inextricably mixed with the native law. Elsewhere, it introduced the habit of legislation.[1]

There was, however, but little legislation in the modern sense during the Middle Ages, either in the Holy Roman Empire or elsewhere. Such enactments as were passed were for the most part designed to affirm existing rules and practices or to remedy abuses in administration. There was no sovereign whose commands were regarded as law, and the general conception was that law embodied the customs and principles of the community.[2] The efforts of Charlemagne and other rulers were powerless so far as systematic legislation was concerned; their achievements were confined to the modification of particular institutions.[3] Even when political authority began to be consolidated in the 12th and 13th centuries we find writers on law explaining that they had to deal mainly with customs and not with rules established by express legislation or embodied in a code.[4]

An essential characteristic of the feudal state as it existed throughout Western Europe and in England after the Norman Conquest was the absence of law-making either by the central assembly or by any of

[1] H. S. Maine, *Early History of Institutions*, p. 21.
[2] Charles Grove Haines, *The Revival of Natural Law Concepts*, pp. 15-16.
[3] The capitularies of Charlemagne and the other Carlovingian kings were of two classes: provisional and absolute. The former were issued to deal with an emergency. The latter comprised only those which confirmed at a general assembly of the people. According to some authorities, the latter class of capitularies alone acquired the name or force of laws of the Empire. George Spence, *An Inquiry into the Origin of the Laws and Political Institutions of Modern Europe* (London, 1826), p. 254.
[4] Sir Paul Vinogradoff, *Customary Law* in *The Legacy of the Middle Ages*, pp. 287-8.

the other organs of government. The law was not made; it consisted of a body of custom which was declared from time to time.[1] The declarations of existing custom which thus constituted the juridical system were records rather than enactments. It was characteristic of all feudal law that it was the law of a Court, and the idea of "making" law was wholly alien to prevailing modes of thought.[2]

The law administered either by way of self-help or by the early Courts was thus virtually all customary law. In the earlier medieval period the presiding judge of an English Court left the question of the custom to be applied to the doomsmen, who comprised either the whole body of suitors of the Court or their chosen representatives.[2] The doomsman who performed this duty can be traced all over Europe. There were *échevins* in France, *Schöffen* in Germany, *laghmen* and *lögsögumathr* in Scandinavia, *asegas* in Frisia[4] Other peoples both in Europe and in the East made use of Elders whose wisdom and learning fitted them, not to discover new principles, but to enunciate and apply existing habits and customs.

What those existing usages were would depend on circumstances. When Bracton asserted that England was governed by unwritten law and custom, and Beaumanoir made a similar claim for France; when Gratian opened his great *Decretum* of the canon law with the statement that mankind is ruled by natural law and by custom, they were not suggesting that the customs of the community, and hence its law, were

[1] C. H. McIlwain, *The High Court of Parliament* (U.S.A. ed.), p. vii.
[2] *Ibid.* p. 46; E. Jenks: *Law and Politics in the Middle Ages*, p. 61.
[3] Sir Paul Vinogradoff, *op. cit.* p. 289.
[4] C. K. Allen, *Law in the Making*, p. 85.

mechanical or automatic practices which remained fixed for all time. Custom was determined by environment, by the moral ideas of a community and the conditions under which the people lived. It was subject to change and improvement, and hence the law was not conceived as something immutable or immobile. The basic principle was that the law embodied, not the conscious and deliberate purposes of a legislative authority, but the habits and usages of the community according to the circumstances of time and place.[1]

The idea of an absolute monarch as the source of law and as superior to the law was wholly alien to medieval civilisation. Bracton's remark that the king is under God and the law epitomised the tradition of all Europe during the Middle Ages. In so far as the law did not consist of the custom of the community, it was held to reflect the will, or to be an express command, of the people.[2] According to the system of feudal jurisprudence, the emperor or king had clear authority to participate in the legislative process, but he did not occupy an isolated position nor possess arbitrary or unlimited power. The ruler acted with the advice and consent of the chief leaders, temporal and spiritual, and behind them loomed more or less vaguely the mass of the people, whose customs lent supreme ultimate sanction to the whole fabric of the law.[3] As late as the 15th century Sir John Fortescue wrote that "a king governing politickly cannot change his laws without the assent of the chief men of his kingdom".[4]

[1] Carlyle, *op. cit.* vol. v, ch. v; J. Sidgwick, *The Elements of Politics* (2nd ed.), pp. 652-3.   [2] *Ibid.* v, p. 83.   [3] *Ibid.* pp. 63, 83.
[4] *De Natura legis Naturae*, ch. xxvi, *Works* (Clermont ed.), i, p. 216.

During the Middle Ages the power of the king was apparently absolute in that he was not answerable to an elected assembly or any other organ of government. But in theory and in practice the royal authority was absolute only in a limited sense, and even then it was not suffered to be arbitrary. The royal will acquired the force of law only if it were expressed for certain purposes and in a particular manner. The ruler, it was said, was bound by the law of God and the law of nature; and the latter had sometimes an awkward habit of resembling the customary common law of the land.[1]

These checks were not mere self-denying ordinances imposed on the king by public sentiment. They were practical safeguards of a substantial character against tyranny. In some cases an explicit ratification was required: in France, for example, the royal ordinances had to be registered by the Parlement.[2] Everywhere it was recognised that the rights possessed by the king as overlord did not confer upon him the ownership of his subjects' property. Hence he could not legally dispose of his vassals' lands and goods. If he attempted to do so the people were strictly within their lawful rights in defying his authority and renouncing their allegiance.[3] We may summarise the position broadly by saying that the king held absolute, but not arbitrary, authority within a carefully defined sphere; and that no governing individual or organ possessed more than limited powers.[4]

---

[1] C. H. McIlwain, *The Growth of Political Thought in the West* (1932), pp. 364-5.
[2] *Ibid.* p. 366.   [3] *Ibid.* p. 368.
[4] J. Sidgwick, *The Elements of Politics* (2nd ed.), pp. 652-3.

In the 12th and 13th centuries a change of profound importance commenced almost imperceptibly to take place. The notion that the essential foundations of law reside in custom began to give way before the conception of law as the purposeful creation of a conscious legislative will.[1] At the same time the assumption that the customs of the community were the ultimate source of authority began to be challenged, faintly at first, by the statement that it was the prince who had the power to legislate and that it was he therefore who must be regarded as the source of law.[2] Thus, at the very time when the idea of sovereignty was making its first appearance in the modern world, the early whispering could be heard of the great discussion concerning the possession of the sovereign power which was eventually to sweep over Europe like a storm and shake Christendom to its very foundations.

The distant murmur of voices came from Bologna, where the civil lawyers had commenced the revived study of the Roman law amid a contagious ferment of intellectual excitement. According to the explicit statement placed in the forefront of Justinian's *Institutes*, the Roman people, who admittedly possessed at one time an unlimited power of making law, had transferred their authority to the emperor, who thus became absolute monarch.[3] This conception, epitomised in the maxim *Quod principi placuit legis vigorem habet*, was utterly remote from the principles and the spirit of feudal jurisprudence.

One of the principles which had to be established before the doctrine of sovereignty could make sub-

[1] Carlyle, *op. cit.* v, pp. 463-4.   [2] *Ibid.* p. 51.
[3] *Institutes*, Book I, 2, vi.

stantial headway was the conception of a nation attached to a particular territory. To enable this to be done it was necessary to eliminate the remaining traces of personal law and the ideas on which it was based.

During the Dark Ages the laws of the various peoples were applicable not to territorial communities but to tribes or groups supposed to belong to the same racial stock. The Lex Salica, for example, which dates probably from the 5th or 6th century A.D., was not the law of a district but of a so-called race. The Swabian, wherever he might be, lived under Alamannic Law. Agobard, bishop of Lyons, remarked that if five men were walking or sitting together each might own a different law.[1]

In the Njals saga we are told how, on a notable occasion, "both sides went to the Hill of Laws, and each, the Christian men as well as the heathen, took witness, and declared themselves out of the other's laws, and then there was such an uproar on the Hill of Laws that no man could hear the other's voice".[2] At the present time among Muhammadans a man's law is normally personal and hereditary. He is a Hanafi or a Malaba because his ancestors were either the one or the other, and on a change of domicile he normally takes his ancestral law with him.[3]

This distinction between men based on the differences in their laws continued for many centuries. By the 9th century A.D. it had become an essential characteristic of social organisation. Under Charle-

[1] Pollock and Maitland, *A History of English Law before the Time of Edward I* (2nd ed.), i, p. 13.
[2] *The Story of Burnt Njal*, tr. Sir G. W. Dasent, ch. 101.
[3] S. Vesey Fitzgerald, *Muhammadan Law*, p. 18.

magne the Romans were governed by Roman law, no matter where they lived, the Franks by the Salic or Ripuarian law, the Burgundians by the Burgundian law, the Lombards by Lombard law, the Saxons by Saxon law.[1] Charlemagne greatly extended the system by introducing it into Italy and other parts of the empire.[2]

Over and above this diversity there were certain unities. Thus the canonical legislation of the Church was the same for all Christendom. The capitularies of Charlemagne were sometimes addressed to all the subjects of his empire. Hence in religious and political affairs a measure of unity prevailed, while in civil and criminal matters each homogeneous group had its separate laws.[3]

Under this system the administration of the different codes had to be kept entirely separate. The records of a judicial proceeding of A.D. 918 show that in Languedoc the Roman, Gothic, and Salic laws were applied by separate judges in separate Courts.[4]

If a man "lived" Swabian law (*legem vivere*), he had the right to be tried by the land of his birth. But this "land", *terra nativitatis suae*, had no necessary relation to the place where he was born. It was the residence of his family in the eye of the law. German families "professed" the law of their original land sometimes for centuries after they had left it. Thus, in the middle of the 13th century Eike of Repgow was able to enumerate all the families who were living Swabian law in Saxony. There were included in the

---

[1] F. Guizot, *Histoire de la Civilisation en France*, 25 Leçon.
[2] H. Hallam, *The State of Europe during the Middle Ages* (London, 1853), i, p. 294.
[3] Guizot, *op. cit.*
[4] Hallam, *op. cit.* i, p. 151 n.

list the Brunswickers who had migrated from Swabia three hundred years previously.[1]

By the 11th century the system of personal jurisdictions had passed its zenith. But though on the decline, personal law persisted to some extent throughout the Middle Ages. Charters embodying the system were issued in the 12th century;[2] and there were cases of persons professing to live by Lombard law very late in the medieval epoch—the last was at Bergamo in 1388.[3]

Feudalism was fundamentally incompatible with personal law. The creation of privileges and customs, the emergence of different degrees of freedom and of different kinds of law for different types of property, the growth of local statutes in the rising cities, the rationalising influence of the Roman law, the replacement of kinship grouping by class divisions—these were the several elements in the feudal era which led to the gradual substitution of territorial law for personal jurisdiction. It was a process of melting-down, of assimilation, rather than of formal enactment. Hence we find that in the medieval empire—as in the British Empire to-day—the king's Court administered different kinds of law in his various territories. In Saxony, the royal Court would be composed mainly of Saxon nobles, and the judgments determined according to Saxon principles. When the king came into Swabia the Court would be mainly Swabian, in Bavaria mainly Bavarian, and so forth.

The system of personal law merely illustrates the

[1] H. A. L. Fisher, *The Medieval Empire*, i, pp. 171-5.
[2] "*Qui professus sum lege Longobardica (aut) lege Salica (aut) lege Alemannorum vivere*", Hallam, *op. cit.* i, p. 151 n.
[3] *Ibid.* p. 294.

well-established generalisation that the basis of early society was personal rather than territorial. To Maine belongs the credit for having emphasised the immense importance of the fact that in more primitive times the relations between man and man could be summed up in the term kinship, with its strong emotional basis in instinct.[1] Early society, he pointed out, commenced with the family. The aggregation of families formed the Gens or House; the aggregation of Houses made the tribe; and from a collection of tribes there was constituted the Commonwealth. The starting-point of the history of political ideas is the assumption that kinship in blood is the only possible ground for community of political functions. The idea that a number of persons should exercise rights in common simply because they happened to live in the same place was "utterly strange and monstrous to primitive antiquity".[2] It was only when the legal fiction that kinship could be extended to a stranger had been invented, and family relations extended artificially by this device, that persons of alien descent became amalgamated with the original brotherhood —made "akin" to the group. The familial origin of society is revealed by the use of such words as mother-country, fatherland, brothers-in-arms.[3]

[1] Maine, *Early History of Institutions*, p. 228. Maine's statement that there was a fundamental assumption that all men not united by blood were either enemies or slaves is highly doubtful; but it need not be examined here, since the accuracy of his generalisation concerning the origin of the State does not depend upon it. The same applies to his doctrine concerning the patriarchal theory of society.

[2] Maine, *Ancient Law*, ch. v.

[3] *Early History of Institutions*, Lecture III. According to Professor Robert H. Lowie, the territorial tie exists in certain primitive societies to some extent side by side with the tie of kinship. In general, however, he supports Maine's statement. *The Origin of the State*, ch. iv.

Nationality is the modern form of kinship; and nationality is the creature of sovereignty, the special form of power whose evolution is here being traced. The revival by the Nazis in Germany of a pseudo-racial basis of society is a reversion to the doctrines, not of the Middle Ages, but of the Dark Ages.

In the Middle Ages, as I have shown, considerable traces persisted of the complicated network of family jurisdictions and personal laws which had survived from an era when the foundations of society were more or less definitely laid in kinship—a condition which had passed away long before the feudal régime. This personal basis had to be completely swept away before nationality and sovereignty could gain a foothold. For both of these forces, as they have appeared in the modern world, rely essentially on territorial principles.

The Church played an important part in the evolution of sovereignty. For centuries the canon law had been maintained as a separate body of law. It was for long a heterogeneous collection of decrees issued by General Councils of the Church, papal decisions and the determinations of local assemblies of bishops. The authentic part gradually became indistinguishable from the legendary or forged portions. The whole thing was muddled and unsystematic in the extreme. In the 12th century Gratian made his famous redaction, which constituted an immense advance on all previous efforts; and this marked a new chapter in the history of the canon law.[1] Thereafter in the Western world the pope slowly acquired a

---

[1] Bede Jarrett, *Social Theories of the Middle Ages*, pp. 6-7.

power of declaring law which in course of time became a power of making law.[1]

The pope was not, however, content with the
power to ordain the law of the Church. He claimed
the right also, on behalf of the spiritual power, to
exercise ultimate control over the temporal authority
in all secular matters. Thus, not only law-making but
the whole business of government, every nook and
cranny of public affairs, were alleged to be potentially
subject in the last resort to the paramount authority
of the Church.

In former times priest and king were one. Now
they had become separate; and a bitter conflict arose
as to whether prince or prelate was supreme. Out
of that conflict and the unforeseen sequel which
followed, sovereignty was born.

A theory of uncontrolled secular authority was
clearly needed to meet the papal claims if they were
to be resisted; some power had to be called into play
to overthrow them if they were to be defeated. The
most obvious seat of an alternative sovereignty was
the monarchy, and this coincided with the new
doctrines which the Roman lawyers were enunci-
ating at Bologna and elsewhere. Practical expediency
pointed in the same direction, for the Crown was the
only authority whose strength could for a moment
be pitted against the papal power. Accordingly, the
royal power was exalted against that of the pope, and
from the 14th to the 16th centuries the unlimited
jurisdiction of the king was asserted with increasing
emphasis and conviction.[2] That this would prove

[1] F. W. Maitland, *Canon Law* in *Collected Papers*, iii, p. 66.
[2] J. N. Figgis, *The Divine Right of Kings*, pp. 91-2. In 1460-61
Sir John Fortescue, a former Lord Chief Justice, declared that although

destructive of popular rights "which nobody claimed and nobody exercised" [1] was not realised. Monarchy was being defended and exalted not for its own sake, but only as an organ of resistance to the papal claims. So men wrote and spoke with an easy mind of the appointment of kings by God and the duty of absolute obedience to their command which that necessitated, a doctrine easily proved by Holy Scripture.

By the close of the 16th century events had done much to strengthen the monarchy and to generate notions of its divine character. The theory of the unlimited jurisdiction of the Crown had been formulated and the obligation not to resist the royal will in any circumstances elaborated with profuse learning.[2]

This theory was not subjected to the test of popular criticism until the following century. A mature and carefully reasoned doctrine of popular control over the king by the people had been worked out two hundred and fifty years earlier by Marsiglio of Padua (1270–1343); and William of Ockham, his famous contemporary, had also developed ideas of a similar character. Marsiglio's great book *Defensor Pacis* is one of the most daring works ever committed to writing by a political philosopher, having regard to the conditions of the time.[3] The conception of popular sovereignty which it expresses entirely outruns the confines of the Middle Ages.

These medieval forerunners of democracy exerted

the king could not change the law without the consent of the chief men of his kingdom, he nevertheless "when laws are deficient can supply their place" (*De Natura legis Naturae*, ch. xxvi, *Works* (Clermont ed.) i, p. 216).

[1] Figgis, *op. cit.* p. 93.   [2] *Ibid.* p. 105.

[3] R. L. Poole, *Illustrations of the History of Medieval Thought*, pp. 267-77; M. Creighton, *A History of the Papacy* (1897), i, pp. 42-46.

little or no influence either on their own generation
or on those which succeeded it. They were too far
in advance of their age; and the march of practical
events was not such as to conduce to their theories
receiving either attention or recognition. For as yet
there was no dispute between Crown and Parliament.
The only authorities who claimed unlimited obedience were the king and the pope. No alternative to
these two extremes of absolute obedience to the prince
or absolute obedience to the Church seemed possible
or practical.[1] The sole question was to whom allegiance was due. If it were owed to the secular power,
then it must be due to the king. It was not until the
17th century, when the chief scene of the discussion
shifted to England, that the rights of the people
against the prince came to be asserted. But when
that great popular movement flared up the principles
which Marsiglio had enunciated were sought, not in
his writings, but in those of later thinkers who had
discovered them anew.

The theory of the Divine Right of Kings belongs
to an age in which religion and politics, theology
and law, were inextricably mingled, when "even for
utilitarian sentiments a religious basis must be found
if they were to obtain acceptance. All men demanded
some form of divine authority for any theory of
government",[2] and the opponents of the theory did
not quarrel with the methods of its advocates. To-day,
with the aid of the vast body of new knowledge concerning primitive peoples, the history of government,
and the early forms of law, which recent research
has placed at our disposal, we can appreciate the immense background of superstition, magic, medicine-

[1] R. L. Poole, *op. cit.* p. 259.   [2] Figgis, *op. cit.* p. 11.

mongering, and religious belief which is secreted in the origins of kingship. Had the exponents of the relatively modern theory of the Divine Right of Kings known of its existence they would doubtless have made use of it to lend the theory a false historical justification. In point of fact they were not able to do so, for they had not the knowledge. Hence they were unable even to claim an organic relation between the magical origin of kingship and the Divine Right of Kings. The theory was perforce reared on the thin milk of the *histoire raisonée* and nourished with scriptural quotations.

The theory of the Divine Right of Kings declared that the prince owed his office to the intervention of God, that his person was sacred, the authority he wielded endowed with supernatural sanction, and his entire reign a direct result of heavenly dispensation. These postulates placed the rulers of the most civilised countries of Europe in the 14th, 15th, 16th, and 17th centuries on a footing essentially similar to that on which the Pharaohs had been placed in Egypt five thousand years earlier, on which the Hindu king had been placed by Manu possibly ten centuries before Christ, on which the Emperor of China was placed until the day of his overthrow. It is reasonable to suppose that there must have been an immense difference between the superstitious belief in the sacred nature of king or chief, deeply felt by the member of a savage tribe, and the adherence of an educated or even illiterate Englishman in the 16th century to the consciously framed theory which assured him that his king ruled by divine right. Nevertheless the immensely important part played by the theory of the Divine Right of Kings in the history of modern Europe during three or four centuries, and the violent repercussions in the world of action to which it gave rise, indicates that it must have inspired a potent emotional belief rather than, or in addition to, a mere intellectual assent.

When the theory of the Divine Right of Kings, and the political activity which was based upon it, came to be recognised and resented in the 17th century as a new form of tyranny, the resistance to the doctrine was at first based not on any doctrine of popular sovereignty, but on the alleged supremacy of the law. The dispute between prince and people, which was later to find expression in the conflict between King and Commons, was at the outset expressed in terms of a struggle·between the Crown and the Law.

In early times, just as priest and king had been one, so had the offices of judge and king been united. A separation had taken place in the latter case as in the former. And now the two were in conflict. The judges, and those for whom they spoke, claimed that the supreme power in the State was the law, and that even the monarch must be subject to its dictates. The royalists, on the contrary, asserted that it was the sceptre which wielded paramount authority. One side had before it "the vision of law conceived as a system existing by Divine Right, its origin lost in the past, independent of circumstances and men's caprice, superior to kings, and controlling Parliament. The other side laid stress on the conception of a sovereign raised high above all laws with power to abrogate them, and who alone can give binding force to enactments and invest custom with legal sanction. The supporters of the Crown are repeatedly found arguing that the King must be before and above the law, or how can it be binding?"[1]

On the surface this disputation may well have appeared to have been an argument as to whether the community should suffer an absolute monarch or abide indefinitely by a system of law the main features of which were fixed in principle and settled in detail.

Actually it was nothing of the kind. The judges not only professed the common law, they were its masters. No one denied their right to interpret the law, and in the right of interpretation lay the power of legislation. The judges declared in effect that all constitutional questions could be settled by a reference to custom. They omitted to point out that they alone were competent to declare the custom.[2]

Looked at from this angle, therefore, the judges and the King were alike contending for sovereign power. Had the judges succeeded in their claim, they would have made themselves the ultimate authority in the State, even to a greater extent than the judges of the Supreme Federal Court of the United States have made themselves wellnigh pre-eminent through their right to interpret the Constitution in terms of the validity of legislation. The king, realising clearly that there must be a sovereign, claimed the position which the judges by implication asserted for themselves.[3]

When the centre of gravity shifted to the struggle between King and Commons, the issue turned on

[1] Figgis, *op. cit.* p. 233.   [2] *Ibid.* pp. 231-2.

[3] For a discussion of the influence of all this on modern public administration see W. A. Robson, "The Committee on Ministers' Powers", *Political Quarterly*, July–September 1932. And see my evidence before the Committee in the Minutes of Evidence, Vol. I.

essentially the same question of sovereignty, although the matter was stated in more explicit and articulate terms. Right up to the Revolution of 1688 Whigs and Royalists were agreed that there must exist a supreme power in the State. The only question was where it should reside.

The king was destined for overwhelming defeat in attempting to match the claims of even divine royalty against the awakening consciousness of popular rights and liberties and the newly realised desire of the people to consent, to advise, to participate in government. But we can now perceive the indirect service performed by the exponents of the Royalist cause in espousing the absolute authority of a monarch ruling by divine right against the successive claims of the pope, the judges, and the people. For out of that great threefold struggle there has emerged the unfettered free secular legislature possessing sovereign power to make new law as a deliberate and conscious process.

The modern world accepts this achievement as a commonplace scarcely deserving of note, but it was utterly beyond the ken of the medieval world, and so strange to the men of the 14th, 15th, 16th, and 17th centuries that they scarcely realised for what they were contending. The movement, in consequence, was disguised and indirect.

If we would appreciate our heritage more vividly, let us compare it for a moment with that other great system which holds sway over the Moslem world. The conceptions by which English or European lawyers are dominated, such as sovereignty, allegiance, nationality, and domicile, are essentially alien to Muhammadan ideas. Although Islam has known many despots, "it has always insisted that sovereignty belongs to God alone, and in theory has never conceded to any human being any greater right than that of enforcing His law and protecting and leading His people. Allegiance, as a counterpart of sovereignty, is due only to God. Nationality is impossible in a world-wide brotherhood, and domicile is unimportant beside religious belief, whether Moslem or idolator".[1] The whole of Western society, on the other hand, has arrived at the stage where at last territorial nations can make their own laws freely through popular representative assemblies or through popularly supported dictators on a purely secular basis without divine assistance or revelation and without reference, if need be, to the immemorial customs of the community.

A greater contrast can scarcely be imagined.

[1] S. Vesey Fitzgerald, *Muhammadan Law: an Abridgment*, p. 26.

PART II
THE LAW OF NATURE

I

THE SCHEME OF THE WORLD

In the preceding pages we have seen how communities came to give themselves laws or to receive them, directly or indirectly, from the supernatural powers who were supposed to govern the universe. We have observed the effects which magic and superstition, people's ideas about religion, about God and the gods, have had on the authority, the substance, and the working of those laws, and, indeed, on the entire mechanism of government. In this part of the work I propose to survey the influence which has been exerted by human laws and political institutions on men's conceptions of the universe and the general order of nature. At times, it will be seen, cause and effect are so closely intermingled that separation becomes almost impossible. In such circumstances one may properly regard the relationship as a series of interactions or an integration.

Every society of human beings has a framework of ideas concerning the general constitution of the universe. This intellectual framework may be simple or complex, true or false, crude or refined, narrow or broad, noble or absurd. But whatever its qualities, the construction of such a framework appears to be an indispensable necessity of human life; and its function is everywhere substantially the same: namely, to enable men and women to interpret in some measure their place in the general scheme of

things, to reconcile their own lives with the phenomena which seem to lie outside those lives, to make
both the individual and the group feel at home in
the world.

This framework of ideas entertained by a given
society or group of thinkers within a society may be
termed their scheme of the world. Its general character is of such importance that a brief indication of
certain aspects of its shape and features at different
times must be given here as a necessary prelude to
what follows.

To the most rudimentary savage mind, the world
is peopled with spirits. On every side the ordinary
objects of everyday life are shifted hither and thither
by mysterious influences. The most commonplace
events are regarded as inspired by supernatural
forces and the processes of nature depend upon the
working of strange and secret powers.[1] These powers
are multitudinous and frequently in conflict. Hence
there can be little unity in nature for savages.[2]
Gradually the anthropomorphic tendency asserts
itself and primitive man attempts to explain the
operations of external nature in terms of the activities
of personified beings whose whims and caprices are
not altogether unlike those which he himself displays.
The dim unseen forces which inhabit springs and
rivers take shape as nymphs and sprites and gods
who govern the waters and the weather as man
himself governs his flock and his family.[3]

There is, in this development, a disguised attempt

---

[1] Julian Huxley, *Essays of a Biologist* (Phoenix ed.), pp. 236-7.
[2] William James, *A Pluralistic Universe*, p. 21.
[3] Thomas Erskine Holland, *Elements of Jurisprudence* (12th ed.),
p. 16.

to establish a definite sequence of cause and effect in the environment, irrational and haphazard though its orgins may be. We find, moreover, that primitive man is able to observe with extraordinary accuracy the beasts and birds and fishes which surround him and to reproduce their forms and habits with superb artistic skill, as everyone who has seen the magnificent cave-drawings and rock-carvings in the Dordogne and elsewhere can testify. Yet despite these powers and aspirations, despite the possession of certain elements which become at a later stage incorporated into the scientific mood, it cannot be said that savage society reveals anything which can properly be termed scientific.[1] The mind of primitive man is moreover enmeshed in those notions of magic which constitute "a spurious system of natural law as well as a fallacious guide to conduct", a false science no less than an abortive art.[2]

The ancient Egyptians conceived the universe in all its parts to be inseparably linked with the life of man. Among Egyptian deities Thoth, the scribe of the gods, occupied a position of special significance. He was believed to be self-begotten; he was supposed to have made the calculations required for establishing the heavens, the stars, and the earth; he was the master of law both in its physical and moral aspect.[3] He it was who spoke the words which resulted in the creation of the universe. It was his knowledge and mathematical powers which measured out the heavens and planned the earth and everything therein. It was his will which maintained the

[1] Charles Singer, *Historical Relations of Religion and Science* in *Science, Religion and Reality*, pp. 88-9.
[2] Sir James Frazer, *The Magical Origin of Kings*, p. 38.
[3] E. A. Wallis Budge, *The Gods of the Egyptians*, i, p. 401.

forces of heaven and earth in equilibrium. It was he who kept the stars in their courses. It was he whose great skill in celestial mathematics assured the proper use of the laws upon which the foundation and maintenance of the universe depends. Thoth, in short, was the heart and tongue of Rā, the great sun-god. In one way he was even greater than Rā, for he represented the reason and the mental powers of the sun-god.[1]

Thoth was also indissolubly connected both from a physical and moral point of view with the goddess Maāt. This deity took her name from a word meaning "that which is straight". The Egyptians employed the word in both its physical and moral senses, and it thus came to mean "right, true, truth, real, genuine, righteous, just, steadfast, unalterable", and so forth. The goddess Maāt personified order and truth, physical and moral law. She was the lady of the Judgment Hall, the symbol of justice who awarded to every man his due. It was she who indicated the regularity with which Rā rose and set in the heavens, and marked out his daily path across the sky from east to west.[2]

Among the ancient Hebrews there was no greater disposition than among the Egyptians to attribute natural events to natural causes. The earlier books of the Old Testament contain no conception of natural law whatever. The more awe-inspiring events such as thunder and lightning, whirlwind and drought, famine and disease, were deemed to be the direct result of divine intervention.[3] A typical attitude is to

---

[1] E. A. Wallis Budge, *The Gods of the Egyptians*, i, pp. 407 408, 421.

[2] *Ibid*. pp. 416-17.   [3] Charles Singer, *op. cit.* pp. 106-7.

be found in Psalm xxix, 3: "The voice of the Lord is upon the waters: the God of Glory thundereth".

A development of great importance introduced by the Jewish outlook was the change from polytheism to monotheism. Hitherto there had existed a world of many gods, each with his own powers and jurisdiction. The god of the mountains, for example, was believed to be supreme master of the heights but utterly impotent in the valleys.[1] The single omnipotent God of Judaism embodied a new sense of the unity and harmony of the universe in all its parts.

Nevertheless the ancient Hebrew was as little able to conceive of the action of natural causes in the sphere of human affairs as he was in the cycle of the seasons or in the outbreak of a thunderstorm. "Alike in the affairs of men and in the processes of nature he was content to trace the finger of God, and this calm acquiescence in supernatural agency as the ultimate explanation of all things presented almost as great an obstacle to the cool concerting of political measures as to the dispassionate investigation of physical forces in the laboratory."[2]

When we arrive at even the earliest Greek era of which we have any detailed knowledge it is impossible not to feel that an enormous intellectual advance is, if not actually made, at any rate in course of preparation. For the first time men are beginning to conceive nature as a system and to study that system as a key to the world-scheme. It is sometimes said, indeed, that the early Greek thinkers devoted themselves entirely to the study of external nature and

[1] Joseph Yahuda, *Law and Life according to Hebrew Thought*, p. 14.
[2] Sir James Frazer, *Folk-lore in the Old Testament*, iii, p. 108.

that it was not until Socrates that the problems of mankind were able to command attention. This is far from the truth. The Pythagoreans, for instance, not only interpreted the universe in terms of Number, but applied that interpretation to legal and political affairs. Thus, they regarded justice as a perfect number: that is, a square number, for a number multiplied by itself is a perfect harmony composed of equal parts. Again, if justice is a square number, it follows that it must be based on the idea of a state consisting of equal parts. Hence a state remains just only so long as its parts remain equal; and justice is the preservation of that equality.[1]

The earlier Greek philosophers may have speculated chiefly about the physical world, but their conclusions about matter were not "mere theories of physical scientists dealing with a problem of chemistry; they were, to those who propounded them, solutions of the riddle of the universe. As such, they applied to the life of man as much as they did to the life of the earth. Conclusions with regard to the elements of physical nature and their mutual relations involved similar conclusions about the elements of man's moral nature and the connexion of those elements—about the elements of the State and the scheme by which they were united."[2]

There was, indeed, a general belief in early times that order in human affairs cohered with order in nature and that both derived their ultimate sanction from a world-order which was one and indivisible.[3]

[1] E. Burle, *Essai historique sur le développement de la notion de droit natural dans l'antiquité grecque* (Trevoux, 1908), p. 86; Ernest Barker, *The Political Thought of Plato and Aristotle*, pp. 19-20.

[2] Ernest Barker, *op. cit.* p. 19.

[3] John L. Myres, *The Political Ideas of the Greeks*, p. 253.

Heraclitus was not speaking figuratively when he said that the Furies would track down the sun if it left its course, nor was Anaximander employing a metaphor in explaining the phenomena of change when he remarked that the physical elements suffer sentence of justice and pay the penalty to each other for their injustice. Anaximander was not arguing from nature to man but from the inevitable law of human conduct to nature.[1]

In the 5th century B.C. a change took place. Hitherto political institutions and human conduct had received from philosophers only so much attention as was warranted by their place in general cosmology. Now came a shift in the centre of gravity and for the first time men began to reflect primarily upon social institutions. Politics occupies the centre of the stage in the Athenian City-State of the later part of the 5th century and men turn to nature chiefly when they need physical examples to support their political theories. The philosophers who occupied themselves with the defence of democracy regarded the chief purpose of the world of matter as the provision of a series of object-lessons for the human race. Thus, the unity of nature indicated the necessity of the State as a condition of human unity.[2]

All this was in striking opposition to the views of the contemporary Sophists, who declared that the State and all the institutions of government are no more than a matter of man-made convention, as contrasted with the universal laws of nature emanating from the gods.[3] In the *Antigone*, Sophocles makes

[1] Ernest Barker, *op. cit.* pp. 22-3.   [2] *Ibid.* pp. 24-5.
[3] Charles Grove Haines, *The Revival of Natural Law Concepts*, p. 5.

the heroine say, in defence of the charge that she has wilfully disobeyed the king's commands: "Nor deemed I that thy decrees were of such force, that a mortal could override the unwritten and unfailing statutes of heaven. For their life is not of to-day or yesterday, but all time, and no man knows when they were first put forth."[1] In Plato a reconciliation is effected between nature and convention. Political thought "has become part of a whole system; and the State appears as a necessary element in the scheme of the world. There is no argument from physical nature to things moral and political; the two are not independent entities, but united as embodiments of one Idea, which constitutes both."[2]

Of Aristotle, the most comprehensive thinker of antiquity, I shall say nothing here. His influence was so vast and pervasive that it will be more convenient to postpone all discussion of his ideas until a later page.

Among the more practical Romans there was, of course, far less speculation about the scheme of the universe than had taken place among the highly imaginative Hellenes. "The world in which the Imperial Roman lived was a finite world bounded by the firmament and limited by a flaming rampart. His fathers had thought that great space peopled by *numina*, 'divinities' that needed to be propitiated. The new dispensation—the *lex naturae* of the world that had so many parallels with the *ius gentium* of the Empire—had now taken the place of those awesome beings."[3] Yet when we come to Cicero we find

---

[1] *Antigone*, p. 450 ff.   [2] Ernest Barker, *op. cit.* p. 27.
[3] Charles Singer, *Historical Relations of Religion and Science* in *Science, Religion and Reality*, p. 106.

once again an attempt to bridge the gulf which seemed to separate the world of man from the world of inanimate matter. "Nothing is so completely in accordance with the principles of justice and the demands of Nature" wrote Cicero "(and when I use these expressions I wish it understood that I mean Law) as is government, without which existence is impossible for a household, a city, a nation, the human race, physical nature and the universe itself. For the universe obeys God; seas and land obey the universe, and human life is subject to the decrees of the supreme law."[1]

The scheme of the world outlined in this passage is in certain respects closely akin to the most typical doctrine of the Middle Ages. Medieval thought regarded the universe as an essential unity, in which every being, whether an individual or a community, could be regarded both as what Gierke called a Partial Whole with a value of its own and as a mere fragment without separate significance. In such a conception every ordered community of human beings took its place as a component part of the world-order established by God, and every group of mortals appeared as an organic member of that divine state, that *Civitas dei*, which embraces both heaven and earth. In medieval eyes the world was a single organism, animated by One Spirit and fashioned by One Ordinance,[2] while the whole universe was considered to be but a single realm under the sovereign rule of God. The relation of temporal monarch to terrestial State was, indeed,

---

[1] *De Legibus*, tr. C. W. Keyes (Loeb ed.), p. 461.
[2] Otto Gierke, *Political Theories of the Middle Age*, tr. G. Maitland, pp. 7-8.

comparable to that believed to be borne by God to the entire world.[1]

St. Thomas Aquinas and the schoolmen developed the idea of the world being under the sway of an eternal law emanating from on high. This law fell into two parts. One part governed the voluntary actions of mankind and was thus the source of moral obligation, while the other part governed the activities of all created things and was in consequence the source of physical necessity. These two parts of the eternal law united in the idea of God as the supreme ruler and law-giver of the universe.[2]

The existence of this eternal law did not for a moment preclude the possibility of miraculous interferences with the course of nature occurring almost as a matter of daily experience. The most conspicuous feature of medieval society was an intense consciousness of the divine presence permeating every aspect of human life. The Law which governed the world was not in any sense impersonal; it was the expression of supernatural purpose, and this, in an unscientific age, was identified with the notion of abnormal and unforeseen interferences in human affairs arising from the direct intervention of the deity. Angels, devils, prayer, and witchcraft were all capable of affecting the behaviour of both inanimate matter and human beings. The largest affairs of men no less than small details of domestic life were equally subject to supernatural manipulation without notice.[3]

It was through spectacles coloured by this funda-

---

[1] Otto Gierke, *Political Theories of the Middle Age*, tr. G. Maitland, p. 30.

[2] John W. Salmond, "The Law of Nature", *Law Quarterly Review*, xlii, p. 134.

[3] Cf. G. N. Clarke, *The Seventeenth Century*, p. 244.

mental belief in miraculous intervention that the men
and women of the Middle Ages looked at life. To us
the universe is a vast process of ordered change and
regular development. To them it was a definite and
almost unchanging creation, formed in a moment out
of nothing and likely to end as suddenly as it began.[1]
Interest in the movements of heavenly bodies derived
mainly from the effect they were supposed to have on
human destinies; and it was not until 1682, when
Halley calculated the orbit of a comet, that people
escaped from the belief that comets portended great
calamities in human affairs and were without natural
cause in the ordinary sense of the term.[2] Chemistry
was studied in order to discover the secret of trans-
muting base metal into gold; botany was pursued to
provide plants suitable for medical and magical purposes; mineralogy offered in the main a knowledge of
the magical properties of jewels. Even as late as the
17th century there was much burning of witches, not
only in Europe, but also in the new world across the
Atlantic.[3]

The abolition of witch-burning came, not from a
humanitarian revolt against the hideous cruelty and
savage injustice of the practice, but from a decline in
popular belief in the efficacy of witchcraft. The work
of Copernicus, of Kepler, Galileo, and Tycho Brahe,
by introducing the conception of natural law into the
stellar universe, had a decisive effect in destroying
the notion that the heavens were the special province
for the operation of supernatural forces.[4] By the end

---

[1] Logan Pearsall Smith, *The English Language*, pp. 230-32.
[2] G. N. Clarke, *op. cit.* p. 245.   [3] *Ibid.* p. 246.
[4] W. E. H. Lecky, *The History of the Rise and Influence of the
Spirit of Rationalism in Europe*, i, p. 282.

of the 17th century the scheme of the world was in its main outline utterly different from that which had moulded the life and thought of the Middle Ages. The modern world was in process of emerging from the womb of time.

The processes of the growth of law and the institutions of government have to a peculiar extent interacted throughout the ages with the various schemes of the universe which men have entertained. In the Middle Ages, for example, it was common for political theorists to find in the relation of the sun to the moon conclusive evidence of the supremacy of the spiritual power over the secular authority—a doctrine sometimes worked out in precise arithmetical proportions.[1] To take another instance, in the 16th, 17th, and 18th centuries three great thinkers applied themselves to the study and practice of the law— Bacon, Leibnitz, and Vico. All three sought a basis for jurisprudence in the order of nature and the constitution of society.[2] Can we fully understand the jurisprudence or political theories of these or any other thinkers without knowing something of the foundations on which it was placed? Conversely, it may also be said that men's ideas of the order of nature can be more clearly comprehended if they are studied in the light of their relation to the prevailing jural and political order or the fundamental concepts on which it is based.

---

[1] According to one calculation the pope was $7744\frac{1}{2}$ times greater than the emperor. Another made the ratio 47 : 1. R. L. Poole, *Illustrations of the History of Medieval Thought*, p. 262.

[2] Sir John MacDonnell, *Great Jurists of the World*, p. 300.

II

NATURE

IN the preceding pages frequent reference has been made to Nature and to natural causes. We must now attempt to give some idea of the meaning attributed to these phrases in past ages. Not that one can hope to accomplish such a task comprehensively, for the thinkers of every epoch have occupied themselves greatly with formulating, amending, refining, changing, expanding and explaining the concept of Nature; and the results of their efforts sprawl over entire literatures. There is still in our own day an immense discussion concerning Nature and her ways.

The term Nature, it has been well said, is one of those fluid, indefinite names under whose shadow great advances of thought have sometimes been made.[1] The vitality of the conception and its derivatives, such as the Law of Nature, is without doubt in some measure due to these very qualities of fluidity and indefiniteness.

It is quite certain that Nature did not mean to antiquity what it means to us who have inherited the notion of evolution. To the Greek, the natural apple was not the wild one from which our cultivated apple has been grown, but rather the golden apple of the Hesperides. The natural object was that which perfectly expressed the idea of a thing. It was the perfect object.[2]

[1] A. R. Lord, *The Principles of Politics*, p. 28.
[2] Roscoe Pound, *Introduction to the Philosophy of Law*, p. 32.

But although the perfect object might be regarded as the most natural, Nature was not regarded as a harmonious order permeating the universe. To the early Greeks it was the State and the customary laws which had come down from time immemorial that seemed fundamental and divine. It was the whole complex of human conduct which seemed to embody inevitable order, and by comparison the life of the earth, with its flux and change, its lightning and tempest, appeared incalculable and indeterminate. It was in human life that all was appointed. "Man lived in a charmed circle of law and custom, but the world around him still seemed lawless."[1]

The Greeks of later antiquity developed a complicated cosmology based on an entirely fallacious system of astronomy. A distinction was drawn between the region lying above the sphere of the moon and the space below it. In the high heavens an unchanging and unchangeable order prevailed. The stars, which were believed to be divine beings endowed with reason, formed part of that eternal order and manifested its static purpose.[2] In the sublunary sphere, which was occupied by the four elements, all was uncertainty and change, and subject to a fluctuating purpose. Here on earth we are beneath the moon and hence in the region of sport and chance.[3] But the life of man was governed by Fate, that

---

[1] John Barnet, *International Journal of Ethics*, vii, p. 332; E. Barker, *The Political Theories of Plato and Aristotle*, p. 28.

[2] A. Bouche-Leclerq. *L'Astrologie grecque* (Paris, 1899), pp. 114-16. Cf. Thomas East Lones, *Aristotle's Researches in Natural Science* (London, 1912), *passim*.

[3] Francis R. Johnson and Sanford V. Larkey, *Thomas Digges, the Copernican System and the Idea of the Infinity of the Universe*, Huntingdon Library Bulletin No. 5, April 1934; Gilbert Murray, *Five Centuries of Greek Religion*, pp. 125, 180.

mysterious and pitiless force which dominated the Hellenic mind. Greek literature is inspired throughout by the consciousness of an inexorable destiny from which all thought of escape is hopeless. Already in Homer the idea is present of women who spin the destiny of men at their birth; by the time of Hesiod the spinsters have been named.[1] In the tragedies of the Greek dramatists man is represented again and again as the victim of some awful unseen power which foredooms him to disaster. "Awful is the mysterious power of fate" wrote Sophocles in the *Antigone*. Even the gods themselves, it was sometimes suggested, were subject to fate. Plato invariably assumes that there is a predestined course of events which determines human affairs, although he does not reveal by what power or in what manner it has been determined.

With Aristotle the distinction between Nature and Convention was clearly formulated for the first time. In a famous passage in the *Nicomachean Ethics*[2] he divides justice into the kind which is in accordance with Nature, and hence universal, and the kind which is conventional, and applicable only to a particular time and place. The higher law, in Aristotle's conception, is unwritten, universal, eternal, immutable, and in accordance with Nature.[3] From it is derived the absolute right which may be contrasted with the right that is merely man-made.[4]

Aristotle steadfastly refrained from setting up an

---

[1] Sometimes the gods themselves do the spinning. Cf. *Odyssey* iv, 207 f.   [2] Chapter 7.

[3] Charles Grove Haines, *The Revival of Natural Law Concepts*, pp. 6-7.

[4] J. Salmond, "The Law of Nature", xlii, *Law Quarterly Review*, pp. 123-4.

antithesis between Nature and Convention. "Every state is the work of Nature," he declared,[1] and yet man's handiwork has contributed to its structure, human art imitating and perfecting the work of Nature. Law, again, is natural, and yet it is enacted by a human legislator. In the Aristotelian doctrine of nature there is the conception of a rational ideal in the universe, which is manifested, though never perfectly realised, in the material world.[2] Hence the law of the state and the law of Nature are one. Yet in the case of actual states we must distinguish between natural and conventional law, between the naturally just and the legally just. The former enjoys a universal and unchanging validity, the latter varies from state to state and depends upon human enactment.[3] Nature in the Aristotelian philosophy is a guiding principle in the universe, and natural law is its expression.[4] In the ideal state the law corresponds completely to nature.

Since Nature was the source of natural law, and the common or universal identified with the natural, the implication followed that if a practice was everywhere in force it must be because it had been taught to all the peoples of mankind by Nature, their universal mother.[5] In this way the Aristotelian view led to

[1] *Politics*, Book I, ch. 11.
[2] F. Pollock, "The History of the Law of Nature: 1", *Columbia Law Review*, pp. 12-13.
[3] E. Barker, *op. cit.* p. 328. For an exposition of other meanings of the term Nature given by Aristotle in his *Physics* see *op. cit.* p. 221, and see also Otto Gierke, *Natural Law and the Theory of Society*, Introduction by E. Barker, p. xxxv.
[4] J. Bryce, *The Law of Nature* in *Studies in History and Jurisprudence*, p. 568.
[5] H. F. Jolowicz, *Historical Introduction to the Study of Roman Law*, p. 103.

the positive conception of Nature considered as the personified universe and in that capacity giving laws to men.[1]

This idea of Nature fulfilling a legislative function for the human race received its full development in the hands of the Stoics, although it was by no means exclusively confined to that school. In Stoicism, Nature or the universe was conceived as a living organism of which the material world was the body, and the Divine or Universal Reason the pervading and controlling soul. In man, as in the universal Nature of which he is a part, Reason is the ruling and guiding force. Hence the end and purpose of mankind is to live in harmony with this world-organism of which he is a part. To live in accordance with Nature was at once the highest virtue, the sum of all the virtues, and the path both of duty and of happiness.[2]

It is impossible to over-emphasise the importance in the subsequent life and thought of the world of the dualism adumbrated by Aristotle between the universal or natural element in law on the one hand and the local or conventional enactments of a particular group of men on the other. It was to this dualism that medieval thinkers inevitably referred when, centuries later, they contrasted natural and divine law with the statutory enactments of a particular community.[3] Nor should we fail to mark the immense influence exerted by the Stoic doctrine in its fully developed form. Since the time of the Stoics, whenever there

---

[1] John W. Salmond, *op. cit.* pp. 124-5.
[2] J. Bryce, *The Law of Nature* in *Studies in History and Jurisprudence*, p. 568; J. M. Baldwin, "Nature" in *Dictionary of Philosophy and Psychology*. Cf. *The Mind of Rome* (edited by Cyril Bailey, Oxford, 1926), p. 489 *et seq.*
[3] Charles Grove Haines, *op. cit.* p. 7; Pollock, *op. cit.* pp. 12-13.

seemed to be a danger of law, politics, or ethics forsaking the principles of inherent right and justice and degenerating into a series of empty formulae existing for their own sake, men have ever and again appealed to Nature; "and by 'Nature' they have meant reason and general principles of right. The appeal to reason and to the sense of mankind for the time being as to what is just and right which the philosophical jurist is always making, and his insistence upon what ought to be law as binding law because of its intrinsic reasonableness, have been the strongest liberalising forces in legal history."[1]

Among the Roman jurists many different meanings were given to the term Nature. It was used to indicate the essential characteristics of an object or a living creature. It was employed to describe the scheme of the entire physical universe. It might denote physical or biological relationships among human beings, as, for example, when the rule that illegitimate children followed the status of their mother was ascribed to Nature. It could mean the general moral sense or good feeling of mankind, as when it was said that Nature requires parents to be supported by their children, that Nature forbids theft, or that Nature makes adultery a disgrace. Above all, it referred to Reason, considered either as a universal principle or as practical common sense. It was this meaning that gave the word Nature its greatest significance in ancient Rome.[2]

---

[1] Roscoe Pound, "Scope and Purpose of Sociological Jurisprudence: 24", *Harvard Law Review*, p. 608.

[2] J. Bryce, *The Law of Nature* in *Studies in History and Jurisprudence*, pp. 586-7. The use of the term to denote the legal consequences of a contract (as in the expression *natura contractus*) is now believed to be a late post-classical conception.

In its more practical applications as a rational
principle Nature could prescribe such definite legal
maxims as that no one should profit through injur-
ing another person, or that he who bears the burden
of a thing should also enjoy the benefits. In its
more philosophical aspects it gave rise to such vast
generalisations as the famous utterance of Cicero,
"Universal Consent is the voice of Nature".[1]

Cicero, a pupil of Posidonius, the leading Stoic of
his day, may be said to have inherited and perpetu-
ated the essence of the Stoic doctrine on the subject
of Reason and Nature. In a characteristic passage he
asks: "What is more true than that no one ought to
be so foolishly proud as to think that, though reason
and intellect exist in himself, they do not exist in the
heavens and the universe, or that those things which
can hardly be understood by the highest reasoning
powers of the human intellect are guided by no
reason at all? . . . And since all things that possess
reason stand above those things which are without
reason, and since it would be sacrilege to say that
anything stands above universal Nature[2] we must
admit that reason is inherent in Nature."[3]

The distinction between Nature and convention
introduced by Aristotle survived without difficulty
the advent of Christianity. In the Epistle to the
Romans (ii, 14-15) St. Paul declares, "For when
the Gentiles which have no law do by nature the
things of the law, these, having no law, are a law
unto themselves; in that they shew the work of the

---

[1] "Omnium consensus naturae vox est", *Tusc.* I. xv, § 35; "Omni
autem in re consensio omnium gentium lex naturae putanda est",
ibid. I. xiii, § 30.
[2] "Nefasque sit dicere ullam rem praestare naturae omnium rerum."
[3] *De Legibus*, tr. C. W. Keyes (Loeb), pp. 389-91.

law written in their hearts". But as the Christian era developed the Greek theory of natural law came into contact with Hebrew theology. The result was that Nature became identified with God, and the law of nature with divine rule. Thus among the fathers of the Church we find Origen (A.D. 185–254) saying, "We may obey the laws of the state only when they agree with the divine law; when they contradict divine and natural law we must obey God alone".[1] St. Augustine (A.D. 354–430) contrasted the temporal law made by man, which governs human States, with the eternal law which proceeds from the divine mind and rules the City of God.[2]

In St. Thomas Aquinas we meet once again the doctrine of the Stoics that reason and nature are one, that they are universal and eternal. "Every act of reason and will in us", writes St. Thomas, "is based on that which is according to nature, for every act of reasoning is based on principles that are known naturally. . . ."[3] There is much else in St. Thomas of great significance on this subject, but it can be more conveniently treated in connection with natural law.

Save for a few minor divergencies, this line of thought continued to be followed in the most civilised countries until as late as the 17th century, when the revolution in scientific knowledge and invention had begun to lay hold of the most deep-rooted and long-established convictions. The comparative slowness, however, with which men of science, pioneers in

[1] W. R. Inge, *Liberty and Natural Rights* (1934), p. 25; Salmond, *op. cit.* p. 130.
[2] *De Civitate Dei*, Book XIX, ch. xvii.
[3] *Summa Theologica*, Part II, 1. 91, 2.

some special field of enquiry, were able to see their
particular discoveries in relation to the general character of the universe, is an interesting feature of
the time. Robert Boyle, for example, highly distinguished as a chemist and general man of science,
published in 1685–86 a volume entitled *A Free Inquiry into the vulgarly received Notion of Nature*.[1]
In this he remarks upon and deplores the large
number of diverse meanings given to the word
Nature. We should, he says, distinguish it from God,
from the essence of things, from the inherent or
original qualities of living creatures, from the internal
principles of local motion, from the fabric of the
world or system of the universe, from the mechanism
or aggregate of powers belonging to a body (especially a living one), and from the phenomena of the
universe.[2] Boyle is, indeed, especially strong on the
negative aspect of Nature—on what Nature is not.
"When water is raised in a Sucking-Pump, 'tis said,
that Nature makes the Water ascend after the Sucker,
to prevent a vacuum; though in reality this ascension
is made, not by such a separate Agent, as Nature is
fancied to be, but by the pressure of the Atmosphere,
acting upon the Water according to Statical Rules,
or the Laws or the Aequilibrium of Liquors, settled
by God among Fluids, whether visible or Pneu-
matical."[3]

Having disposed of the notion of Nature as a
separate agent or entity responsible either directly
for the behaviour of water or for the rules of causation laid down by God, Boyle then proceeds to enunciate his definition of Nature. The most proper use of

---

[1] The first draft of the work had been dictated in 1666.
[2] *Op. cit.* (1st ed.), pp. 27-30.   [3] *Ibid.* pp. 253-4.

the word, he observes, is for the purpose of distinguishing between the universal and the particular nature of things. And, he continues, "Of universal nature, the notion I should offer should be . . . that Nature is the aggregate of bodies, that make up the world, framed as it is, considered as a principle, by virtue whereof they act and suffer according to the laws of motion prescribed by the Author of things. Which description may be thus paraphrased; that nature, in general, is the result of the universal matter, or corporeal substance of the universe, considered as it is contrived into the present structure and constitution of the world, whereby all the bodies that compose it, are enabled to act upon and fitted to suffer from one another, according to the settled laws of motion." In contradistinction to this, "the particular nature of an individual body consists in the general nature, applied to a distinct portion of the universe: or rather supposing it to be placed, as it is, in a world, framed by God, like ours, it consists in a convention of the mechanical affections . . . of its parts . . . convenient and sufficient to constitute in . . . its particular species . . . the particular body they make up, as the concourse of all these is considered as the principle of motion, rest and changes in that body".[1]

The obscure idea described in so laboured and tortuous a manner appears to be almost equally useless both to philosophy and science. Boyle's main object seems to have been to prevent the concept of nature from infringing on the jurisdiction of God on the one hand, or from being identified with scientific law on the other. The limitation of his outlook is only

[1] *Op. cit.* (1st ed.), pp. 71-3.

fully disclosed, however, when he explains that in his discussion of nature all reference to "the rational soul or mind of man" will be rigorously excluded, and that he will consider the world "as it once really was towards the close of the sixth day of the creation, when God had finished all his material works, but had not yet created man".[1]

The *Tractatus Theologico-Politicus* of Spinoza was published in 1683, two years before Boyle's work was presented to the public. Yet with its clearness and simplicity, its unity and comprehensiveness, Spinoza's view of Nature might have come centuries later. To Spinoza, Nature is God.[2] He speaks about the "order of Nature", and says that the physical laws are what we know about the operations of the divine mind. He does not, moreover, admit that there are two distinct systems of law in the universe, one applicable to inanimate nature and the other referable to human beings. He provides an interpretation that unites the physical laws which regulate matter according to scientific principles with the laws of the mind which act in accordance with what it thinks to be reasonable.[3] For man, observes Spinoza, in so far as he is a part of nature, constitutes a part of the power of nature. Whatever, therefore, follows necessarily from the necessity of human nature (that is, from nature herself, in so far as we conceive her acting through man) follows necessarily from human power.[4]

---

[1] *Ibid.* p. 26.
[2] "The eternal and infinite Being, which we call God or Nature" (*Ethics*, Part IV, *Works* (tr. R. H. M. Elwes), ii, p. 188. See also ii, p. 68.
[3] Cf. G. N. Clarke, *The Seventeenth Century*, p. 259.
[4] *Tractatus Theologico-Politicus. Works*, ed. R. H. M. Elwes, i, p. 57.

To come upon Spinoza after reading Boyle is like discovering a well-marked path after wandering for hours in a trackless forest. When Kant asked us to relate "the starry heavens above and the moral law within";[1] when Wordsworth wrote that Nature comprehends all that is

> In the round ocean, and the living air,
> And the blue sky, and in the mind of man;

when the Duke of Argyll, writing in 1866, urged that Nature be understood in the widest sense as including, not merely physical matter, but the whole mental world in which we ourselves live and move and have our being, and first and foremost our own Mind and Will[2]—philosopher and poet and statesman were but echoing in a slightly more developed form the words which Spinoza had written nearly two hundred years earlier.[3] When Professor Whitehead observes that "Nature is a system"[4] one feels that there is an unbroken cord which binds Spinoza to some of the best thought of our own day.

Thus Nature has meant many different things during the past ages of human history. We are accustomed to say that Nature is the universal mother of mankind. It would be nearer the truth to say that Nature resembles a department store from which each generation has taken the particular kind of concept

---

[1] *Critique of Practical Reason* (tr. T. R. Abbott, 1889), p. 260.
[2] Duke of Argyll, *The Reign of Law* (5th ed.), pp. 5-6. The lines of verse are from Wordsworth's "Tintern Abbey".
[3] "Nature's laws and ordinances . . . are everywhere and always the same, so that there should be one and the same method of understanding the nature of all things whatsoever, namely, through nature's universal laws and rules" (*Ethics, op. cit.* pp. 128-9. Cf. Sir F. Pollock, *Spinoza* (2nd ed., 1912), pp. 199-20).
[4] A. N. Whitehead, *The Concept of Nature*, p. 146.

it needed. The important thing to note, however, is that at all times Nature has been regarded as an objective reality, a definite fact to be reckoned with.[1] Whether conceived as the embodiment of universal reason or as inferior to divine revelation, whether viewed as a moral rule of life to be followed by rational beings or as the opposite of convention, the idea of Nature has in all its guises implied the notion of an objective order in the universe which could be studied and comprehended by man but which lies entirely outside his power to alter in even the slightest degree. It was this conception which gave significance and force to the distinction between natural law and civil law to which we can now turn our attention.

[1] A. R. Lord, *The Principles of Politics*, p. 29.

III

THE LAW OF NATURE

THE Greeks of antiquity were deeply impressed by the great variety of laws in force among the numerous communities with which they came in contact; and they discussed at length the great question whether justice and right are purely relative arrangements changing with time and place, or whether behind the apparent flux and diversity there exist ultimate principles of right and wrong possessing eternal validity. The Sceptics held the former view, but from the time of Socrates onwards the notion of an underlying natural justice dominated the great thinkers of the age. Both Plato and Aristotle spoke of a law of nature to which all rational beings must everywhere conform.[1] The Stoics emphasised the ethical aspect of the Aristotelian conception of natural justice and in their hands it became a guiding principle immanent in the universe. This immanent principle was identified with reason and its expression was manifested in natural law.[2] Natural law, it was said, is binding on the entire human race and is therefore universal. It is of perpetual validity and its character changes not with time and place.

These speculations of the Greek philosophers came to have great practical importance among the Roman lawyers. The Roman tribunals exercised supreme

[1] Sir Paul Vinogradoff, *Commonsense in Law*, pp. 235-7.
[2] Charles Grove Haines, *The Revival of Natural Law Concepts*, p. 9.

jurisdiction over a large variety of peoples, and in the course of their work they were confronted with a heterogeneous collection of laws and customs and enactments. To reduce this chaotic mass to some kind of order was not an academic exercise in intellectual abstraction, but an urgent task of immediate practical importance. In this way the great jurists came to seek a unifying principle underlying the diverse phenomena with which they had to deal. This led them to grasp eagerly at the Greek theory of a Law of Nature which served to provide a rational basis for all particular laws.

Thus we find the jurist Gaius beginning his celebrated *Institutes* with a passage which closely follows Aristotle:

> All peoples who are governed by laws and customs apply partly their own law, partly law which is common to all mankind; for the law which each people has made for itself is peculiar to that people and is called its *ius civile*, the special law of the State; but that which natural reason has appointed for all men is in force equally among all peoples, and is called *ius gentium*, being the law applied by all races. Thus the Roman people applies partly its own law, partly that common to all men.[1]

Wardship was described by Gaius about A.D. 150 as an arrangement founded on natural reason, and the *Institutes* of Justinian also refer to natural law in this case.[2] The jurist Paul observes that since leases are

[1] Cf. H. J. Jolowicz, *Historical Introduction to the Study of Roman Law*, p. 104.
[2] Gaius 1, 189; Just. 1, 20, 6.

suggested by nature, and are to be found in the law of all nations, a particular form of words is not required to effect a valid transaction. Consent alone is sufficient. The same applies in the case of sale.[1]

The Stoic doctrine of a ubiquitous Law, divine in character and emanating from the universal Reason, was a liberating and enlarging conception in the hands of the Roman jurists. It was a corrective and expansive force, not only in abolishing obsolete practices but also in creating new rules of law appropriate to the needs of the time.[2] Prior to the recognition of Nature as a source of law, both the practice and the study of the law were of a crabbed practical character devoid of any philosophical interest in the moral principles underlying all law and government.[3] The idea of the Law of Nature introduced a guiding principle which conformed with practical common sense, with the best side of human nature, with morality, above all with reason.[4] Cicero himself declared that "true law is right reason in agreement with Nature".[5] Nature and utility were united, and Rome's local code became the law of the world.

The Law of Nature as such did not, however, have any legal validity in the Roman tribunals. *Jus naturale* comprised, strictly speaking, the rules of conduct which could be rationally deduced from the general conditions of human life.[6] So much of those rules as had been actually applied by all civilised people con-

---

[1] Vinogradoff, *op. cit.* pp. 236-7.
[2] J. Bryce, *The Law of Nature* in *Studies in History and Jurisprudence*, p. 593.
[3] W. Warde Fowler, *Social Life at Rome*, p. 107.
[4] Bryce, *op. cit.* p. 589.   [5] *De Rep.* III, 22.
[6] Sir F. Pollock, "The History of the Law of Nature: 1", *Columbia Law Review*, pp. 14-15.

III THE LAW OF NATURE 215

stituted the *ius gentium*, and it was this *ius gentium* which was legally enforced.[1] Thus the *Institutes* of Justinian (2. 1) declare that by natural law running water and the sea are common to all, so too are rivers and harbours; and by the law of nations ships from all parts may be moored there. The *jus gentium* came to be regarded as universal and as implanted in man by Nature. Hence it was frequently regarded by some of the most eminent jurists as equivalent to the *ius naturale*.[2] Gaius, as we have seen, described *ius gentium* [3] as "that which natural reason has appointed for all men". There was, however, no uniformity of practice in this respect, and the texts sometimes identify the *ius naturale* with the *ius gentium* and sometimes distinguish it.[4] The law of nations might approximate to the Law of Nature, but it could never become synonymous so long as slavery remained one of the essential foundations of Roman society. For slavery was a universal institution in the ancient world and therefore part of the *ius gentium*. But philosophers had observed—and it did not require a philosopher to make the observation—that it was contrary to nature.[5]

Broadly speaking, *ius naturale* was a philosophical

[1] For a very interesting use of *ius gentium* in a modern case, see *"In re* a reference under the Judicial Committee Act 1833 and *in re* piracy *jure gentium"*, *Times* newspaper 4th and 27th July 1934. The question was whether robbery is an essential element in the crime or whether a frustrated attempt to commit a piratical robbery is not equally piracy *jure gentium*.

[2] W. W. Buckland, *The Main Institutions of Roman Private Law* (1931), p. 9.

[3] *Ante*, p. 196.

[4] Buckland, *loc. cit.*; A. R. Lord, *The Principles of Politics*, pp. 30-31.

[5] Even Aristotle, in his famous defence of slavery, did not attempt to justify *de facto* slavery.

doctrine possessing an ideal or abstract character,[1] while *ius gentium* was a body of legal rules recognised by the Courts, expounded by the jurists, and normally deriving its essential justification from natural law. According to Bryce, there was a tendency to employ the term *ius naturae* or *naturale* when emphasising the rational basis of a rule, and to use the expression *ius gentium* when dealing with its practical application.[2]

In addition to the *ius naturale* and *ius gentium* there was also the *ius civile*. This was no more than the body of local laws and customs operating in a particular community. By virtue of its merely local character, the *ius civile* presented a striking contrast to both *ius naturale* and *ius gentium*. Cicero inferred that what is part of the law of nations (*ius gentium*) should also form part of the law of each particular State (*ius civile*), although the converse would of course not follow, since there are many matters in which, as Aristotle had pointed out, nature is indifferent and each community free to lay down its own rules.[3]

[1] "*Jus naturale* is always a general legal ideal. It is, in its essence, the Stoic ideal of a common law of all humanity, which is a law of Reason and Nature. It is permeated by the Stoic principle of equality; *omnes homines natura aequales sunt*—they are equal persons in the great court of Nature. It is not a body of actual law, which can be enforced in actual Courts. It is a way of looking at things—a spirit of 'humane interpretation' in the mind of the judge and the jurist—which may, and does, affect the law which is actually enforced, but does so without being actual law itself. No Roman jurist ever asserted that Natural Law overrode concrete and positive law, as was asserted in the Middle Ages and afterwards; all that they did was to allow their idea of Natural Law to affect the actual law when it came to be applied in the Courts" (Ernest Barker, Introduction to Otto Gierke, *Natural Law and the Theory of Society* (1934), p. xxxvii).   [2] Bryce, *op. cit.* p. 585.
[3] H. J. Jolowicz, *Historical Introduction to the Study of Roman Law*, p. 103.

The *ius naturale* was the peculiar and exclusive possession of the human race: an isolated statement in Justinian's *Institutes* extending it to the animal kingdom is discredited by modern scholars as a mere rhetorical flourish without significance.[1] The *ius gentium* was the common law of mankind—its generality being indeed the mark of its authentic character. In this capacity it was applied by the Roman Courts to persons who had no citizenship of any city. Between A.D. 212 and 217 the Emperor Caracalla conferred Roman citizenship on all the subjects of the empire. This enormously reduced the number of non-citizen subjects or *peregrini*, and thereafter everyone in the Roman world, with the exception of foreigners, criminal outcasts, and the lowest species of freedmen, enjoyed the full benefits of the civil law. This greatly weakened the practical importance of the distinction between *ius gentium* and *ius civile*, so far as the persons subject to each were concerned.[2] But for centuries the conception of the Law of Nature exercised a dominating influence in moulding the substance of the law. It left its mark on the relations of parents and children, of patrons and freedmen, of masters and slaves. The law relating to property, inheritance, obligations, and procedure were similarly affected. In every sphere the Law of Nature exercised a softening and humanising influence.

Under the aegis of the Christian Church the Law of Nature became at first identified with the law of God. At a later stage it was once again accorded a separate

---

[1] Di. 1. De Just. 1, 3; Sir F. Pollock, *op. cit.* pp. 14-15; Jolowicz, *op. cit.* p. 105.
[2] Bryce, *op. cit.* pp. 586, 588-9.

existence, but subordinated to the divine law of which it was made to form a part. The conception of the Law of Nature persisted with considerable force all through the Dark Ages and the Middle Ages into the modern world. But during the course of its journey it underwent more than one transformation, and the context in which it was set received profound changes.

The early Christian fathers, such as Origen, St. Ambrose, and St. Jerome, accorded an important place in their system of thought to the doctrine of natural law. They contrasted its universality with the temporary character of mere man-made enactments, and spoke of it as equivalent to the law of God.[1] Isidore of Seville, in the first half of the 7th century, remarked that "All laws are either divine or human. The divine rest upon Nature, the human upon custom; and the latter accordingly differ among themselves. . . ." This statement acquired fame through being incorporated, during the 12th century, in the introduction to Gratian's celebrated redaction of the canon law. Gratian himself wrote in the preceding paragraph of the Decretum, "Mankind is ruled by two things, natural law and customs. Natural law is that which is contained in the law and the gospel, whereby everyone is commanded to do to another that which he would have done to himself." This identification of the law of nature with the law of God and the golden rule turned out to have far-reaching consequences.[2]

The medieval canonists, like the Fathers of the

---

[1] R. W. and A. J. Carlyle, *History of Medieval Political Theory in the West*, i, p. 23 *et seq.*

[2] Carlyle, *op. cit.* ii, pp. 28, 98, 102, 105, 113.

Christian Church, were primarily concerned with the divine and eternal laws of the universe which had been revealed to man and over which he had no control. They accordingly contended that the Law of Nature was a particular part of the law of God regarded from a certain aspect. St. Thomas Aquinas taught that, in addition to natural law, there is also human law and divine law. The necessity for divine law, he said, arises from four causes. First, because man is destined for an end of eternal bliss which he cannot attain through the exercise of his natural faculties alone. It is therefore necessary that in addition to natural law and human law he should be guided to this beatific end by a law given by the deity. Second, on account of the uncertainty of human judgment there arise diverse and contrary laws, and in order to avoid this uncertainty it is necessary to have a supreme and infallible guide to conduct. Third, since human law cannot adequately control interior acts, it was necessary for God to provide a divine law for this purpose. Fourth, human law cannot hope to punish or prohibit all evil deeds, for if it attempted to do so it would also abolish many good things and hinder the common welfare; hence, in order that no evil may remain unforbidden and unpunished, it is necessary for the divine law to supervene whereby all sins are forbidden.[1] As regards natural law, wrote St. Thomas, the rational creature, being subject to divine providence, has a share of Eternal Reason "whereby it has a natural inclination to its proper act and end: and this participation by the rational creature in the eternal law is called the Law of Nature". The natural law, he concluded, is

[1] *Summa Theologica*, Part II, 1 Q 91, art. 4.

"nothing else than the rational creature's participation in the eternal law".[1]

We can see from these characteristic passages the
way in which the Law of Nature was ascribed to the
revealed law of God. We can see also the relation
between the two. The law natural is implanted in
natural reason for the pursuit of worldly ends, while
the law divine is revealed by God to man in a supernatural way for transcendental purposes.[2]

This philosophy contained two important implications. One was that Nature is assumed to be a reasonable product of God's will. The will of God is recognised as a reasonable will and human reason can
properly claim the right to interpret it.[3] The other
was that a dichotomy was established which distinguished the actions of rational beings from all other
activities and processes. To man the eternal law says
"You ought"; to the rest of nature it says "You must".
Man alone possesses the prerogative of freedom, and
is able in consequence to break the precepts of this
eternal law; but all other created beings must render
it perfect obedience.[4] The medieval idea of the Law
of Nature as a guide to conduct, discernible to the
rational being and to none other, further emphasised
the distinction between mankind and the rest of the
universe.

The doctrine of the law natural continued to play
a part in the domain of practical affairs during the
Middle Ages of even greater importance than it had
in the days of ancient Rome, for its influence spread

[1] *Summa Theologica*, Part II, 1 Q 95, art. 2.
[2] Cf. O. Gierke, *Political Theories of the Middle Age*, tr. by F. W.
Maitland, p. 75.
[3] A. R. Lord, *The Principles of Politics*, p. 32.
[4] Salmond, *op. cit.* pp. 132-4.

from the field of legal institutions to the entire realm of political institutions and royal authority.

"Every law framed by man bears the character of a law exactly to that extent to which it is derived from the Law of Nature. But if on any point it is in conflict with the Law of Nature, it at once ceases to be law; it is a mere perversion of a law." So wrote St. Thomas Aquinas [1] in the 13th century. In doing so he was merely expressing the received opinion of the time that civil law is subject to the overriding authority of natural law.[2] The conviction which this idea carried is shown by the fact that Philip the Fair of France, when he proposed to liberate the serfs under his jurisdiction in A.D. 1311, declared that "every human being formed in the image of Our Lord ought by natural law to be free".[3] Again, when Edward III of England submitted a document to the pope for the purpose of establishing his claim to the French throne, in the course of which he argued that the descendants of women could succeed to the property or throne of a male ancestor, he declared that he was basing his contentions on natural law, although in fact the power of women to transmit rights of inheritance to their descendants was pure Roman law of recent origin not specially connected in any way with the Law of Nature.[4] There might be much controversy as to the precise origin of the Law of Nature and the exact source of its binding obligation, but all men were agreed that natural law existed, that it provided an authentic and compelling rule,

[1] *Summa Theologica*, Part II, 1 Q 95, art 2.
[2] R. W. and A. J. Carlyle, *A History of Medieval Political Theory in the West*, v, p. 80.
[3] Cf. Bryce, *op. cit.* p. 596.
[4] H. S. Maine, *International Law*, pp. 20-21.

and that its authority derived from a transcendental power which no one dare question or disobey. Men believed that "before the state existed the *Lex Naturalis* prevailed as an obligatory statute, and that . . . from this flowed those rules of right to which the state owed even the possibility of its own rightful origin. And men also taught that the highest power on earth was subject to the rules of Natural Law. They stood above the Pope and above the Kaiser, above the Ruler and above the Sovereign People, nay, above the whole Community of Mortals. Neither statute nor act of government, neither resolution of the people nor custom, could break the bounds that were thus set. Whatever contradicted the eternal and immutable principles of Natural Law was utterly void and would bind no one." [1]

It followed from this that no king or ruler, in the exercise of his authority, could lawfully infringe the dictates of the Law of Nature. Any attempt to do so, whether by executive act or legislative decree or statute, was to be treated as void and illegal by every judge, magistrate, or public officer who was charged with the application of the law. [2]

That this was not merely the fine-spun dogma of sheltered monks and power-hungry ecclesiastics is clearly shown by the utterances of a hard-headed practical English lawyer like Sir John Fortescue, Lord Chief Justice under Henry VI, who in 1460–1461 issued a treatise on the Law of Nature intended to prove that a ruler cannot succeed to a throne by the female line. In the first part of the work he quaintly explains that during the 3644 years which

[1] Otto Gierke, *Political Theories of the Middle Age*, tr. by F. W. Maitland, p. 75.   [2] *Ibid.* p. 84.

elapsed between the time when Adam and Eve were driven out of Paradise and the moment when the Israelites received from Moses the law written by the Lord, the human race was governed by the Law of Nature.[1] Since the coming of Christ, however, continues Fortescue, natural law is that which is contained in the revealed law and in the Gospel, and in particular the golden rule which bids us do unto others as we would have them to do unto us.[2] This law is supreme. "For no edict or action of a king, even if it hath arisen politickly, hath ever escaped the vengeance of divine punishment, if it hath proceeded from him against the rule of Nature's Law."[3] It would almost seem as though the punishment of kingly violations of Nature's Law is itself part of the Law of Nature, although Fortescue is careful to declare that the power of punishing an erring ruler rests in the hands of God.

In the 16th century a change of emphasis, slight in itself but pregnant with possibilities, can be noticed in the treatment of the Law of Nature. Hitherto the term had connoted a body of commandments expressing the will of God in regard to the conduct of rational creatures, a rule of life superior to individual desires and temporary exigencies.[4] Despite all the vicissitudes which the conception had undergone in the course of its long journey from the time of the later Roman Republic, there had remained the idea of an ultimate principle of fitness with regard to the nature of man considered as a rational or social being,

[1] *De Natura legis Naturae*, Part I, ch. iv.
[2] *Ibid*. chs. iv and v.
[3] *Ibid*. Part I, ch. xxvii. *Works* (Clermont ed.), i, pp. 89, 218-19.
[4] Cf. Oxford English Dictionary: "Law" (9); R. H. Tawney, *Religion and the Rise of Capitalism*, p. 62.

which is, or should be, the justification of all positive law.[1] Now, however, in 1531, we find St. German in the *Doctor and Student* explaining that "The lawe of nature . . . consydered generally . . . is referred to all creatures as well reasonable as unreasonable . . . the lawe of nature specially consydered, whiche is also called the lawe of reason, perteyneth onely to creatures reasonable, that is man. . . . And it is written in the herte of every man". Hooker, in 1594, writes of the spirit borrowing the canons of Reason from the school of Nature, and refers to the "Law rational, which men commonly use to call the Law of Nature, meaning thereby the Law which human nature knoweth itself in reason universally bound to, which also for that cause may be termed most fitly the Law of Reason".[2] This law of Reason or human nature comprised the body of principles which men have recognised by the light of their intelligence to be eternally binding upon them. These laws are moreover "investigable by Reason, without the help of Revelation supernatural and divine".[3] Hooker's general conception was that man learns from Nature through the exercise of his reason, Nature being the instrument of God.[4]

From this type of approach there began to emerge a separation between the Law of Nature and the divine authority with which it had been associated throughout the Middle Ages. The element of rational per-

---

[1] Sir F. Pollock, "The History of the Law of Nature: 1", *Columbia Law Review*, p. 11; A. R. Lord, *The Principles of Politics*, pp. 28-9.

[2] *Ecclesiastical Polity*, i, viii, § 9.

[3] *Ibid.* § 8-9.

[4] "The general and perpetual voice of men is as the sentence of God himself. For that which all men have at all times, Nature herself must needs have taught; and God being the author of Nature, her voice is but his instrument" (*ibid.* § 2).

ception gradually enlarged while the element of holy revelation dwindled. Even if the divine will was considered to be the ultimate source of natural law, and God the legislator who formally enacted it, human Reason was still regarded as the only source from which knowledge of this law could actually be obtained.[1] The conception of the Law of Nature began to stand on its own feet once again in the guise of an appeal to right reason,[2] looking on the one hand to the phenomena of the world, and on the other hand to the spirit of rationality. Both aspects indicate that we are on the threshold of the modern world.

This transformation was, of course, a gradual and somewhat confused process; and as in the case of all developments in human thought, it is possible to find repeated reversions to an earlier outlook.

Moreover, between the 16th century and the modern world there sprawled the powerful and unpleasant figure of Thomas Hobbes, whose whole political and moral philosophy was built on a special conception of the Law of Nature. Hobbes was born in 1588 and his principal work was done in the middle of the seventeenth century.

Law, said Hobbes, is of two kinds, divine and human. Divine law is twofold: natural or moral, and positive. Natural law is that which God has declared to men by their natural reason; and it is identical with the moral law or the sum of moral philosophy. Positive law is that which has been revealed by the word of prophecy. All human law is civil; and civil law may again be divided into sacred and secular.[3]

[1] Otto Gierke, *Natural Law and the Theory of Society*, 1500-1800 tr. E. Barker, i, p. 98.   [2] A. R. Lord, *op. cit.* pp. 29-30.
[3] Thomas Hobbes, *Philosophical Rudiments concerning Government and Society* (Molesworth ed.), ii, pp. 47, 49, 50, 187.

Civil and natural law, explained Hobbes, are not different kinds of law, but different parts. The part which is written is called civil, the part which is unwritten natural.[1] "The Law of Nature, and the civil law, contain each other, and are of equal extent. For the laws of nature, which consist in equity, justice, gratitude and other moral virtues on these depending, in the condition of mere nature . . . are not properly laws, but qualities that dispose men to peace and obedience."[2] The Law of Nature is therefore a part of the civil law in every commonwealth in the world.

The first and fundamental dictate of right reason, that is, the Law of Nature, declared Hobbes, is "to seek peace, where there is any hopes of obtaining it, and where there is none, to enquire out for auxiliaries of war".[3] Other laws of Nature are to fulfil contracts, to keep trust faithfully, not to permit a benefactor to suffer from the confidence which he reposes in you, to render oneself useful to others, to practise the quality of mercy.[4] A law of Nature is, indeed, a precept or general rule, found out by reason, whereby a man is forbidden to do anything which is destructive of life or an impediment to its preservation.[5] Such laws of nature are immutable and eternal. What they forbid can never be lawful, nor what they command unlawful. For pride, ingratitude, breach of contract, inhumanity and contumely will never be lawful, nor the contrary virtues unlawful "as they are considered in the court of conscience, where only they oblige and are laws".[6]

[1] *The Great Leviathan*, p. 254.   [2] *Ibid.* p. 253.
[3] *Government and Society. Works*, ii, pp. 13, 16.
[4] *Ibid.* pp. 29, 35-7.   [5] *Leviathan*, p. 116.
[6] *Government and Society. Works*, ii, p. 46.

From time to time in the course of his works
Hobbes was careful to identify the law natural with
the eternal law of God,[1] but it is abundantly clear
that the main emphasis of his docrine was to make
the Law of Nature an essentially intellectual construction comprising the rational conduct which he
considered most likely to preserve and maintain
human life. He took the instinct of self-preservation
as a basic fact and formulated a rational code intended to ensure its successful functioning. The core
of his teaching is to be found in a passage in which he
says that "True reason is a certain law; which, since
it is no less a part of human nature, than any other
faculty or affection of the mind, is also termed
natural. Therefore the law of Nature, that I may
define it, is the dictate of right reason, conversant
about those things which are either to be done or
omitted for the constant preservation of life and
members as much as in us lies."[2] This was an essentially secular formulation; and it is this which is fundamentally significant in the Hobbesian discourse.
Thenceforth, no prominent thinker is found associat-
ing the natural law with the commands of the
deity. One can appreciate the gulf which separates
the medieval schoolmen from the author of *Leviathan*, despite all his professions of adherence to the
Christian religion and his frequent reference to the
gospels, when one finds a cleric like Bishop Berkeley
repeating in 1712 the Hobbesian dogma that "self-

---

[1] *E.g.* "Princes succeed one another; and one judge passeth, another cometh, nay, heaven and earth shall pass, but not one tittle of the
law of nature shall pass; for it is the eternal law of God" (*Leviathan*,
p. 264).

[2] *Government and Society. Works*, ii, pp. 15-16.

preservation is . . . the very first and fundamental law of Nature".[1]

The *Leviathan, or the Matter, Form, and Power of a Commonwealth* was first published in 1651. The identification which it preached between the pursuit of political self-interest (in terms of subordination to dominant authority), the comfort of the flesh, and the Law of Nature, was paralleled by an equally convenient harmony of a similar kind which was already overcoming all resistance in the economic sphere. By 1660 the pursuit of economic self-interest was not only acknowledged to be the Law of Nature, but it had come to be associated with the working of the providential plan, which was but another name for the law of God.[2] In this way the intellectual foundations were laid for that vast economic transformation of society which for want of a better name is called the Industrial Revolution.

But the secularised version of natural law was also put to other and better uses. Hugo Grotius was born at Delft five years before Thomas Hobbes. His great work, *De Jure Belli ac Pacis*, published in 1625, is generally recognised to have provided the principal basis for public international law in the modern world. It was translated into almost all the languages of the civilised world and as many as seventy-six editions have seen the light of day. No law book, it has been said, has achieved such international fame since the days of the great Roman jurists.[3]

---

[1] *Passive Obedience*, § 33.
[2] R. H. Tawney, *Religion and the Rise of Capitalism*, p. 259.
[3] Cf. a review by Professor Winfield of the translation issued by the Carnegie endowment in *Journal of Comparative Legislation and International Law*, xi, Part I.

In the prolegomena to his treatise, Grotius laid down the principles of a science of natural law which he subsequently employed as the foundation of his system of international law.[1] The Law of Nature to which he thus appealed for the purpose of determining legal relations in the international sphere was not in any sense the product of an abstract rationalism. He sought for it in the utterances of poets and philosophers, in the pronouncements of historians and men of letters, in the teaching of Roman law and historical precedent. These diverse sources supplied him with material to demonstrate the agreement of mankind concerning certain rules of conduct and contributed in various measure to the natural law which he defined as "the dictate of right reason".[2]

Writers in every country up to the end of the 18th century, and outside England nearly all authorities down to the present time, agree in recognising the Law of Nature as the ultimate source of International law.[3] We are to-day, indeed, enjoying the benefits of many practices and institutions which are descended from the principles and customs of previous generations who looked to the direction of the Law of Nature as a guide to conduct. A great part of the law of nations which now prevails is indisputably derived from the practices of bygone rulers and nations who constantly appealed with deeply held conviction to the law natural. "We must either admit", says Sir Frederick Pollock, "that modern International law is a law founded on cosmopolitan principles of reason,

---

[1] Walter Schücking, *Introduction to Pufendorf: De Officio Hominis* (ed. Classics of International Law).
[2] *De Jure Belli ac Pacis*, i, 1. 10; A. R. Lord, *op. cit.* pp. 31-2.
[3] Sir F. Pollock, *Essays in the Law*, p. 63.

a true living offshoot of the Law of Nature, or ignore our own most authoritative expositions of it." [1]

The influence of the Law of Nature, both in theory and in practice, was by no means confined to the regulation of international relations. On the theoretical side it spread, in the hands of Pufendorf, over the entire fabric of the legal structure. Pufendorf was Professor of the Law of Nature and of Nations at Heidelberg in 1661, and in 1670 went to Sweden as Professor of Natural Law in the University of Lund. His chief work was brought out nearly half a century after the *De Jure Belli* of Grotius. In its original form only two chapters out of the total of thirty-five are concerned with International law, a fact which indicates the wide range and application of the concept of natural law. [2] In this treatise Pufendorf develops the idea that the fundamental Law of Nature is that every man shall cherish and maintain sociability to the utmost possible extent. From this it follows that all things which necessarily and universally promote that sociability are understood to be ordained by natural law and all things which impede or destroy it are forbidden. [3] The laws which indicate how people should conduct themselves so as to conduce to sociability are natural laws.

Pufendorf, like Hobbes, to whom he was much indebted, explained at length the manner in which his doctrine submitted all mankind to the jurisdiction of God. [4] But he was denounced and attacked by divers pastors and professors in Germany and

---

[1] Pollock, *Essays in the Law*, p. 67.

[2] The work in its original form was entitled *De Jure Naturae et Gentium*. A subsequent abstract was entitled *De Officio Hominis et Civis Juxta Legem Naturalem*.

[3] *De Officio Hominis*, ch. iii, p. 809.   [4] *Ibid.* p. 10.

Sweden for having divorced natural law from theology [1] His critics were perfectly correct from their
own point of view in suspecting the ultimate implications of his work, although he was merely adding
a few extra blows of the hammer to the wedge which
Hobbes had already driven in.

On the practical side, the influence of the Law of
Nature was no less wide in scope. In the domain of
private law the twin ideas of reasonableness and
natural justice, of which it was the progenitor, leapt
into fresh activity, and created or modified whole
bodies of doctrine.[2] The law merchant, formulated to
a large extent by Lord Mansfield, claimed to be
founded on usages which the general reason of mankind had approved as rational; and it was independent of any particular code of local law. In this sense
it was a branch of the Law of Nature and was constantly described as such.[3] The conception of the
"reasonable man", which plays so important a part
in most departments of Anglo-American law, both
civil and criminal, and the rules of Natural Justice,[4]
which form a conspicuous feature of English administrative law and judicial procedure, can also be
ascribed to the practical application of the Law of
Nature.

The following is an example of a yet more direct
application. In 1786 the island of Penang, at that
time neither settled nor cultivated, was ceded by a
native raja to the East India Company. The juris-

[1] Coleman Phillipson, *Pufendorf* in *Great Jurists of the World*,
p. 307.
[2] Sir F. Pollock, *Essays in the Law*, pp. 62-3.
[3] *Ibid.* p. 68.
[4] Cf. W. A. Robson, *Justice and Administrative Law*, pp. 149,
169 *et seq.*

diction of the Governor-General and Council of
Bengal was not accepted, and for some years there
was scarcely any positive law in force in Penang. In
1800 a form of regular government under the Bengal
Presidency was provided for the island, and instructions were sent to the first Lieutenant-Governor to
frame regulations for the administration of justice.
He was directed to adopt native law "tempered by
such parts of the British law, as are of universal
application being founded on the principles of natural
justice".[1] Three years later the judicial officer of the
island reported that the only law he could discover
to direct his efforts was the Law of Nature, and this he
found inadequate as a guide for determining questions
relating to inheritance. The position was rectified a
few years later by the establishment of a regular
Court operating under a charter from the Crown.
The Law of Nature has played a prominent part in the
legal system of the Straits Settlements right up to the
present time, through the operation of a rule whereby native customs are recognised unless contrary to
"justice and general public policy".[2]

The transformation of the Law of Nature, a juristic
expression, into the laws of Nature in the scientific
meaning of the term, was a gradual and subtle
process.

We have seen how the Law of Nature was regarded
as that part of the divine law regulating human
conduct which men could discern by the light of
their reason. The use of the expression to denote a

---

[1] R. St. J. Braddell, *The Law of the Straits Settlements* (Singapore,
1915), pp. 8-9; Sir Frederick Pollock, *Essays in the Law*, pp. 76-7.

[2] W. J. Napier, *An Introduction to the Study of the Law administered in the Colony of the Straits Settlements* (Singapore, 1898),
pp. 32, 39.

theoretical principle deduced from particular facts, applicable to a defined group or class of phenomena, and expressible by the statement that a particular phenomenon always occurs if certain conditions are present, was first used by men who regarded such laws of Nature as commands imposed by God upon matter. It is worth noting that the phrase was employed with reference to a particular science or field of enquiry long before it was used in the more generalised sense as meaning the order and regularity of the entire universe, of which the laws of Nature are but the expression.[1]

The factors which contributed to the transformation of the concept from its former meaning of an ideal norm of human conduct have already been surveyed in the preceding pages. We have seen how the Law of Nature conveyed the notion of universality, of a rule independent of time and place. We have noticed the emphasis it laid on the idea of fundamental principles underlying diverse particular manifestations. We have remarked its indissoluble connection with rationality and its final emergence as the very embodiment of human reason. We have observed its long association with the will of God and the gradual weakening and ultimate destruction of that link. These were the principal strands in the evolving thread of discourse which enabled men of science to appropriate the expression the Laws of Nature, with all that it implies, as the most significant phrase in their vocabulary.

The seeds of this tremendous change were clearly germinating in the 17th century. Spinoza, writing in 1670, said that "the word law, taken in the abstract,

---

[1] Cf. O.E.D., "Law", iii; also *Laws of Nature.*

means that by which an individual, or all things, or as many things as belong to a particular species, act in one and the same fixed and definite manner, which manner depends either on natural necessity or on human decree. . . . For example, the law that all bodies impinging on lesser bodies lose as much of their own motion as they communicate to the latter is a universal law of all bodies and depends on natural necessity. So, too, the law that a man, in remembering one thing, straightway remembers another either like it, or which he had perceived simultaneously with it, is a law which necessarily follows from the nature of man." [1]

The influence of these conceptions is clearly reflected in the poets of the day, who then as always were quick to apprehend and absorb the general ideas of the time. Matthew Prior (1664–1721) declared that

> From Nature's constant or eccentric laws
> The thoughtful soul this general inference draws
> That an effect must presuppose a cause.

John Gay (1688–1732), easily given to satire and ridicule, was serious when he wrote

> He who studies nature's laws
> From certain truth his maxim draws.

Dryden, the Poet Laureate (1631–1700), was not merely translating Virgil [2] when he proclaimed

> Happy the Man, who, studying Nature's Laws,
> Thro' known Effects can trace the sacred cause.

It is not to be supposed that even the most edu-

---

[1] *Tractatus Theologico-Politicus. Works*, tr. R. H. M. Elwes, I, p. 57.

[2] *Georgics*, ii, 490. Cf. Lucretius, *De Rerum Natura*, iii, pp. 37, 38.

cated men of the age were all aware of the general drift of thought. One of the most interesting examples is the case of Robert Boyle, who is, of course, justly celebrated for his scientific work. By a curious irony the author of Boyle's Law protested vigorously against the expression Laws of Nature being applied in any manner whatever to physical matter. For, said he, since a law is a notional rule of acting according to the declared will of a superior, only an intellectual being can be capable of receiving and acting by a law.[1] This scientific pioneer was prepared to go to great lengths in applying a purely juristic interpretation of natural law to physical phenomena. The inconsistency to which he was driven is illustrated by his statement that we should distinguish between "the laws of Nature, more properly so-called, and the custom of Nature, or, if you please, between the Fundamental and General constitutions among Bodily Things, and the Municipal laws . . . that belong to this or that particular sort of Bodies". Thus, when water falls to the ground it may be said to do so by virtue of the custom of nature, that being its usual conduct, whereas when it ascends by suction in a pump, that may be ascribed to "a more catholick law of Nature, by which 'tis provided, that a greater pressure, which in our Case the water suffers from the weight of the incumbent Air, should surmount a lesser, such as is here the Gravity of the Water, that ascends in the Pump or Pipe".[2]

Even in the 18th century the question was not entirely settled. When David Hume, for instance, said that "a man, in conjoining himself to a woman,

[1] Robert Boyle, *A Free Enquiry into the vulgarly received Notion of Nature* (1685-86), pp. 41-2.   [2] *Ibid.* pp. 256-7.

is bound to her according to the terms of his engagement: in begetting children, he is bound, by all the laws of nature and humanity, to provide for their subsistence and education",[1] it is by no means clear whether he is using the term "laws of nature" to mean a moral norm of conduct or a description of the way in which things must inevitably occur.

Broadly speaking, however, the issue was decided, and in the 17th century natural law passed from the domain of the jurists, the theologians and the political philosophers, in whose keeping it had lain for so long, into the hands of the men of science. It only remained for John Austin to set the seal of his barren hand on a *fait accompli* by rejecting, as ambiguous and misleading, the appellation Law of Nature to denote the whole or a portion of the laws set by God to man.[2] Thus passed a great tradition.

One further development remains to be noticed. This was the extension, during the 19th century, of the concept of the laws of nature in its new guise to embrace not only the whole universe of physical matter, but also the sphere of social phenomena and human conduct. This tendency has been well described by Dean Roscoe Pound. "All phenomena were determined by inexorable natural laws to be discovered by observation. Moral and social and hence legal phenomena were governed by laws as completely beyond the power of conscious human control as the movements of the planets. We might discover these laws by observation of social phenomena and might learn to submit to them intelligently

[1] *Of Polygamy and Divorces* in *Essays and Treatises* (4th ed.), i, p. 256.
[2] J. Austin, *Jurisprudence*, ii, p. 88.

instead of rashly or ignorantly defying them. But we could hope to do no more. Except as he could learn to plot some part of the inevitable curve of legal development and save us from futile flyings in the face of the laws by which legal evolution was inevitably governed, the jurist was powerless." [1]

This was the age, not only of a rigid and inflexible jurisprudence, but also of a mechanical and immutable system of political economy. Malthus associated economics with laws of nature not in the traditional juristic meaning of the term but in the newer sense in which the expression was used in the physical sciences.[2] He spoke of the "fixed laws of our nature",[3] and referred to "necessity, that imperious all-pervading law of nature"[4]

Richard Cobden, in his free trade speech in 1844, demanded that the people should have corn at its "natural price" in the world market and that every source of supply should be freely opened "as Nature and Nature's God intended it to be"[5] John Stuart Mill conceived that the laws of production were analogous to the laws of nature applicable to physical phenomena; in his view it was only the laws of distribution which could be regarded as man-made and, therefore, subject to modification by human agency.[6] His outlook was far more humane than that of most of his contemporaries, but its foundations were by no means secure.

---

[1] *An Introduction to the Philosophy of Law*, pp. 54-5.
[2] J. Bonar, *Philosophy and Political Economy* (1922), p. 385.
[3] *Essay on the Principle of Population*, 1798 (1st ed.), pp. 11-12.
[4] *Ibid.* p. 15.
[5] *Speeches by Richard Cobden*, ed. J. Bright and Thorold Rogers, i, p. 105.
[6] Bonar, *op. cit.* p. 387.

The economic doctrine which did most to produce and prolong misery in the 19th century, was the "iron law of wages". The parentage of this principle is not easy to discover. Turgot, Adam Smith, Ricardo, each contributed something to its procreation, though innocently and indirectly, for neither they nor any of the other classical economists ever committed themselves explicitly to the doctrine proclaimed by the "iron law".[1] Yet somehow it emerged from the statements of the economists concerning wages, subsistence, and population; and to the popular consciousness there seemed to be no more characteristic and authentic conclusion to be drawn from the principles of political economy than the assertion that even the most intolerably low wages and utterly miserable conditions of existence were in accordance with the immutable laws of the universe. It thus appeared that any attempt to improve working-class conditions constituted a futile effort to defy the commands of Nature. It was for this reason that Ferdinand Lassalle put in the forefront of his Working Men's Programme of 1862 a denunciation of the "iron and inexorable law" whereby the average wages of labour remain always reduced to the bare subsistence necessary for maintenance and reproduction.[2]

These and other incidents in the development of "the dismal science" during the earlier part of the

[1] Turgot, *Reflexions*, vi; Edwin Cannan, *A Review of Economic Theory* (2nd imp.), pp. 337, 341-5; Palgrave, *Dictionary of Political Economy* (1923), ii, p. 678; Gide and Rist, *A History of Economic Doctrines* (tr. Richards), p. 361; Alfred Marshall, *Principles of Economics* (8th ed.), p. 508; L. H. Haney, *History of Economic Thought* (1922), p. 269.

[2] Palgrave, *Dictionary of Political Economy* (1923), ii, p. 567; Gide and Rist, *op. cit.* p. 361.

Industrial Revolution led to, or condoned, much human suffering which might have been alleviated or avoided. But from one point of view the movement of thought which underlay them betokened a wider synthesis than any which had hitherto prevailed. For it revealed an attempt to bridge the gulf which once again separated mankind from the physical universe. At one period in the ancient Hellenic world "Man lived in a charmed circle of law and custom", and all around the world was lawless.[1] In the opening years of the 19th century it was Nature which presented the spectacle of an ordered world and only man was lawless. The task of the Victorian age was so to widen the concept of Nature as to bring the activities of the human race once more within the jurisdiction of her laws.

[1] *Ante*, p. 200.

IV

NATURAL RIGHTS

THE Law of Nature, during the latter part of its long career, gave birth to the idea of the State of Nature on the one hand and to the conception of Natural Rights on the other.

It is not too much to. say that these twin ideas proved to be the most powerful political forces in the modern world. They provided the intellectual ammunition for the revolt against absolute monarchy which culminated in the French Revolution and led to the subsequent downfall of the legitimist system throughout Europe; they were invoked by the rebellious North American colonists when they founded the republic of the United States; they led to the liberation of the individual from a mass of age-long restrictions in which he was everywhere embedded; they were the progenitors of the nationalism and the claims to self-determination which still surge around us with undiminished vigour; and finally, from their union have been derived many of the assumptions on which socialism, liberalism, and fascism are based.

There was no inevitable connection between the Law of Nature and these formidable offspring. Neither logic nor necessity dictated their procreation. But once they had come into existence no one could seriously doubt their parentage. The line of descent is clear beyond a doubt. Before, however, we attempt to trace the family relationship between the Law of

Nature, the State of Nature, and Natural Rights, I propose to enquire into certain linguistic developments, certain errors of the tongue, whereby some fundamental ideas were expressed in words which entirely changed their meaning.

One of the most important words in the vocabulary of ancient Greek thought was *physis*, which represented a kinetic idea of change or process. The poet Sophocles, when he described Eteocles as "more recent in *physis*" than his elder brother, used the word to indicate human growth; but he also employed it to denote the behaviour of inanimate matter, as, for example, the process which makes the seas continue to be as they are, or in a term of abuse such as "You would provoke the *physis* of a stone" —that is, drive it to behave in an abnormal manner.[1] Herodotus similarly employed the word to connote both biological and geological processes. In one place he refers to certain Spartans as men "well begotten in *physis*, and risen to the first place in wealth"; in another, he remarks that Egypt is "land additionally acquired by the Egyptians or a gift of the river . . . for the *physis* (mode of growth or extension) of the land of Egypt is as follows. . . . The *physis* by which the Egyptian territory grows larger is a 'pouring forward' "—by which he meant a process of sedimentation.[2]

To the early Greek scientists the word *physis* was even more valuable than to the poets and the historians as an instrument for interpreting the general principles underlying all phenomena. "Physis meant at first *growth* or *development*, the essential element

---

[1] J. L. Myres, *The Political Ideas of the Greeks*, p. 268.
[2] *Ibid.* pp. 260-61; *Herodotus*, 2. 5; 7. 134.

of all existence, and it was specially applied to all living things. Gradually there dawned on the Greek mind the idea that this growth proceeded according to definite rules which differed in different cases but in which a certain common character might be distinguished. By a simple process of transference *physis* came to be regarded as this rule or manner of development itself, and so it came to mean something very near to what we should now call a natural law."[1] In a treatise on epilepsy (the so-called sacred disease) written towards the end of the 5th century B.C., which is said to be the first work bearing the distinctive marks of the scientific spirit as contrasted with the religious outlook, we can see a particular application of *physis* in the field of medicine:

"Surely then this disease has its *physis* and causes whence it originates, even as have other diseases, and it is curable by means comparable to their cure. It arises like them from things which enter and quit the body, such as cold, the sun, or the winds, things which are ever changing and are never at rest. Such things are divine or no—as you will, for the distinction matters not—nor is there need to make this distinction anywhere in nature, wherein all things are alike divine and all are alike human, for have not all a *physis* which can be found by those who seek it steadfastly."[2]

Physis, then, was the process of growth or development. The formulation by mankind of such growth, or, indeed, the formal description of any custom, habit, regularity of behaviour, or manner of occur-

[1] Charles Singer, *Historical Relations of Religion and Science* in *Science, Religion and Reality*, p. 93.
[2] *Ibid.* pp. 95-7. The passage as given above has been abbreviated and paraphrased by Professor Singer, *op. cit.*

rence, was denoted by *nomos*.[1] The word *nomos* meant any custom or usage, whether in the external world or in the relations of human beings to one another. A trifling practice such as wearing a beard, no less than the imposition of the death penalty for murder, was equally *nomos*.[2] The term was specially used, however, in connection with human laws. The early codes of the City-States, with the single exception of the Draconian compilation of Athenian case-law, were described as *nomoi*, which were conceived as a body of rules of conduct exerting both restraint and compulsion, at once penal and remedial.[3] The *nomos* was on its juridical side the mean, the common measure which procured the greatest sum of equity, the impartial rule which restrained individual or collective passions, the master who opposed excesses of liberty.[4] The word embodied and explained all that reverence for law as the crystallisation of immemorial custom which was so conspicuous a feature of Greek society.

The words *physis* and *nomos* underwent a significant transformation in the hands of the Romans. The Greek term *physis* was mistranslated by the Latin word *natura*, which means the act of being born, as contrasted with the process of growth or development. Thus the essential meaning of *natura* ends just where that of *physis* begins.[5] As a result the emphasis of men's thoughts was shifted from the laws underlying the processes of change to the far less fertile idea of origin. An illustration of the stagnant pool

---

[1] J. L. Myres, *The Political Ideas of the Greeks*, pp. 264, 278.
[2] Henri Beer, Foreword to G. Glotz, *The Greek City*, p. xvi n.
[3] J. L. Myres, *op. cit.* p. 243.
[4] G. Glotz, *The Greek City*, p. 136.
[5] J. L. Myres, *op. cit.* p. 385.

into which speculation ran in consequence of this verbal error is provided by the work of Lucretius in the 1st century B.C. His treatise *De rerum natura*— "On the Origin of Things in General"—is a philosophical attempt to explain the entire workings of the universe on a particular hypothesis concerning its origin.[1]

The Greek *nomos* was in its turn mistranslated by the Latin *lex*. The derivation of the word *lex* is obscure. It may come from *legere* (to read) and thus be associated with a written ordinance, or from *ligare* (to bind) and hence be connected with the idea of a covenant. But without any doubt it specially connotes statute law, as contrasted with *ius*, which included customary and other types of law. In its most general sense *lex* meant an enacted law, rule or decree.[2] It could also denote a covenant or agreement.

The writings of Cicero reflect the juridical and ethical theories of Greece expressed in the language of Rome.[3] But a fundamental change was involved by that change of language. In every matter the consent of all peoples is to be considered as the law of nature, wrote Cicero,[4] using the phrase *lex naturae* to convey the notion of natural law. But it was a fundamental mistake for the Romans to translate

---

[1] Charles Singer, *op. cit.* p. 94 *et seq.* Cf. Tenney Frank, *Life and Literature in the Roman Republic*, pp. 238-41.

[2] The statute, *lex*, was a written enactment made on the proposal of a magistrate who had obtained favourable auspices and was authorised by the *comitia* of the people to publish it under his own name, provided it received the *patrum auctoritas* from the Senate. J. Declareuil, *Rome the Law-giver*, pp. 18-19. Cf. H. J. Jolowicz, *Historical Introduction to the Study of Roman Law*, pp. 83-4. As to the legislative process see *ante*, p. 36.

[3] Salmond, "The Law of Nature, xlii", *Law Quarterly Review*, p. 128.

[4] *Tusc.* I, 13, 30.

physis by *natura* and *nomos* by *lex*, and much confusion was created by superimposing the Latin
conceptions of origin and contract or enactment on
the Greek notions of process and formula. Fifteen
hundred years of obscure and perverted thinking
took place before the Hellenic ideas of process and
its formulation were recovered and the spirit of
scientific enquiry enabled to resume its task once
again.[1]

Among the Roman jurists we meet also with the
expression *Jus naturale*, which they employed when
referring to the rules of conduct that could be rationally deduced from the general conditions of human
life. *Jus* really means that which is morally binding,
whether written or unwritten, be it natural, human or
divine. *Jus naturale* is that which, because it is good
and just, possesses in and of itself the principles of
law: in short, the Right of Nature. There was, however, a "convenient ambiguity" about *Jus* whereby it
could mean not only right and law, but also "a right"
—that is, an actual legal right possessed by a particular individual or class, and capable of being
enforced in the Courts of Law.[2] It was this ambiguity
which ultimately produced the doctrine of Natural
Rights.

The distinction between *ius* and *lex* became recognised to an increasing extent with the passing of the
Middle Ages. The former, wrote Sir John Fortescue
in the 15th century, represents everything that is
good and equitable. But all such is not *lex*, although
law ought properly to be equal and good. Hence "it
is not convenient to call all *ius* law; for every man

[1] J. L. Myres, *The Political Ideas of the Greeks*, pp. 385-8.
[2] Roscoe Pound, *An Introduction to the Philosophy of Law*, p. 42.

who seeks to have back what is his own before a judge hath the right (*ius*) but not the law (*lex*) of claiming it".[1] Hobbes, again, distinguishes the Right of Nature (*ius naturale*), which is the liberty each man has to use his own powers for the purpose of preserving his life, from a law of nature (*lex naturalis*) which is a definite precept or general rule, founded on reason, by which a man is forbidden to commit any act which may lead to his destruction. Thus, *ius*, or right, is the freedom to do or to forbear, whereas *lex*, or law, binds one to a particular obligation.[2]

Law, in its Latin garb, connoted some kind of positive commandment which had been definitely enacted in one way or another. It implied command and obligation, no matter whether the enacting power were God alone, human reason, or the divine power working through and in conjunction with the rational intelligence of man. Sir Isaac Newton, whose *Principia* was published in 1687, described his famous laws of motion as *Lex I*, *Lex II*, etc., and called them collectively *leges*. The English word law was not applied to natural phenomena before the Restoration; and the laws of nature were regarded, by those who first used the expression in a scientific sense, as enactments imposed by God upon matter.[3] The far-reaching importance of this notion of command and obedience in the physical realm will be discussed in a later part of the work.

We can now see, after this somewhat lengthy excursion into the history of certain words and phrases, how and why it was that there emerged from the idea

---

[1] *De Natura legis Naturae*, ch. xxx (Clermont ed.), I, pp. 222-3.
[2] Thomas Hobbes, *Leviathan* (Molesworth ed.), p. 116.
[3] Cf. Logan Pearsall Smith, *The English Language*, pp. 218-20.

of the Law of Nature the notion of Natural Rights: that is, of rights possessing inherent validity by virtue of their own essential justice and moral force. The innate strength of such Natural Rights thus came to be, to those who recognise their authority, in no sense dependent upon the extent to which they are reflected, neglected, or opposed by the actual law. It may be truthfully said, indeed, that the appeal to Natural Rights has been the most powerful weapon for opposing existing law and government ever forged by the human intellect. Whenever multitudes of men and women have suffered deeply from oppression or felt passionately about some form of injustice, they have invariably claimed its removal in terms of Natural Right. Whenever a community has resisted the prevailing political and legal order, they have usually done so on the ground that it violated the Rights bestowed by Nature. Whenever a governing class or a ruler has sought to uphold a questionable authority in the face of wavering allegiance, it has invoked Natural Right or its *alter ego* Natural Justice. Whenever the framers of a revolutionary constitution have desired to place the seal of ultimate sanction upon their handiwork, they have announced its conformity with the dictates of Natural Right. Natural Rights, it has been remarked, are the court of appeal for all who think that they suffer injustice.[1]

John Locke, and most of the publicists of the 17th and 18th centuries who derived the theory of Natural Rights from the Law of Nature, regarded the doctrine

[1] W. R. Inge, *Liberty and Natural Rights* (1934), p. 23. The use of Natural Rights has not been confined to those who desire to effect radical changes in the existing order. In the hands of Blackstone, for example, the doctrine was employed for conservative ends. *Ibid.* p. 29.

as an appeal to freedom. And such it was, even when the freedom demanded was selfish and materialistic in character. In the 17th century, for example, Natural Rights were invoked by the proponents of the rising individualism of the time as a reason why the moral restraints upon cupidity which had prevailed throughout the Middle Ages should be swept away and economic self-interest be given an entirely free hand.[1] In 1604 we find a Committee of the House of Commons asserting that since merchandise is the principal trade of the country, it is "against the natural right and liberty of the subjects of England to restrain it into the hands of some few".[2]

Later in the 17th century the English sects who preached and practised resistance to kings and magistrates sought to justify their actions in terms of Natural Rights, which they identified in varying measure with reason, the inner light, and Christian revelation. Complaint was made against the Levellers in Cromwell's time that "be the Lawes and customes of a Kingdom never so plain and cleer against their wayes, yet they will not submit, but Cry out for natural rights derived from Adam and right reason".[3]

It was, however, in the 18th century that Natural Rights exerted their most powerful influence. The Declaration of Independence by the American Colonies in 1776 and the Declaration of the Rights of Man by the National Assembly in France were two events of world-shattering importance which not only

---

[1] R. H. Tawney, *Religion and the Rise of Capitalism*, p. 180.
[2] *Commons' Journals*, 21st May 1604, vol. i, p. 218. Quoted by Tawney, *op. cit.* p. 179.
[3] C. Becker, *The Declaration of Independence* (1922), p. 34.

breathed the spirit of Natural Rights but were deliberately expressed in terms of the doctrine. The framers
of the Declaration of Independence solemnly proclaimed that the American colonists were assuming
among the powers of the earth "the separate and
equal station to which the Laws of Nature and of
Nature's God entitle them". The famous document
then went on to declare "these truths to be self-
evident, that all men are created equal, that they are
endowed by their Creator with certain unalienable
rights, that among these are life, liberty, and the
pursuit of happiness". Government is instituted
among men to secure these rights and "whenever
any form of government becomes destructive of
these ends, it is the right of the people to alter
or to abolish it, and to institute new government. . . ."

Jefferson explained later in a letter to Lee that the
Declaration aimed neither at originality of principle
nor of sentiment. "It is intended to be an expression
of the American mind. . . . All its authority rests then
on the harmonising sentiments of the day, whether
expressed in conversation, in letters, printed essays,
or the elementary books of public right, as Aristotle,
Cicero, Locke, Sidney, etc."[1]

These "harmonising sentiments of the day" comprised the notion that there is a natural order in the
world to which everything is properly subject, including all the political and social relations of mankind. The laws or principles of this natural order
are clearly revealed to the human mind and cannot
be confused or mistaken for anything else. Every
human being has an inherent Right conferred by

[1] *The Writings of Thomas Jefferson* (1869), ii, p. 407.

Nature to have the laws and political institutions under which he lives conform to these principles.[1] How these ideas could be reconciled with slavery was not and could not be explained.

The *Déclaration des Droits de l'Homme et du Citoyen* was issued in 1789. In it the representatives of the French people solemnly proclaimed the "Natural, inalienable, and sacred Rights of Man" (*les Droits naturels, inaliénables et sacrés de l'homme*). Article I stated that men are born and remain free and equal in rights. Social distinctions can be founded only on the common good. Article II declared that the end of all political association is the conservation of the Natural and imprescriptible Rights of man. These Rights are liberty, property, safety, and resistance to oppression (*la liberté, la propriété, la sûreté, et la résistance à l'oppression*).

The action of the American colonists, no less than that of the National Assembly in France, commended itself warmly to the radical mind of Jeremy Bentham. But the sentiments which inspired them seemed to him the height of absurdity. "Natural Rights is simple nonsense," he wrote, "natural and imprescriptible rights, rhetorical nonsense — nonsense upon stilts."[2] In his view it is not the rights of man, but their non-existence, which cause government to be established. It has always been desirable that rights should exist, but they do not exist unless they are expressly established.[3] "Who can help lamenting", he said of the Declaration of

---

[1] Becker, *op. cit.* pp. 26-7.
[2] J. Bentham, *Anarchical Fallacies. Works* (ed. Bowring), vol. ii, p. 501.
[3] *Panomial Fragments. Works*, vol. iii, p. 219.

Independence, "that so rational a cause should be rested upon reasons, so much fitter to beget objections, than to remove them?"[1]

Yet for all the scorn which Bentham poured on the revolutionary doctrines of the day, the Utilitarian philosophy of which he was the chief author had much in common with the theory of Natural Rights. Both are formed on the idea of universal reason. They both lead to much the same conclusions though perhaps by different routes. To the greater part of mankind, however, the idea that each individual possesses, by the mere fact of being alive, innate moral rights based on equity and justice arising from the very essence of human existence, is infinitely more attractive and inspiring than the laboured ratiocination contained in Bentham's awkward phrases.

It was through the doctrine of Natural Rights, then, that the principles of the Law of Nature, which for two thousand years had operated as a series of beneficent but peaceful maxims, became in the last quarter of the 18th century a mass of dynamite that shattered an ancient monarchy and shook the civilised world to its very foundations.[2] Liberty, Equality, and Fraternity, said Lord Bryce, are virtually implied in the Law of Nature in its Greek guise no less than in its French dress. The same might be said of the right to life, liberty, and property. These implications were embedded even in the Roman conception, but they lay so deep down

---

[1] J. Bentham, *An Introduction to the Principles of Morals and Legislation. Works*, vol. i, p. 154.

[2] J. Bryce, *The Law of Nature* in *Studies in History and Jurisprudence*, p. 599.

and were overlaid by so vast a mass of positive legal rules and monarchical institutions that their presence was unsuspected. Hence no hint of the tremendous possibilities which they contained served to awaken apprehension or mistrust.

Even in the 19th century the influence in practical affairs of Natural Rights and Natural Justice was still considerable. The Indian Civil Procedure Code, 1882, provided that a foreign judgment shall not operate as a bar if in the opinion of the Court which deals with the question it is "contrary to natural justice", and this remains substantially the law to-day.[1] The British Order in Council for Southern Rhodesia of 20th October 1898 directed the Courts in that territory to be guided in civil cases between Kafirs by native law, "so far as that law is not repugnant to natural justice or morality, or to any Order made by Her Majesty in Council". The mills of the British Empire grind exceedingly slow, but it was no small triumph for the Law of Nature to be placed, after two thousand years of variegated history, on an equality with an Order in Council of good Queen Victoria.

The "principles of natural justice" so far as the practical operation of English Law is concerned at the present time, have come to consist in the main of a series of well-established rules which the Courts require to be observed in the letter and the spirit by

---

[1] Code of Civil Procedure, Part I, s. 14. For the present law see R. Satyamurti Aiyar, *The Code of Civil Procedure* (as modified to July 1930), sec. 13 (2nd ed., Madras, 1930). In British India, again, the Courts have from time to time been directed to apply "the principles of justice equity and good conscience in cases where no positive law or usage is available to be applied to the case in hand". C. P. Ilbert, *The Government of India* (3rd ed., 1915), p. 360.

any person or body exercising functions of a judicial
or even an administrative character. These include
such provisions as the requirement that the judge
must not be personally interested in the subject-
matter of the dispute; that he must hear both sides
before determining the issue, and that each party
must know the case he has to meet.[1] This modern
idea of Natural Justice within its very narrow field
takes account of Nature in a way closely resembling
that which prevailed in the ancient world: the natural
is that which accords with what is supposed to be
the true and universal reason of mankind. Professor
C. K. Allen uses the phrase in a similar sense in a
contemporary work when he expresses regret that
the English system of equity should have developed
"on lines which often seem to be the opposite of
natural justice".[2]

Broadly speaking, however, the conception of
Natural Right or Natural Justice long ago lost its theoretical importance in England and the British Empire, despite its continuing influence in practical
affairs. In this respect there is a striking contrast
between England and most of the other European
countries. In the Continental schools *droit naturel* or
Naturrecht has remained one of the great and vital
topics of discourse among jurists and philosophers,[3]
and many of the leading intellects have been and
still are devoted to the study of the moral and social

---

[1] See my *Justice and Administrative Law*, p. 169. The practice of
the Judicial Committee of the Privy Council in appeals on criminal
matters from various parts of the British Empire is of great interest in
this connection.

[2] *Law in the Making*, p. 229.

[3] Cf. Sir F. Pollock, *Introduction to the History of the Science of
Politics*, p. 110.

conditions of universal significance which determine the evolution of the law. In England, on the contrary, legal speculation has lain dormant for nearly a century, apart from the occasional contribution of a great pioneer like Sir Henry Maine [1] or a brilliant historian like Maitland. On the whole, English legal thought since Bentham has run in narrow grooves, remaining crabbed and "practical" in the worst sense of the word, unimaginative and devoid of any philosophic, ethical, or sociological background. John Austin is a perfect example to illustrate the tendency on its analytical side, while from the historical standpoint the undue eminence accorded to Blackstone may be regarded as an indication of the flatness of the surrounding country. It is scarcely too much to say that jurisprudence hardly exists in Great Britain. Philosophy and law are barely on speaking terms, while sociology and law are strangers who have never even met.

This unfortunate state of affairs is largely due to the fact that when in the 17th century the Law of Nature passed from the realm of the jurists and the political philosophers to the domain of the men of science, its former guardians lost all interest in the concept of Nature, that great beacon whose rays have illuminated for twenty centuries the hard and stony path along which the thinker struggles on his lonely journey. Because English lawyers no longer sought the light of nature,[2] they remained virtually in-

---

[1] See my essay on "Maine To-day" in *Modern Theories of Law*.

[2] A significant illustration of the attitude of modern English judges is contained in *In re King and Co.'s Trade Mark* (1892), 2 C.D. p. 479. The case concerned the jurisdiction of the High Court of England to rectify the register kept under the Patents Acts 1883–88. "The Act of Parliament", said Lord Justice Lindley in the Court of Appeal, "says

different to the great discussion concerning Natural
Rights and Natural Justice which took place on the
continent in the 18th century.

No one who is at all conversant with the methods
of modern science, and sympathetic to its aims and
spirit, would desire for a moment to revive the con-
fident *a priori* deductive rationalism of the natural-
law writers of the 17th and 18th centuries. To do so
would undoubtedly be a retrograde step. We cannot assume that the alleged principles of natural law
are self-evident, and assert as dogmatic truths such
propositions as "All men are equal before the law" or
"All men have the right to life and to the product of
their labour" any more than we can assume that
there are eternal and self-evident principles operating
in the physical world whereby "the whole is greater
than any part" or "the cause must be equal to the
effect".[1] Every statement, whether relating to the
social relations of human beings or to the phenomena
of the physical world, must be tested for its certainty,
accuracy, universality, and coherency. But to admit
this does not imply that it is desirable for jurisprudence and political science to be divorced from
the study of Nature. To realise the full extent of the
loss which law has suffered one has only to turn to
the popular text-book on *Jurisprudence* by T. E.
Holland, which is still widely used in British universities and law schools.

A right, says Holland, is in general one man's

nothing whatever about the method of procedure to rectify the register.
. . . The rules do not prescribe how the applications are to be made.
We are left entirely to the light of nature. What is the light of nature?
I mean English nature and English notions of justice and of what
is right."

[1] Morris R. Cohen, *Reason and Nature*, p. 413.

capacity of influencing the acts of another, by means of the opinion or force of society rather than by his own strength. "A 'right' is thus the name given to the advantage a man has when he is so circumstanced that a general feeling of approval, or at least of acquiescence, results when he does, or abstains from doing, certain acts, and when other people act or forbear to act, in accordance with his wishes; while a general feeling of disapproval results when anyone prevents him from so doing or abstaining at his pleasure, or refuses to act in accordance with his wishes. *Further than this we need not go.* It is for psychology to enquire by what, if any, special faculty the mind is capable of affirming or denying the existence of rights." [1]

If Natural Rights are unsubstantial, these rights of Holland's are mere shadows, phantom skeletons in the lawyer's cupboard devoid of life and blood. If Natural Rights are based on false history, this analysis is based on no history at all. If the exponent of Natural Rights seeks to trace the ultimate sanction for the legal order to a universal moral consciousness the existence of which is doubtful, the author of *Holland's Jurisprudence* is content to hand over the essential problems of his subject to the adherents of another discipline without making even the feeblest attempt to solve them. If the doctrine of Natural Rights falls into the error of postulating a universal and ubiquitous faculty of reason which prescribes rules and institutions that vary with time and place, English lawyers during the past hundred years have escaped this pitfall only at the price of avoiding all speculative

---

[1] *Jurisprudence*, p. 82. See p. 86 for a further explanation of a right. (The italics are mine.)

reflections of any kind whatever, believing themselves thereby to be more "practical" and business-
like, more truly professional and more firmly rooted
in reality.[1] In the last resort, however, is there anyone
so essentially unpractical as the professional specialist
who knows nothing and cares less about the philosophical and historical foundations of his subject?

[1] Dean Inge has recently observed that though the appeal to Natural
Law leaves many problems unsolved, "the advantage of admitting that
things are right or wrong absolutely, and are not merely made right or
wrong by Parliament or public opinion, is incalculable" (*Liberty and
Natural Rights*, p. 34). The defence is worth quoting, but the modern
doctrine of Natural Rights has no need to call in aid "absolute" ethical
values. It is essentially relative to the possibilities and antecedents of
any given situation.

V

THE STATE OF NATURE

CLOSELY allied with the doctrine of Natural Rights was the idea of a State of Nature, and it is to this that we can now turn our attention.

The Law of Nature (*ius naturale* or *lex naturae*) of the Romans had no connection whatever with a State of Nature.[1] The jurists of ancient Rome never interested themselves at any time in the conditions of primitive communities other than those of the less civilised peoples with whom they came into contact; nor did they associate Natural Law with a particular time and place.[2] The early Fathers of the Church, the canon lawyers and theologians of the Middle Ages, were equally unaware of any possible connection between the law natural and a pre-social condition of mankind. There is, indeed, no inevitable relationship between the two conceptions, although they have in fact had an historical association.

The first attempt to establish a connection was probably that made by Francisco de Vitoria (*c.* 1483–1546), Professor of Theology at Salamanca and one of the founders of International Law. The discovery

[1] Seneca conceived a State of Nature in which mankind originally lived as a Golden Age not unlike that postulated by the Christian Fathers to have existed before the Fall. But this ideal condition had no relation either to historical or contemporary realities, or to *ius naturale*. R. W. and A. J. Carlyle, *A History of Mediaeval Political Theory in the West*, i, pp. 23-5, 117.

[2] Otto Gierke, *Natural Law and the Theory of Society*, 1500–1800, introd. by Ernest Barker, vol. i, p. xxxvii.

of America towards the end of the 15th century
brought the most civilised nations of western Europe
into contact with the primitive Indian tribes of the
new world. The question arose in a sharp practical
form whether these barbarous heathen communities
could be regarded as possessing any rights in their
dealings with the conquering invaders. Francisco
and certain other great Spanish jurists of the day
declared unequivocally that the relationship must
inevitably be governed by Natural Law and Christian
duty. In a treatise specially devoted to the subject,
On the Indians recently Discovered, Vitoria insisted
that the same rules of justice expressed in the same
rules of law were applicable alike to the civilised
nations of Europe and to the primitive peoples of
America—indeed to all other peoples of the world.[1]

This view was supported by a wealth of learning
culled from the law and literature of the ancient
world. The whole earth, said Vitoria, is in some sort
one republic; and he enunciated for the Spanish
settlers a policy of trusteeship or mandate not fundamentally dissimilar from that which is at last beginning to gain recognition in our own day. The humane
doctrine which Francisco proclaimed was ignored by
the statesmen and buccaneers of his age; but it was
nevertheless destined to live through the centuries.[2]

With the approach of the modern world political
thinkers and jurists lost touch with these ideas arising
out of the early voyages of discovery. There emerged
in place of them a series of doctrines concerning a so-

[1] *De Indis Noviter Inventis*; James Brown Scott, *The Spanish
Origins of International Law: Francisco de Vitoria and his law of
Nations* (London, 1934), pp. 63, 163, 386.

[2] *De Indis*, sec. iii; Scott, *op. cit.* p. xxxvii; A. Zimmern, *Quo
Vadimus?* (Oxford, 1934), p. 15.

called State of Nature, which related, not to the conditions known to prevail among aboriginal peoples of whom observation had been actually made, but to the hypothetical condition in which the human race was supposed to exist before any social arrangements or political institutions had been established.

In the 17th century, Filmer, Locke, and Hobbes all made extensive use of this hypothetical State of Nature to support their respective political philosophies, and each of them sought to base the commonwealth on certain consequences alleged to arise from this rudimentary condition. The dualism inherent in Aristotle's separation of Nature from convention[1] took shape after the Reformation and was clearly embodied in Locke's theory of the social compact and his doctrine of Natural Rights existing prior to government or law.[2] Locke contended that the "State of Nature has a law of Nature to govern it, which obliges everyone, and reason, which is that law, teaches all mankind who will but consult it, that being all equal and independent, no one ought to harm another in his life, health, liberty or possessions."[3] This invention of a pre-social condition of existence served to confer upon mankind certain Natural Rights whose authority was claimed to be anterior in point of time and superior in validity to any which could be derived from human laws or the institutions of civil government. It also enabled Locke to demonstrate to men and women their irrevocable title to vindicate these Natural Rights

[1] *Ante*, p. 201 *et seq.*
[2] Charles Grove Haines, *Revival of Natural Law Concepts*, p. 23.
[3] *Second Treatise on Government*, sec. 6; see also sec. 87.

by resisting tyranny and all forms of absolute monarchy.

Nature and the Law of Nature began to assume a new garb in the hands not only of Locke, but also of his conservative opponents such as Filmer and Hobbes. The newly conceived State of Nature led to the identification, for the first time, of the natural with the primitive. It required but another step, and a logical one at that, to arrive at the idealisation of primitive Nature expressed in so compelling a manner by Jean Jacques Rousseau. To live in accordance with Nature had been to the Stoics the sum of all virtue two thousand years earlier; and by Nature they had meant the universal divine reason implanted in man. Rousseau's war-cry was the Return to Nature; but by this he meant a condition of extreme simplicity, a way of life at once primitive and ideal: opposed alike to the artificial existence he saw around him, the established political order and even the culture which was supposed to be its rarest fruit. Rousseau elevated the State of Nature to "the splendour of a lost paradise." He saw it as a condition in which human beings were unfettered by social restraints and hence free and equal.[1]

Between these two conceptions of the life according to Nature a great gulf seems to yawn. And yet they are more nearly related than might at first appear. For Locke, Rousseau, and nearly all the thinkers of the 17th and 18th centuries regarded primitive man as being a strictly rational creature. They made Natural Law and Natural Rights, indeed, the outcome of the essential reason with which man-

[1] Otto Gierke. *Natural Law and the Theory of Society*, 1500–1800 (tr. E. Barker), p. 101.

kind is imbued. From this point of view Rousseau and the forerunners of his school were not revolutionary innovators but the conservators of an ancient doctrine. Grotius himself had remarked that human nature is the mother of natural law, and, through contractual relationships due to the exigence of society, the great grandmother of civil law; while Pufendorf insisted that one must consider the natural state, not of animals governed by mere impulse, but of man endowed with reason, the controller of all his other faculties, which even in the State of Nature has a common, steadfast, uniform standard to go by.[1]

What the philosophers of the 18th century did was to popularise and emphasise the theory, the origins of which lay far back in the remote past, that in one respect every human being is alike, that there is a faculty that all men share and which is precisely the same in every individual. This faculty is Reason, or *le bons sens*. It is the *'intelligence humaine'* of which Descartes speaks when he says *"Les sciences ne sont rien autre chose que l'intelligence humaine qui reste une et toujours la même quelle que soit la variété des objets aux quels s'applique"*. Descartes did not mean to suggest that everyone has an equal share of this faculty of human intelligence, but only that its form or character is the same in everyone. The "reasonable man", whose standard of conduct constitutes a norm by which every litigant in the English Law Courts is liable to be judged at the present time, is based on exactly the same hypothesis.

From the middle of the 17th century, when the

[1] Coleman Phillipson, *Pufendorf* in *Great Jurists of the World*, pp. 314, 324; Grotius, *Proleg.* 16.

doctrine of natural law became associated with the notion of the State of Nature, its influence increased both in scope and in intensity. The principles enunciated by John Locke secured widespread acceptance both in England and in the American colonies, while on the continent the writings of Rousseau swept all before them. Only on a few rare occasions in history have the doctrines of an abstract theorist exercised the irresistible power over the thoughts and actions of men which the ideas of Rousseau acquired in the 18th century. To them must be ascribed, more than to any other single intellectual force, the tremendous explosion of the French Revolution, which transformed European society root and branch.

The voluminous discussion which raged for more than a century on the subject of the State of Nature, and the character of the natural law which prevailed therein, was sustained by the practical importance of its conclusions. To-day the arguments seem dogmatic, unhistorical, fantastic, absurd. But those who participated or listened to them felt they were moving in a world of discourse which bore directly on all the great political and legal problems of the day. The power of the prince, the rights of the people, the privileges of the aristocracy, the position of the Church, the functions of government, the status of the peasant, the right to property, freedom of speech —all were referred to the pre-social condition in which man was originally supposed to live, the compact he made when agreeing to enter into community with his fellows, and the consequences which could be said to flow therefrom.

The adherents of the theory were unanimous that "the transition from a State of Nature, exclusively

controlled by Natural Law, to the conditions of
political life, had always been made in obedience to
immutable natural rules, and that the union of men
in a political society, and the erection of a political
authority, had always taken place in virtue of the
same eternal principles. . . ."[1] The actual law claiming authority in human society was held to be unable
to affect in the slightest degree the impregnable
foundations of natural law. Men therefore looked
to the dictates of a Law of Nature, enthroned high
above the whole fabric of historically established
law,[2] for guidance or direction in the solution of all
the fundamental problems arising from the relation
of king and people, of citizen and society, of government and group.

[1] Otto Gierke, *Natural Law and the Theory of Society, 1500–1800*
(tr. E. Barker), vol. i, p. 39.
[2] *Ibid.*

VI

REASON, LAW, AND GOD

THE association of a Universal Reason with the laws and political institutions of mankind has been a matter of great importance in the history of ideas. Among the Greeks the notion found explicit expression in the works of both Plato and Aristotle. If we wish, says Plato, to name States after their rulers, the true State ought to be called by the name of the God who rules over wise men; for ultimately it is reason which predominates, as expressed in law, and reason is God.[1] Aristotle, in the *Politics*, observes that he who bids the law rule makes God and Reason supreme, but he who entrusts man with supreme power adds an element of the beast; for desire is a wild beast, and passion perverts the minds of rulers, even when they are the best of men. The law is intellect free from appetite.[2] Thus Plato and Aristotle were agreed that Reason and God are one, and law the expression of Reason.

Demosthenes was a pupil of Plato, and in his ora-

[1] Plato, *Laws*, pp. 713-18. Cf. E. Barker, *The Political Thought of Plato and Aristotle*, p. 190.

[2] *Politics*, Book. III, ch. xvi. Cf. the declaration in the Constitution of Massachusetts (framed in 1779-80), article xxx: "In the government of this commonwealth, the legislative department shall never exercise the executive and judicial powers, or either of them: The executive shall never exercise the legislative and judicial powers, or either of them: The judicial shall never exercise the legislative and executive powers, or either of them: to the end it may be a government of laws and not of men".

tion in the case of Aristogeiton he declared, "This is law, to which it is proper that all men should conform, for many reasons, chiefly because every rule of law (*nomos*) is a discovery and gift of the gods, an opinion of sensible men, a restitution of things done amiss, voluntary and involuntary, and a general compact of the community in accordance with which it is proper for all in that community to live". This statement, which clearly identifies the divine will, human reason, and the law of the State, was prefixed to the Digest of Justinian in the 6th century A.D., and thus formed part of the contribution made by Greek thought to Roman law. The only change introduced was the replacement of the Olympian "gods" in the original by the "God" of Christianity.

Cicero had elaborated the same doctrines in the first century B.C. "Since there is nothing better than reason, and since it exists both in man and God," he wrote in his most celebrated treatise, "the first common possession of man and God is reason. But those who have reason in common must also have right in common. And since right reason is law, we must believe that men have law also in common with the gods."[1] Law, continued Cicero, is right reason applied to command and prohibition.[2] Furthermore "those who share law must also share Justice; and those who share these are to be regarded as members of the same commonwealth. If indeed they obey the same authorities and powers, this is true in a far greater degree; but as a matter of fact they do obey this celestial system, the divine mind, and the God of transcendent power. Hence we must now conceive

[1] Cicero, *De Legibus* (Loeb), pp. 323, 2.
[2] *Ibid.* p. 333.

of this whole universe as one commonwealth of which both gods and men are members."[1]

When the Roman law revived after the long gloom of the Dark Ages it was the predominance of Reason in its system and method that made the study of it in the newly founded universities of Europe an intellectual adventure of outstanding significance. Roman law became a stimulating force in the centres of Western learning from the 11th century onwards very largely because it upheld the conception of law as a reasoned systematic whole, to be developed by scientific interpretation.[2] Without it the laws of the European countries might have been no more than a medley of local customs.

In the Middle Ages, as we have already observed, men's thoughts were concentrated on the idea of the law of God and its supremacy over all other enactments.[3] This did not preclude a widespread controversy among the Schoolmen as to whether the essence of divine law is Will or Reason: that is, whether it derives its authority from the mere fact of being a divine command, or whether its essential force inheres because it embodies the dictate of Reason as to what is right, the role of the deity being that of teacher rather than of law-giver.[4] But each of these doctrines led ultimately to the identification of law with Reason, for the will of God was in any case assumed to be a reasonable will and human reason could properly claim to interpret it.

St. Thomas Aquinas laid special emphasis on the

[1] *Ibid.* p. 323.
[2] F. de Zulueta, *The Science of Law* in *The Legacy of Rome*, p. 177.
[3] O. Gierke, *Political Theories of the Middle Ages*, tr. by F. W. Maitland, p. 172.
[4] *Ante*, p. 202 *et seq.*

view that since man is a reasoning animal his nature must tend towards a rational good. The laws of human society must therefore above all else deal with the pursuit of this rational good.[1] A law, said Aquinas, is "nothing else than an ordinance of reason for the common good, made by him who has care of the community, and promulgated".[2] The eternal law which governs all things is the expression of the Reason of God, the supreme law-giver. That part of it which is not revealed, but discerned by man through his own intelligence, may be termed Natural Law. It is the outcome of human reason, which is itself created and directed by Divine Reason.[3]

The Reformation produced a conflict between law and religion of an almost unprecedented character and extent. The antagonism between lawyers and clergy which arose in the 16th century resulted in a contrast being drawn by Catholic theologians between the cramping narrowness of "legalism"—a term of reproach addressed to the secular law—and the spiritual freedom of the Church.[4] The Protestant jurists and publicists replied to this assault by preaching the doctrine of a divinely ordained State and a Law of Nature divorced from theology. In this way they formulated a philosophy of law and politics suited to the needs of the age. The system of Natural Law thus created was based mainly on rational foundations and embodied that unlimited belief in Reason which marked the Renaissance. It permitted

[1] Bede Jarrett, *Social Theories of the Middle Ages*, p. 13.
[2] *Summa Theologica*, First Part of Part II, Q 90, 4.
[3] J. Bryce, *The Law of Nature* in *Studies in History and Jurisprudence*, pp. 594-5.
[4] J. Bryce, *The Relations of Law and Religion* in *Studies in History and Jurisprudence*, p. 638.

the jurists of each country to claim the right to interpret the Law of Nature by the light of their own intelligence, just as Protestant theology allowed each Christian to interpret the gospels to the satisfaction of his own reason and conscience.[1]

The culmination of this approach is to be found in Pufendorf, who explained that there are three sources from which men derive knowledge of their duty, and of what is commanded in this life as being morally good or forbidden as being morally bad. The first of these sources is the light of reason, from which flow the commonest duties, especially those which produce sociability. The second is the civil law, which determines the duties of man in so far as he is subject to the jurisdiction of a particular State. And thirdly there is the particular revelation of divine authority, from which spring the duties of a Christian.[2]

A few years later we find the French philosopher Nicolas Malebranche declaring that the general laws in accordance with which God regulates the course of the world are similarly revealed by Reason, Experience, and Scripture. The general laws of the communication of motion, by which fire is made to burn and the sun to illuminate; the laws of the conjunction of soul and body, by which speech, feeling, imagination, walking, and so forth are effected and man united to the other works of God; and "the laws of the union of the soul with God, with the intelligible substance of the Universal Reason" whereby the mind is able to think of whatever it desires and to discover truth—these laws, said Malebranche, flow

---

[1] Roscoe Pound, *Introduction to the Philosophy of Law*, p. 39.
[2] Samuel von Pufendorf, *De Officio Hominis et Civis*, Introduction, ix.

from the twin founts of Reason and Experience. From Scripture flew the general laws of Nature and grace which give good and bad angels power over inferior bodies, and enable devils to tempt us and angels to defend us; and secondly, the laws through which Jesus received supreme power in heaven and earth over both mind and body.[1]

The significant fact is that Pufendorf, writing on law and social institutions, and Malebranche, reflecting on metaphysics and religion, both derive the laws which they postulate from the threefold sources of Reason, Experience, and God. At the moment when they wrote the modern world was emerging from the womb of time; human laws and scientific laws had alike been placed for the most part on a secular foundation, and Universal Reason was coming to be recognised as the sovereign lord of mankind. But in the background there remained a residuum of unexplained physical phenomena on the one hand and of moral obligation on the other. In this province the God of Christianity held sway as a kind of residuary legatee unaided by either Reason or Experience.

In the first part of this book an attempt was made to show the association, during all the earlier stages of human history, of the laws and political institutions of mankind with the divine or supernatural forces of the universe. We saw that magic is the parent of both law and science, since the medicine-man is at once the early law-giver, the embryonic scientist, and the priest. He explains natural phenomena, such as

[1] Nicolas Malebranche, *Dialogues on Metaphysics and Religion* (published 1688), tr. M. Ginsberg (1923), pp. 336-7.

thunder and lightning, disease and pestilence, famine and drought, in terms of magic and superstition; and he bases the legal code on these same forces, using as his strongest appeal the alleged need to appease evil spirits. Thus human law and natural law are alike rooted in magic, religion, and superstition.

This second part has been devoted to an account of the life-history of the idea of natural law, from the days when it had an essentially jural and humanistic meaning to the time when it came to connote the laws relating to the universe of science. We observed the various changes which took place in the concept of Nature; we saw Natural Law become embalmed in the religious doctrine of the Middle Ages; we traced the gradual emergence of Reason as the authentic source of law, alike for the laws which govern society and for those which rule physical matter. Universal Reason either supplants the divine element or else is identified with God and the divine authority.

There are many different conceptions of the nature of juridical law. "Each shows us a picture of some ultimate basis, beyond reach of the individual human will, that stands fast in the whirl of change of which life is made up. This steadfast ultimate basis may be conceived as the divine pleasure or will or reason, revealed through a divinely ordained immutable moral code. It may be put in the form of some ultimate metaphysical datum which is so given us that we may rest in it forever. It may be portrayed as certain ultimate laws which inexorably determine the phenomena of human conduct. Or it may be described in terms of some authoritative will for the time and place, to which the wills of others are subjected, that will deriving its authority ultimately and

absolutely in some one of the preceding forms, so
that what it does is by and large in no wise a matter
of chance."[1]

The liberation of the human mind from the cramping influence of religious assumptions respecting the
nature of the universe; the destruction of authori-
tarian dogmas concerning the sanctity of law and the
behaviour of physical matter; the banishment of
sprites, demons, angels, gods, witches, and wonder-
workers of all kinds to the realm of myth and legend;
the substitution of rational analysis for a belief in
supernatural intervention and miraculous interfer-
ence in the affairs of daily life; the awakening of a
spirit of patient and impartial enquiry into the processes of Nature; the belief that the behaviour of all
phenomena is subject to the operation of known or
knowable causes and effects; the recognition that the
laws of man are what men make them and the laws
of Nature what men discover them to be: all this constitutes a supremely important movement in the
evolution of the human race. It forms, one may say,
the most essential step towards freedom and knowledge and power that the human mind has yet taken.

No less impressive is the craving to discern some
ultimate foundation of truth and certainty on which
to rest the laws of Nature and of man. All through
the ages and still to-day men have sought a rock
upon whose stubborn sides the waves of doubt and
disbelief could beat in vain and on whose surface the
ravages of time would leave no mark. To discover
by the light of reason a substratum of ultimate and
unchanging truth, and to know, again by reason,

[1] Roscoe Pound, *An Introduction to the Philosophy of Law*,
p. 70.

that it would stand for all time impregnable against
the assaults of reason: such was the aim of the
ancient Greek philosophers who lived and held their
discourse more than two thousand years ago. Such
is still the aim of those who hold aloft the torch of
reasoned thought to-day.

PART III
THE NATURE OF LAW

I

THE REALM OF LAW

In this concluding part I propose to survey and analyse the relationship existing between contemporary science and contemporary law. We shall confront the laws of nature with the laws of man, and seek to discover whether all kinship between them is past; or whether the vital blood-tie of a common ancestry still provides an indissoluble bond underlying all the vast divergencies which appear on the surface. The answer to this question may provide a clue to the deepest and most fascinating of all problems: the relation between human existence and the world of external nature.

The domain of science has been enormously extended during the past three hundred years, and particularly during the last century. The older disciplines of astronomy, physics, mathematics, biology, and chemistry have immensely widened their scope and outlook, while a whole series of newer studies, such as geology, anthropology, economics, biochemistry, and sociology, have established themselves as separate sciences. Furthermore, a very large part of the mental world, both conscious and unconscious, has been added to the material subjected to scientific investigation. Every group of living organisms or inanimate matter, every phase of human life, whether individual or social, every stage of past or present development, is swept into the far-flung net of the scientist. The unity of science consists, indeed, in its method rather than in its subject-matter, for the material is co-extensive with all that we know of the universe.

Our conception of the universe itself has been radically transformed by the great scientific movement of the modern world. For us the universe is very different from what it was for our great-grandfathers; and in all probability it will undergo large changes for our great-grandchildren. The universe is a variable quantity, varying with the capacity of our organs of sense-perception and the powers of our instruments of observation.[1] The wellnigh unimaginable dimensions of the more remote stellar distances and the imperceptibly small world of the electron have entered our mental horizon only in recent decades. "Every great advance of science", it has been said, "opens our eyes to facts which we had failed before to observe, and makes new demands on our powers of interpretation. This extension of the material of science into regions where our great-grandfathers could see nothing at all, or where they would have declared human knowledge impossible, is one of the most remarkable features of modern progress."[2] Many people have come to believe that there is no sphere of life in which science may not one day shed her light.

The word Law, in its scientific sense, has come to mean a theoretical principle deduced from particular facts, applicable to a defined group or class of phenomena, and expressed by the saying that a particular phenomenon always occurs if certain conditions be

---

[1] Karl Pearson, *Grammar of Science* (3rd ed.), p. 15.
[2] *Ibid.* p. 14.

present.[1] Thus, Newton's first law of motion states that a body continues in its state of rest or of uniform motion in a straight line unless acted on by some external force. Scientific law applies to all the uniformities, successions, and similitudes comprised in the order and regularity of Nature. The essence of science is, indeed, the search for, and discovery of, the laws of Nature defined in this way. Much scientific work consists of little else than the systematic collection and recording of observations, not far removed from the attainments of the savage. "But behind the vast systematic collection of observations that occupies the main scientific effort throughout the ages there is a motive, an inspiration, that is absent from the savage mind. It is just that motive which makes science. The scientific motive is provided by a conscious faith in the existence of general laws underlying the multiplicity of phenomena. Science is the purposeful search for such general laws that can then be used to link together the observed phenomena. The savage has none of this faith, this aspiration. If he had, he would cast off his magic and cease to be a savage." [2] This faith is consciously held. It is different from reason.

The basis of the scientist's creed is, then, a belief that natural phenomena behave in an orderly manner and are susceptible of being resumed in terms of general principles. The conviction that we live in an ordered world is no new one. It existed long before science was born. But in former ages it was connected with religious doctrines concerning

[1] O.E.D., "Law", 11.
[2] Charles Singer, *Historical Relations of Religion and Science* in *Science, Religion and Reality*, p. 89.

God and human destiny, whereas to-day it is derived
from a reliance on the intellectual works of man—
especially these of Isaac Newton.[1] "The restless
modern search for increased accuracy of observation
and for increased detailed explanation is based upon
unquestioning faith in the reign of Law. Apart from
such faith, the enterprise of science is foolish, hopeless."[2]

The faith of the scientist has been abundantly
justified in the two hundred and fifty years which
have elapsed since Newton accomplished his great
work. On every side there are indisputable indica-
tions that the reign of law is co-terminous with the
realm of science. There is clear evidence of natural
law among living creatures no less than in physical
matter. The inheritance of biological characteristics,
the processes of digestion, the migration of birds, the
atomic weight of chemical elements, the vagaries
of the weather, are no longer supposed to be
due to a series of fortuitous occurrences but are
known to be subject to the operation of natural law.
Newton himself placed in men's hands "a law whose
writ was universal. The law of the heavens was now
the law of the earth."[3] Since that time men have
found law wherever they have sought it, provided
they looked with sufficient skill and patience. From
laboratory and observatory, from breeding station
and experimental farm, from clinic and research
institute, a stream of results has continuously poured
forth, surpassing all expectation both in theory and
in practice, transforming the thoughts of men no less

---

[1] J. W. N. Sullivan, *Limitations of Science*, p. 284.
[2] A. N. Whitehead, *Adventures of Ideas*, p. 173.
[3] Singer, *op. cit.* p. 146.

than the material environment in which they live, and bringing to men of science both a reward for their labours and support for their faith.

The goal of science is nothing less than the complete interpretation of the universe. Such an aim is at once remote and ideal; it serves but to mark the general direction in which scientific investigation tends to move.[1] The immediate object of science, as distinct from its ultimate aim, is to discover laws by which the facts of experience may be summarised in an effective and succinct manner. The statement of a scientific law enables us to formulate our experience in a generalised way without loading the mind with descriptions of particular events in space and time.[2] Only by the resulting economy of effort is the human mind released from a morass of detail and enabled to undertake the vast soaring flights to which we have now become accustomed.

The method pursued by the scientist consists of the collection and classification of relevant facts, of an analysis of their relationships and finally in "the discovery by aid of the disciplined imagination of a brief statement or formula, which in a few words resumes a wide range of facts".[3] A well-known example of such a formulation or law is the principle of Archimedes that when a body is immersed in water it loses weight equal to the weight of the water which it displaces.

According to Professor Karl Pearson, the classification of facts and the formation of absolute judgments upon the basis of the classification, constitutes

---

[1] Karl Pearson, op. cit. p. 14.
[2] A. D. Ritchie, Scientific Method, p. 55.
[3] Karl Pearson, op. cit. p. 77.

the essential aim and method of modern science.[1] "The man who classifies facts of any kind whatever," he wrote in *The Grammar of Science*, "who sees their mutual relation and describes their sequences, is applying the scientific method and is a man of science",[2] whether the facts relate to the past history of mankind, the social statistics of a great city, the atmosphere of the most distant stars, or the digestive organs of a worm. It is not the facts themselves which make science, but the method by which they are dealt with.

In his insistence on the need for "the disciplined imagination" as an aid to the discovery of scientific laws, Professor Pearson struck a note which has been emphasised again and again by subsequent thinkers. No one believes that the laws of nature "emerge", like a chick from an egg, from facts which have been collected and classified, no matter how long the process of incubation may be prolonged. Nor does anyone suppose that it is possible to lay down mechanical rules which will enable the industrious apprentice to make discoveries like those of Clerk Maxwell or Pasteur. The process of discovering natural laws has rightly been called an art.[3]

On the other hand, the preoccupation of the scientist with the laborious collection and classification of facts postulated by Professor Pearson has been somewhat discredited by more recent enquiries into scientific method by philosophers and psychologists. The actual procedure of natural science, observes one contemporary critic, involves constant reliance on

[1] Karl Pearson, p. 6.   [2] *Ibid.* p. 12.
[3] A. D. Ritchie, *Scientific Method*, p. 53. Cf. Graham Wallas, *The Art of Thought, passim*; H. Poincaré, *Science et Méthode*.

principles, and is incompatible with the assumption made by John Stuart Mill that only particulars exist in nature.[1] How else, indeed, can one appreciate which facts are relevant to the subject matter of the enquiry? The number of collectible facts is infinite, and there must clearly be some principle by which to distinguish those that are potentially useful to the investigation from those which are without value.

The modern tendency is to emphasise the importance of system, rather than the mere collection of facts, in scientific work. "The best single term for describing the general character of science as opposed to common sense is system"[2] declared the late L. T. Hobhouse. In science, he continued, system becomes the explicit purpose. Science is systematic because in the first place it seeks to be complete and to examine a subject not for the sake of any practical interest but solely in order to understand its essential nature; and secondly, because this task of understanding involves a comprehension of the real underlying connection of things. Science may be distinguished from ordinary common-sense knowledge by the rigour with which it subordinates all other considerations to the pursuit of certainty, exactness, universality, and system.[3] Ordinary common-sense knowledge is by comparison disconnected, fragmentary, chaotic, or illogical. "Science is devoted to the ideal of system, in which these defects are overcome. Indeed . . . we may well maintain that the one essential trait of developed science is system" and all other traits are incidental

---

[1] Morris R. Cohen, *The Place of Logic in the Law* in *Law and the Social Order*, pp. 171-2.
[2] L. T. Hobhouse, *Mind in Evolution* (3rd ed.), pp. 366-7.
[3] Morris R. Cohen, *Reason and Nature*, p. 83.

to it.[1] Another contemporary exponent of scientific method tells us that the more developed sciences constantly endeavour to link up systematically such laws or regularities as they have already discovered. The greater the knowledge already possessed, the more possible is the interconnecting of it into a coherent system likely to be; and the farther this process of systematisation proceeds, the deeper becomes our insight into natural phenomena.[2]

Such, then, are the general characteristics of the scientific movement which has created the body of natural law on which Western civilisation depends for its material support no less than for its intellectual nourishment. That movement is said to have started with the publication of such works as the treatise on the sacred disease in the 5th century B.C., and there are traces of the first dim stirrings of the scientific spirit to be found even in scriptural writings like the book of Job.[3] But it is the past three centuries that have witnessed the great quickening of the scientific temper and the reaping of the main harvest of new knowledge and ideas.

One of the chief contributory factors to the powerful impulse that has enabled science to sweep all before it in the modern world has been the increasing extent to which the laws of nature have been formulated in quantitative terms. Among the ancient Greeks the Pythagoreans taught that nature could be resolved into mathematical forms. But in actual practice it was found impossible to formulate definite

---

[1] Morris R. Cohen, *Reason and Nature*, p. 106.
[2] A. Wolf, *The Essentials of Scientific Method*, p. 89.
[3] Charles Singer, *Historical Relations of Religion and Science* in *Science, Religion and Reality*, p. 107.

laws of a mathematical character, and in the latter part of the 15th century Nicholas of Cusa said the task was beyond human capacity. Kepler's three laws of planetary motion mark, indeed, the first occasion on which the laws of nature were expressed in mathematical terms.[1] This event wrought a profound revolution in scientific enquiry and paved the way for Newton's still greater achievement in reducing all the phenomena of nature with which he dealt to mathematical laws. The extent to which contemporary scientists are dominated by the quantitative element is demonstrated by Sir Arthur Eddington's remark that the cleavage between the scientific and the extra-scientific domain of experience is not a cleavage between the concrete and the transcendental but between the metrical and the non-metrical.[2]

In contrast with this fundamentally narrow view of the realm of law we find a distinguished sociologist suggesting that the laws of nature may be arranged in inverse order of their dependence upon quantitative exactness. The law of applied physics which expresses the behaviour of a moving stone is more complex than the law of abstract physics which ex-

---

[1] Kepler's three laws were as follows:

(*a*) Planets move in elliptic orbits having the sun for one of their foci.

(*b*) The velocity of a planet is such that an imaginary line joining the moving planet to the sun sweeps out equal areas in equal intervals of time.

(*c*) The squares of the times which any two planets take to complete their revolutions round the sun are proportional to the cubes of their mean distances from the sun.

[2] *The Nature of the Physical World*, p. 275. Contrast H. Dingle, *Astronomy and Scientific Ideas* in *Science To-day* (1934), p. 287: "We have no right to assume that nature, by a self-denying ordinance, has limited her phenomena to those which can be described by mathematical processes; still less can we say that nature, or God, must be fundamentally mathematical."

presses the relations between the three sides of a triangle. Similarly, the organic law exposing the mode of growth of a plant is more complex than the law determining the movements of the stone. The psychical law expressing the growth of mind, is again more complex than the law of vegetative growth. The stone is no more than a physical object and therefore subject only to physical law; the plant is a physical object and something more (though not by mere addition) and hence subject to organic law; while man is an organic object and something more besides, and is in consequence subject to physical law, organic law, psychical law, and social law. Man as a social being is thus in a sense "the focus of all the laws of the universe". These laws, from the point of view of our knowledge, take on more and more the aspect of tendencies as we pass from pure physics to sociology. There are no "iron laws" of society.[1]

This analysis presents certain difficulties which its author has not completely overcome. But that is equally true of all the attempts to define in comprehensive terms the domain of science. One may suggest, however, that any interpretation which seeks to comprehend all parts of our experience in terms of the same fundamental type of natural law is infinitely more satisfying to our feelings than any explanation, however apparently logical, which divides up phenomena into the metrical and non-metrical, the scientific and religious, the factual and the artistic, or any similar dichotomy. In case anyone may imagine that feelings are unworthy of consideration on the higher levels of scientific discourse or irrelevant as a criterion of validity in such a matter as this, I may refer to the

[1] R. M. Maciver, *Community* (2nd ed.), pp. 15-16.

remarks made by Albert Einstein in a lecture delivered at Oxford. "Any scientific system", said he, "can be considered from two aspects—its power to cover known facts and to predict new ones, and its logical form as a system of relationships. From this latter point of view our understanding of a theory is enhanced if its axioms or hypotheses are few in number, simple in form, and in addition appear as natural. But the decision of what is natural is a matter of feeling, and hence the valuation of a new theory, which is not yet in conflict with any facts, remains to some extent a matter of feeling."[1]

The development of science clearly owes a good deal to the application of the impartial methods of thought which were first evolved in the Courts of Law. If it is significant that we use the word Law to denote both a rule of conduct for human beings and a description of the way in which the stars behave, it is also worth noticing how frequently we hear men of science employ other legal phrases as, for instance, when they say that there is no "evidence" to support So-and-so's theory; that in the speaker's "judgment" such and such a contention is nonsense. It is not merely the phraseology of the Law Courts which is borrowed but also the attitude of mind and the traditions which have slowly been developed in the judicial system. "The classification of facts and the formation of absolute judgments upon the basis of this classification —judgments independent of the idiosyncrasies of the individual mind—essentially sum up the aim and method of modern science", writes the author of *The Grammar of Science*.[2] With the exception of the last

---

[1] Report of Rhodes lecture on "The Theory of Relativity", *Times*, 11th May 1931.   [2] P. 6.

two words, the passage might be taken from a manual for the conduct of judges in the execution of their official duties.[1] The necessity for the man of science to strive for self-elimination in his work, to arrive at opinions unbiassed by personal feeling and supported by arguments as true for other persons as for himself, is recognised by all who have devoted themselves to the pursuit of scientific truth.

The two or three centuries during which the scientific movement has expanded in so remarkable a fashion have also witnessed an extraordinary extension in the scope and ramifications of human laws and government. Piracy has been suppressed and an ordering of the seas effected. Highwaymen have been exterminated and an ordering of the roads achieved. The activities of men below the surface of the earth has been reduced to some kind of order by means of elaborate mining laws. An ordering of the heavens has been established by international conventions and national laws of the air. On the surface of the earth the reign of law has been extended from one department of life to another. Health and education, commerce and industry, agriculture and fishing, banking and insurance, partnership and joint-stock corporation—all are now subject in greater or less degree to the jurisdiction of the law. Social control has been imposed all along the line, imperfectly and insufficiently in many cases no doubt, but nevertheless comprehensively. The nations to-day not only recognise the bonds of their own laws, but also, in such matters as extradition, those of each other. There is, furthermore, the recognition, immeasurably

[1] For an analysis of the Judicial Mind see my *Justice and Administrative Law*, ch. iv.

weaker than it should be but nevertheless much stronger than it was in any preceding age, of a body of international law to which all the separate communities owe a common allegiance and whose provisions may in some degree be applied by a world court.[1]

Much of this imposing structure of human law is due to the enlarged scale and increased complexity of life that have been brought about by the growth of scientific law. Thus, the public health code is a direct result of the development of bacteriology and preventive medicine during the past century, while the law relating to railways is as much an immediate consequence of the engineering knowledge which made mechanical traction possible as the railways themselves.

It is by no means easy to realise fully the ramifications of the jural order to-day. If one stands in a city street watching the traffic go by, the law seems to impinge on each motorist, *qua* motorist, at only about half-a-dozen points: he must obey the rule of the road; he must obtain a licence for the car and its driver; he must light his lamps at night; he must not drive negligently; he must not park his car in forbidden places; he must observe certain speed limits and insure himself against third-party risks. This appears to be the sum of a motorist's legal obligations. But to appreciate the influence of the law in its true perspective one should consider the enormous legal framework which enabled the car itself to be produced. The machinery of production included not only the physical equipment and the raw materials

[1] Cf. A. Fachiri, *The Permanent Court of International Justice* (2nd ed., 1932), *passim*.

but also the law of patents securing property rights in inventions and legal provisions of many other kinds designed to stimulate activity or ensure peace and safety in industry. The ownership of raw materials and finished goods; the enforcement of certain standards of commercial honesty; the securing to workers, managers, entrepreneurs, and rentiers of their respective wages, salaries, commissions, profits, and interest; the regulation of the relations between employee and employer, vendor and purchaser, banker and customer, landlord and tenant—all this and much else had to be regulated by the law before the production of the motor-car was effected.

A change in the system of production would change the substance of the law, but not its volume or complexity, for these are due essentially to the highly organised character of our society. A socialistic régime, for example, would transfer much private law to the realm of public law; but there would be no golden age of legal simplicity. The extension of governmental functions, whether under dictatorship or democracy, and whether in the direction of communism or state-supported capitalism, tends to expand rather than reduce the volume of the law.

The point I am trying to make is that we have moved far away, once and for all, from the time when the law consisted merely of a few simple rules of conduct, enjoining a man not to take another's life, nor steal his goods, nor commit adultery, and apart from which the father had absolute power over his children, the husband complete dominion over his wife, the chieftain or king undisputed lordship over his subjects.

The growth of all this legal tissue may be regarded

from one point of view as disclosing Law in the scientific sense. The science of comparative law, it is said,
would have been in vain if the law were an accidental
creation, the sport of chance, for in that case the
study of peoples would reveal laws but not Law; it
would exhibit a chaotic profusion of detail, a chaos
of particulars without organisation or regular development. There is, however, ground for believing
that the law is not a chance product but the result of
a reasonable impulse innate in human beings, a
sociological process arising from the material and
spiritual needs of mankind. It is possible, therefore,
that, like other evolutionary processes, it has its own
principles and laws,[1] which in time we may apprehend more fully than at present. It is worth noting
in this connection that periods of emotional excitement, such as those which result from war, revolution, or civil commotion, are invariably times of
lawlessness and legal anarchy.

---

[1] Josef Kohler, *Evolution of Law* in *Primitive and Ancient Legal
Institutions*, ii (edited by J. H. Wigmore and A. Kocourek), pp. 4-5.

"COMMAND" AND "OBEDIENCE"

In tracing the expansion of natural laws and survey-
ing the ever-widening sphere of human laws we have
seen that, whatever else it may involve, the word Law,
both in science and in jurisprudence, denotes order.
Scientific law reveals the existence of order where previously there was thought to be only fortuitous occurrence or supernatural intervention. Jural law ensures
order where otherwise there might exist only chaos.

Much confusion both in jurisprudence and in
science results, I believe, from the false importance
given to the ideas of "command" and "obedience" in
connection with law. This arises from the obsolete
conceptions whose history has already been traced
in the preceding pages. On the one hand there was the
idea of a divine law-giver imposing an inspired code
on a submissive, reverential, and awe-stricken community; on the other, the notion that the stars in their
courses and all the other phenomena of the universe
are subject to the omnipotent and autocratic rule of a
deity who compelled them to behave in exactly the
manner they do.

So far as jurisprudence is concerned, high-water
mark was reached in the English-speaking world by
John Austin, who founded his entire system on a
framework of compulsion and fear of punishment.
Every law or rule is a command, said Austin, and
a command is distinguished from other significations
of desire by the power and purpose of the party com-

manding to inflict an evil or pain in case the desire
be disregarded.[1] If there exists neither the power nor
the intention to inflict harm in case of non-compliance, the expression of a wish is not a command.
Hence the power and intention to inflict evil are
essential elements of a command. The evil to be incurred for disobedience was called by Austin the
sanction, while the liability to suffer such evil in case
of non-compliance created in his eyes a duty to obey
the command. Command and duty, he declared, are
correlative: wherever a duty lies, there a command
has been signified, and *vice versa*.[2] The rules set and
enforced by public opinion, fashion, honour, or other
forces—and including specifically a great part of
international law—were in his view not to be treated
as law but should be regarded as positive morality.
The recurring processes of vegetable growth or
decay, the sequences in the behaviour of the lower
animals, can, he asserted, only be termed laws in a
metaphorical sense, because there must be a rational
intelligence to apprehend the command and a will on
which the sanction can operate before Law can properly be said to exist. These conditions are not
present in such cases.

The unpleasant brew which John Austin prepared
from such characteristically Victorian ingredients has
for many years been rejected by the great majority
of jurists both at home and abroad.[3] But despite
the fact that the Austinian doctrine is generally discredited as a system of jurisprudence, the dogmas of

---

[1] John Austin, *Jurisprudence*, Lect. I, ii, pp. 90-91.
[2] *Ibid.* Lect. I.
[3] A sympathetic account by a contemporary writer is contained in
Modern Theories of Law (Oxford, 1933): "Austin To-day", by C. A.
W. Manning.

command and obedience, which played so important a part in his teaching and that of his forerunners, have penetrated deeply into many unsuspected channels of contemporary thought.

In the physical sciences, remarked Holland, law is used to denote the order or method of the phenomena of the universe, a use which would imply that "this method is imposed upon the phenomena either by the will of God, or by an abstraction called Nature".[1] The word "imposed" clearly suggests a command; but it is scarcely worth while dwelling upon the implications of this, for Holland goes on to say that the first step to be taken in order to remove ambiguity from the term law for the purposes of jurisprudence is to discard the meaning in which it is employed "by a mere metaphor" in the physical sciences, and to adopt as its proper meaning that which it bears in what he was pleased to call "the practical sciences".[2] Sir Frederick Pollock, the doyen of English jurists, has in most of his work sedulously avoided the pitfalls of the Austinian philosophy, yet in one notable passage, where he explains the manner in which the phrase "laws of nature" has come into common use, he remarks: "The powers of nature always behave in the same way, and this readily suggests to our mind a constraint which is always present and always efficient".[3] And a little later he quotes with approval a remark[4] to the effect that when law is applied to any other object than man, it ceases to contain two of its essential ideas, namely, disobedience and punishment.

[1] T. E. Holland, *Jurisprudence*, p. 18.   [2] *Ibid.* p. 19.
[3] *The Laws of Nature and the Laws of Man* in *Essays in Jurisprudence and Ethics*, p. 43.
[4] *Ibid.* p. 44. The remark in question was made by Edward Christian, Downing Professor of Laws (*d.* 1823), editor of Blackstone's *Commentaries* from 1793.

Men of science in our own day have in many cases absorbed the Austinian assumptions in a naïve and uncritical manner. When Karl Pearson, in his *Grammar of Science*, wrote that "the civil law involves a command and a duty; the scientific law is a description, not a prescription",[1] his ready acceptance of Austin's formula might be ascribed to a pardonable unfamiliarity with juristic material. But eminent contemporary scientists, working in what are regarded as the most severely disciplined and objective departments of study, have seen fit to apply the Command and Obedience concept to the very processes of Nature themselves.

Some things never happen in the physical world because they are impossible, writes Sir Arthur Eddington, others because they are too improbable. "The laws which forbid the first are the primary laws; the laws which forbid the second are the secondary laws."[2] Elsewhere he defines the identical laws of Nature as those obeyed as mathematical identities in virtue of the way in which the quantities obeying them are built.[3] In another passage in the same well-known work, he remarks that we cannot assimilate the laws of thought to natural laws, for they are laws which ought to be obeyed, not laws which must be obeyed. Hence the physicist must accept the laws of thought before he accepts natural law.[4]

Similar language is employed by Sir James Jeans. From the single supposition that the motions of the stars are governed by either Newton's or Einstein's law of gravitation, he tells us, we can prove the

---

[1] 3rd ed. p. 87.
[2] A. S. Eddington, *The Nature of the Physical World*, pp. 75-6.
[3] *Ibid.* p. 244.   [4] *Ibid.* p. 345.

theorem of the equipartition of energy to be true. "No subtle statement of exact conditions is required, the mere law of gravitation, together with the supposition that the stars cannot exercise free will as to whether they obey it or not, are enough."[1] The theorem of the equipartition of energy, Sir James Jeans goes on to explain, is that if we put any miscellaneous collection of stars into space, then after they have interacted with one another for a sufficient length of time, "those which started with more than their fair share of energy will have been compelled to hand over their excess to stars with lesser energy, so that the average energy of all the different types of stars must necessarily become reduced to equality in the long run".[2] This theorem arises from "a well-established law of nature" which provides that "no molecule is allowed permanently to retain more energy than his fellows; in respect of their energies of motion, a gas forms a perfectly organised communistic state, in which a law, which they cannot evade, compels the molecules to share their energies equally and fairly".[3]

It is obvious that there is a conscious and slightly humorous vein of anthropomorphism running through these passages, which are taken from expositions intended for the general intelligent reader rather than the technical specialist in astronomy and physics. But after due account has been made for this and the limitations of language in general, the significant fact remains that all these phrases which have been borrowed from the terminology of jurisprudence and politics, such as "forbid", "obey", "compel", "allow",

[1] Sir James Jeans, *The Universe Around Us*, p. 158.
[2] *Ibid.* p. 158.   [3] *Ibid.* p. 156.

are taken straight from the outworn Austinian creed which regards command and obedience as the essence of law. I cannot believe that fallacious and discredited legal notions can be of genuine assistance to scientists, even for the purposes of metaphor, no matter whether they are seeking to think clearly about the problems which confront them or endeavouring to expound the existing body of knowledge to a wider public. If one looks at any of the classic laws of Nature, such as Newton's law of gravitation (every mass tends towards every other with a force varying directly as the product of the masses and inversely as the square of their distances apart) or Boyle's law (the volume of a gas varies inversely with the pressure, the temperature remaining the same), all this talk about "fairness" and "evasion" and "obedience" seems to be an irrelevant and anachronistic intrusion, reminiscent of the days when Herbert Spencer used to speak of the folly of our legislators in trying to repeal by Act of Parliament a law of Nature.[1]

So far as human laws are concerned it is scarcely necessary, at this time of day, to expose the manifest falsity of the Austinian theory. I do not propose therefore to embark upon the tedious task of demonstrating its shallowness, its lack of historical background, its want of psychological insight, its juridical inadequacy. It must be obvious that mere force in possession is not law; that duress and coercion, command and obedience, do not by themselves constitute law. Law, it has been wisely said, denotes something more than these crude facts: it involves a settled state

[1] Herbert Spencer, *Ethics*, Part III, p. 546. Cf. David G. Ritchie, *Natural Rights*, p. 46.

of affairs, a common consciousness of consent, an ordered unity.[1] If this were not so, there would be no way of distinguishing Athens of the Periclean age from the pathological despotism of the craziest tyrant in contemporary Europe or central America.[2]

In contrast to the concept of Command and Obedience, I believe that it is more helpful to start with the fact that law is essential for all forms of co-operation between human beings. It is impossible to co-operate in any field of endeavour without agreeing to submit to a common rule of conduct; and sanctions need not necessarily play any part at all in such an agreement. It is absurd to pretend that an English merchant in the 17th century was not bound to abide by the rules of the law merchant until Lord Mansfield had told him that he was so bound.[3] Custom grows up by conduct and it is unconvincing to say that people who follow a recognised custom are, until the Courts have given it their blessing, following nothing more substantial than a rule of morality. It is, therefore, a mistake to emphasise the element of express sanction by Law Courts and governmental institutions. The great majority of

---

[1] Bede Jarrett, *Social Theories in the Middle Ages*, p. 2.

[2] A recognition of the truth of this statement underlies the uneasy attempts of the apologists of the Nazi régime in Germany to prove that even the worst excesses of the Government are juridically valid. An example of this is a defence by Professor Karl Schmitt of the official massacre of 30th June 1934. The Leader (Herr Hitler), writes Schmitt, "in virtue of his leadership, protected the law from the gravest abuse by directly creating law as supreme law lord. The real leader is always Judge as well. To separate and oppose leadership and judgeship is to make of the Judge either a counter-leader or the tool of a counter-leader, and to lever the State out of its socket with the help of justice. Hitler's judgeship springs from the same legal source from which comes the law of all peoples—the nation's right to live" (*Times*, 28/7/34).

[3] C. K. Allen, *Law in the Making*, p. 29.

customs are essentially non-litigious in origin. They arise not from a conflict of rights, but from the convenience of society and of the individual.[1] A great many laws and customs are sanctioned physiologically or psychologically, by forces coming from within the individual. To overlook this is to neglect one of the most important aspects in the sociological analysis of law.[2]

Once we recognise the mistake of concentrating attention on the litigious aspect of law, we can widen our outlook so as to embrace an immense vista of human activity which would otherwise remain beyond the horizon. Instead of being chained to the Sophistic way of thinking which splits "the confused intricate mass of the universe", or whatever part of it one is studying, into two sharply divided sections in which all the complex facts are labelled as either one thing or its antithesis,[3] one can envisage all the gradations which mark the development from early growth to maturity. Hence instead of postulating that there is either law or an absence of law, that what is enforceable by the Courts of Justice is law and that all else is not law, we can find room in our conception of law for the gradual emergence of various forms of co-operative practices and customary conduct which is the stuff from which the legal fabric is woven.

Let me illustrate my theme with one or two examples of the growth of legal tissue in recent years.

---

[1] *Ibid.*
[2] B. Malinowski, Introduction to *Law and Order in Polynesia* (1934), p. xxxviii.
[3] David G. Ritchie, *Natural Rights*, p. 24.

In 1901 the British Engineering Standards Committee was set up as the result of a motion passed by the Council of the Institute of Civil Engineers. Its object was at first the limited one of arranging a series of standard rolled sections of iron and steel; but the need for systemisation in other branches of engineering soon became obvious and the work of the Committee extended in many directions. The Institute of Civil Engineers invited the councils of other engineering societies to co-operate with them, and the Standards Committee thus came to be formed of representatives of the respective Institutes of Civil Engineers, Mechanical Engineers, Naval Architects, Electrical Engineers, and the Iron and Steel Institute. By the action of the main Committee, a large number of sectional and sub-committees were formed, and the membership of these was widened to include representatives of the Board of Trade, the War Office, Admiralty, India Office, the shipping registration societies, trading associations, railway companies, and manufacturers.[1]

The formation of the Engineering Standards Committee was a voluntary effort to introduce order into a sphere of affairs which was more or less chaotic and which stood in urgent need of intelligent regulation.[2] The economic advantages of standardisation have become widely recognised since the Committee began its work. In the United States of America Mr. Hoover, during his term of office as Secretary for Commerce in the Harding and Coolidge ad-

[1] W. C. Unwin, "Standardisation and its Influence on Engineering Industries", *Proceedings of the Institute of Civil Engineers*, clxxvii, p. 93.
[2] Sir John W. Barry, "Standardisation of Engineering Materials", *Proceedings of the I.C.E.*, vol. cciv.

ministrations, promoted an extensive standardisation movement not only in engineering but also in a whole series of other industries. Many other countries have now established Standards Associations. There are large potential gains to be derived from further standardisation on an international scale, but this has been impeded hitherto by national and economic rivalry.[1]

In the sphere of international standardisation the League of Nations has, however, achieved some notable successes. A conspicuous example is the case of insulin, in regard to which agreement was reached shortly after the remedy became available for everyday use in medical practice.

Prior to 1923 various methods were employed for testing preparations of insulin and for expressing its activity in terms of animal reaction. A conference convened by the Health Organisation of the League decided that the unit to be generally adopted should be that laid down by the Insulin Committee of Toronto University in terms of the production of a stated degree of hypoglycaemia in rabbits. Practical difficulties arose in carrying out this decision owing to the diverse conditions under which the agreed standard unit would have to be tested in the various countries. The Conference thereupon agreed that the most effective method of defining and stabilising a unit would be to arrange for the preparation of insulin in

---

[1] Unwin, *loc. cit.* At the invitation of the B.E.S.A. an unofficial conference was held in 1921 of secretaries of Standards Associations of various countries. It was agreed that exchange of ideas was beneficial, but no one was in favour of international standardisation.—*The Times*, 16th May 1921. For international standardisation a common system of weights and measures is necessary and this does not exist at present.

a dry stable form, the unit to be determined in terms of this standard preparation, which would act as a convenient currency by means of which the unit could be transmitted to every country concerned. By 1924 the preparation of a dry, stable standard had been completed and samples distributed to various laboratories in the different countries. A second Conference was convened by the Health Organisation of the League in 1925, at which the dry preparation of insulin was accepted as the international standard preparation. The result of this was that henceforth a unit of insulin has had a uniform significance throughout the world, and the risk of confusion between different types of unit has been avoided.[1]

Co-operation of this kind, whereby people agree upon the meaning to be attached to certain terms, or upon the conduct to be observed in certain matters by themselves or those whom they represent is, I submit, a type of activity which indubitably deserves to be regarded as legislative. Whether it concerns a concourse of nations or a small community or the members of an industrial or professional group; whether there are sanctions or a complete absence of formal penalties; whether there are obligations involved of a type which would be recognised and enforced by Courts of Justice or only a reliance on mutual honesty, good faith, and an intelligent perception of the advantages of co-operation, such forms of social intercourse, when crystallised into definite rules of agreement and conduct, and accepted by the persons or institutions whom they are intended to bind, are clearly entitled to be considered as law in

[1] League of Nations, *Biological Standardisation of Insulin: Preparation of an International Standard.*

a strictly realistic sense of the term. As such they deserve the serious attention of jurists.

The organic view of the living tissue of the law here put forward is in accord with the illuminating work on primitive law which has recently been accomplished by anthropologists engaged on field work.

In the promotion of co-operation among savages, no less than in the maintenance of their system of property rights, the corner-stone of the social edifice consists of "a definite system of division of functions and a rigid system of mutual obligations, into which a sense of duty and the recognition of the need of co-operation enters side by side with the realisation of self-interest, privileges, and benefits".[1] Among the Trobriand islanders, we are told, the people adhere to the dictates of custom, or what may properly be termed law, because they know that by so doing they will themselves in the near future be entitled to demand a counter-service and will need to rely on the same law.[2]

Primitive communities are frequently devoid of judicial institutions such as Courts, judges, public prosecutors, and the machinery of enforcement. Yet they may nevertheless have clearly discernible laws, and those laws may be followed with a high degree of loyalty. To look for organs of Command and Obedience among such peoples is a hopeless quest. The only fruitful line of approach is to examine on the one hand the positive inducements which compliance with the law secures, and on the other the deprivations and hardships which result from non-compliance. Reciprocal advantages and the incidence of

---

[1] B. Malinowski, Introduction to H. Ian Hogbin, *Law and Order in Polynesia*, p. xl.   [2] *Ibid*. p. xli.

complementary legal obligations are the rewards for
him who follows the common rule; rebukes, reprisals,
and disservices the consequences of contravention.[1]

The conclusion to which the careful study of
retarded peoples has led a distinguished contemporary anthropologist is that, among primitives, law
ought to be defined by function and not by form; in
other words, that attention should be directed towards the underlying arrangements, the sociological
realities, which secure compliance with the law rather
than towards the source from which it emanates or
the form which it assumes.[2]

My own observations of legal and administrative
institutions in developed societies have led me by an
entirely independent path to a similar view. At
present jurists tend to lay emphasis almost exclusively on form and origin as the sole criteria which
rules, customs, and practices must pass before they
can be considered to partake of the character of law.
Arrangements or principles which cannot claim
judicial enforcement or legislative authority are
denied legal status. This I regard as an altogether
unreal approach. There is a vast amount of authentic
legal tissue which lies outside the jurisdiction of the
Courts and beyond the ken of legislative assemblies
and Government departments. To ignore it is to shut
one's eyes to much that is highly significant and
interesting in the evolution of law. To consider legal
institutions without taking into account the processes
of growth and decay to which they are subject, or the
social realities which underlie the outward forms, is
to approach the subject with one's eyes half closed.

[1] B. Malinowski, Introduction to H. Ian Hogbin, *Law and Order in Polynesia*, pp. xxv-xxxvi. [2] *Ibid.* pp. xxix and xliii.

III

LAW AS A PATTERN OF CONDUCT

WE have seen that one of the most important functions of law is to give precise content to our vague ideas and thereby to make human co-operation possible. By defining the essential characteristics of a trust or a contract of marine insurance, the law insists that a particular relationship or transaction shall mean the same thing to every member of the community. The laws of tennis define the game so that it is played under the same rules all over the world. This process of intellectual clarification exerts a powerful influence in promoting uniformity or consistency of conduct, even when no coercive pressure of any kind is brought to bear upon people in order to make them adopt one course rather than another. Thus the law may be said to shape our destinies quite apart from any hope of reward or fear of punishment which it may hold out.

Human laws consist, then, of rules; and a rule may be equally a guide to thought or a direction as to conduct. A direction is by no means necessarily a command. It may be a mere declaration of the consequences of particular acts—a legal signpost indicating where the various roads lead. The old-fashioned idea of law as a menacing system of threats and punishments is as obsolete to-day as the Victorian theology which taught religion in terms of a fire-and-brimstone Hell.

Many of our law students are nevertheless still absorbing doctrines of the type laid down by Holland, who in his 'standard' text-book invited them to believe that "Jurisprudence is specifically concerned only with such rights as are . . . enforced by the power of a State. We may therefore define a 'legal right' . . . as a capacity residing in one man of controlling, with the assent and assistance of the State, the actions of others. That which gives validity to a legal right is, in every case, the force which is lent to it by the State."[1] One hopes that an increasing number of those students will have the curiosity of mind to enquire in exactly what sense the pedestrians who have a legal right to use the public highways, and who are run over by thousands every year while doing so, may be said to "control, with the assent and assistance of the State", the actions of the motor-car drivers who kill or injure them. Particular drivers or their employers may be liable to pay damages for negligence (usually through an insurance company) or even to suffer imprisonment in case of manslaughter, but the accident statistics show that this has no discernible effect in "controlling . . . the actions of others".

Again, I may have a legal right to the undisturbed possession of my house or flat. But if a burglar arrives armed with a revolver, that right does not endow me with the "capacity" to control his action either with or without the assent and assistance of the State.

It is more realistic to consider jural law as a formulation of the pattern of social behaviour, a view comparable to the conception of scientific law as a

[1] T. E. Holland, *Jurisprudence*, p. 83.

formulation of the pattern of physical behaviour. Whatever law may have been in the past, in the modern world it is undeniably something agreed upon or "sanctioned" by public opinion. The support given to its authority by the myriad individuals, corporations, groups, and institutions in the community may be conceived as the separate threads in a fabric which together make up the pattern. When a large number of the threads fall away, the pattern becomes indistinct or blurred, and finally it disappears altogether. This is an exact analogy of what happens in a community when allegiance to the law is undermined either in regard to a particular matter, as in the case of prohibition in the United States, or in general, as in the case of Southern Ireland prior to the establishment of the Irish Free State.

It requires an undue and unreal insistence on the purely formal aspect of the juridical order to enable Sir Frederick Pollock to say that "the law would still be a law if no single person obeyed it on any one occasion".[1] The relevant question is not whether the law is "obeyed", for often there is nothing to "obey", but whether the pattern of social conduct which it formulates is substantially reflected by the actual behaviour of the community. Who can "obey" the law relating to wills, for example? If a testamentary disposition does not fulfil the prescribed requisites (such as those relating to witnesses) there is no valid will and the estate is distributed according to the principles of intestacy. Again, how can anyone "obey" the law relating to blackmail, since it merely defines the crime and prescribes its punishment? What is

[1] Sir F. Pollock, *The Laws of Nature and the Laws of Man* in *Essays in Jurisprudence and Ethics*, p. 44.

essential is that, when an offence is committed, everyone who may be able to assist in the discovery and prosecution of the criminal shall be willing to contribute his or her part. If there is a substantial lack of the support necessary to ensure this, the law of blackmail ceases to be a formulation of the pattern of conduct of the community in regard to the matter with which it deals, and it may eventually pass into the realm of mere myth or legend.

It is important to distinguish between the pattern of conduct displayed by the actual behaviour of human beings and the formulation of that pattern contained in the law.[1] A law or a code of laws or a form of government are not the actual relations of human beings, but rather the conditions and consequences of the relationships.[2]

To what extent do legal rules affect the actual conduct of our lives? It is quite impossible to answer this question in a satisfactory manner. One might equally well ask to what extent the pattern of behaviour influences the law. There are interactions continually going on between law on the one hand and innumerable physical, psychological, economic, moral, and political forces on the other. All these forces, and many others, become merged in the pattern of conduct which forms the end-result of the interactions, and it is impossible to calculate the amount of pressure exerted by any one of them separately. Most people prefer to believe that their actions are dictated by considerations of morality or

---

[1] Mr. Jerome Frank in his *Law and the Modern Mind* fails to grasp this distinction. Cf. A. L. Goodhart, *Modern Theories of Law* (1933), p. 8.

[2] R. M. Maciver, *Community* (2nd ed.), p. 7.

economic advantage or a sense of honour or public spirit rather than by the pressure of legal obligation. If you ask a man why he keeps his financial engagements he will probably assert that he does so from motives of honesty, or because it is good business, or because he wishes to maintain an honourable reputation. In all likelihood he will omit all mention of the legal obligation. This does not mean that the law of contract is an insignificant influence either in his case or in that of anyone else. Indeed, its very correspondence with his feelings or motives or convictions is a mark of its importance and excellence.

It is important that there should be a broad correspondence between the social conduct actually followed by the community and the pattern or design which is formulated by the law. The law will fail to retain support if it lags too far behind actual practice and equally so if it pushes too far ahead. In the former case it will be abandoned by people whose standards have advanced to a stage substantially beyond that attained by the legal system; in the latter it will be disregarded by those whose reach does not extend as far as the grasp of the law.

The relation between human laws and social conduct is essentially dynamic: it changes almost from day to day. Many jurists have endeavoured to dispose of the matter by asserting that custom is a source of law—or *the* source of law. It is true that a rule of conduct may be from one point of view a law and from another point of view a custom. It is equally obvious that an habitual practice does not cease to be a custom when it is reduced to writing and clothed with the authority of the law. But the time-honoured statement that law is based on custom overlooks the

fact that customs may themselves be largely established or influenced by the law.

Custom, said Bacon, is the principal magistrate of
man's life.[1] There is truth in the remark; but it is
misleading to employ the word as though it refers
to a single homogeneous type of usage when in
fact it covers an immense variety of different kinds
of practices. Some customs, like that of going into
mourning after a bereavement, are of immemorial
antiquity; others, such as wearing a wig (still practised
by judges and barristers in England), are relatively
modern. Some customs are purely irrational, as, for
example, the English practice of cutting short the
tails of dogs. Others are rational, or at any rate were
rational in origin, such as the custom which requires
a man accompanying a lady in the street to walk on
the outside of her.

Many customs sprang from purely superstitious
beliefs: that is, from false reason. To this class belong
such practices as that of throwing an old shoe after
the bride and bridegroom or showering them with
rice or grain[2] (often replaced to-day by confetti).
Some customs serve a useful purpose in society,
many are quite useless, while others again are posi-
tively harmful. To lump together all these diverse
types of habitual conduct under the generic heading
of custom, and then to declare it to be a source of law,
is seldom illuminating and is more often misleading.

It is clear that most customs arise from individual
habits which have become generalised in a particular
class, group, or community. Thus the habitual con-

---

[1] *Essays* "Of Custom and Education".
[2] E. Westermarck, *History of Human Marriage* (5th ed.), ii,
pp. 471, 476, 484, 539, 541.

duct of the individual develops into a custom of the group.[1] Hence custom may be regarded as public habits.[2]

These habits have usually grown up to meet the needs incidental to particular situations. The rule of the road arose out of the need to avoid collisions with wheeled traffic. Consequently, as new situations arise there is a continual growth of new customs or the adaptation of existing ones. While this process of devising and adapting is always going on with varying degrees of success, social life everywhere remains littered with a vast accumulation of customary forms of conduct which have lost all their meaning and utility but are none the less reverently or mechanically obeyed. It is usual to speak of custom as though it had in every case come down to us from before the dawn of history. It is therefore desirable to emphasise the newness of many customary forms of conduct. Nearly all the modern inventions, from sanitary appliances to the telephone and the motor-car, have led to the creation of genuine and authentic customs.[3]

In so far as a custom is devised to satisfy a specific need or overcome a particular difficulty, there tends to be created a social interest in its maintenance and generality. This is revealed by the indignation or resentment which is engendered by a breach of the accepted mode of conduct, leading in extreme cases to some kind of protest, which may take various forms, ranging all the way from a private boycott in

---

[1] W. G. Sumner, *Folkways* (1907), p. 3.
[2] E. Westermarck, *The Origin and Development of the Moral Ideas* (2nd ed.), ii, pp. 118-19.
[3] W. G. Sumner, *op. cit.* p. 19.

well-to-do circles of the man who refuses to wear evening-dress clothes to a public rebuke administered by an exponent of conventional opinion in the pulpit or on the platform to the woman who remarries three weeks after her husband's death.

Custom is thus for the most part something more than the mere repetition of a certain mode of behaviour. It is a rule of conduct; and the reprobation which may be called forth by the transgression of it indicates an element of morality. Some customs are, of course, morally indifferent; but many others are regarded as moral rules involving questions of right and wrong conduct.[1] Where the social interest served by a public habit presses sufficiently hard, or where its moral implications give rise to powerful emotions in the event of contravention, custom easily passes into law.

On the other hand, custom and law are sometimes in conflict with one another, a most conspicuous case being the attempt in the United States to impose a statutory prohibition on the drinking of alcoholic liquor in the face of a widespread custom of immemorial antiquity. It is by no means always the case, however, that custom, whether in harmony or in conflict with the law, is anterior in point of time. For example, the custom prevailing in England and other countries whereby a capital sentence is not carried out in the case of certain categories of persons, such as young people or pregnant women, is an administrative usage of much later date than the law whose provisions it modifies.

The notion that custom represents the unconscious

---

[1] E. Westermarck, *Origin and Development of the Moral Ideas*, ii, pp. 118-19, 163.

wisdom of the centuries or that it invariably embodies a sort of blind impulse which has been crystallised through the ages is manifestly an over-simplification even where it is not actually false. The maintenance of many customs requires, indeed, that people shall make a conscious effort to stifle their impulses to act in a contrary manner. This is by no means necessarily a bad thing, for one of the fundamental objects of law is to prevent people from following some of their impulses and to encourage them to follow others. The control of certain impulses, the transmutation of their destructive and selfish elements into creative and socially desirable forces, is or should be one of the primary aims of law.

The extent to which impulse may be restrained by a respect for the law was illustrated by an incident which occurred a few years ago in Manchester. An attack was made one day by robbers on the premises of a firm of jewellers, as a result of which the shop window was smashed and a tray of rings scattered in the street among the crowd. Despite the ease with which the rings might have been stolen, every one of them was returned to the owners, who took occasion to thank the public for its honesty in the face of tempting circumstances.[1]

In a leading article commenting on this incident the *Manchester Guardian* remarked that "while we may congratulate ourselves on such a confirmation of our belief that the majority of people respect the law because they see the sense of the law, it is plain that we have not yet exorcised the fallacy of natural lawlessness from our view of groups and nations. We still believe that if valuables were scattered in a similar

[1] *Manchester Guardian*, 21st November 1927.

way before the nations of the world there would be an outbreak of thieving. But is man organised necessarily man brutalised? An ancient and ugly tradition suggests that he is. But if we can break that tradition as individuals surely we can break it as members of nations. If the State is maintained by the mutual confidence of those who can see the reason of right, why should not the Society of States abandon its wretched routine of terror and distrust?" [1] This is the argument put forward more than two thousand years ago by Plato in the *Crito*, where the laws speak to Socrates, who feels that he is called upon to exercise a high degree of public-spirited conduct because the laws are good and he has lived under them. The argument runs thus: By good laws, by a good State, psychological impulses may be evoked that will produce good behaviour.

The Platonic dialogue was discourse on the highest plane concerning the relation between law and the pattern of conduct. Not less relevant, from a practical point of view, is the Baconian insistence on custom. If we will recognise that law forms habit no less than habit forms law, and if we will mould our laws and revise our customs so as to emphasise the rational element in both, the march of reason and the pattern of social conduct might leap forward together towards distant goals which at present seem but far-off dreams of remote splendour.

[1] *Manchester Guardian*, 21st November 1927.

IV

THE INTERACTIONS OF LAW AND SCIENCE

In an earlier part of this work I surveyed the intimate relationship which had subsisted, among both primitive and civilised peoples, between law on the one hand, and magic, superstition, and religion on the other. Since the scientific renaissance in the 17th century, the centre of gravity has gradually shifted from these precursors of science to science itself. The relations of scientific thought to jurisprudence and politics has not, however, attracted the attention it deserves. I shall endeavour to indicate here some of the more conspicuous interactions, without pretending for a moment to give an exhaustive account of the matter.

An outstanding feature of the scientific progress of the 17th century was the great advance in mathematical knowledge which was achieved. This had a profound influence on the social sciences. The idea became prevalent that legal certainty was attainable by the methods of mathematics,[1] and this led to the

---

[1] This conception is still held to-day by some judges. During the hearing in the Court of Criminal Appeal of the appeals of three men sentenced to death for the murder of a retired druggist named Smith in July 1928, the Lord Chief Justice (Lord Hewart) was reported as follows: "It had also been said that the evidence for the prosecution was circumstantial. So it was; but it did not depend on the observations of one witness. It was the evidence of circumstances which, taken together by undesigned coincidence, was capable of proving a proposition with the accuracy of mathematics. It was no derogation of evidence to say it was circumstantial." The appeals were dismissed. *Rex v. Taylor, Rex v. Weaver, Rex v. Donovan: The Times,* 31st July 1928.

era of legal codes. "It was believed that the one and only legal rule for every possible situation could be written off in advance by a proper combination of axiomatic first principles with the same accuracy as the answers to all the problems in the Euclidean geometry. Law ceased to be an instrument for working towards certainty—it became certainty itself."[1] This idea persisted into the following century. David Hume, in an essay bearing the significant title "That Politics may be reduced to a Science", declared that "so great is the force of laws, and of particular forms of government, and so little dependence have they on the humours and temper of man, that consequences almost as general and certain may be deduced from them, on most occasions, as any which the mathematical sciences afford us".[2]

The most important scientific event in the 17th century was, of course, the discovery of the solar system by Isaac Newton.[3] One of the two most important political events which occurred in the 18th century was the founding of the United States of America. These two events, utterly unrelated as they may appear, had in fact a distinct connection. For the Government of the United States, as the late President Wilson pointed out when he was still a university professor, was constructed upon a theory of political dynamics which was essentially Newtonian in its assumptions. The Whigs in England had already sought to regulate the arbitrary powers of the king and to balance executive, legislature, and

---

[1] John Dickinson, *Administrative Justice and the Supremacy of Law in the United States*, p. 45 n.
[2] David Hume, *Essays Moral and Political* (1742).
[3] The *Principia* was published in 1687; the *Optics* in 1704.

judiciary by means of a series of checks and counter-
poises which Newton might easily have recognised as
an application to political institutions of his own interpretation of the movements of the heavenly bodies.[1]

In the hands of the revolutionary statesmen who
founded the American commonwealth the Newtonian
conception of checks and balances was pushed to extraordinary lengths. It resulted in a Federal Constitution which was intended to limit the activity of
each part and to allow no organ to dominate the
whole. The President is balanced off against Congress, Congress is balanced against the President,
and each is balanced against the Courts.[2] John Adams
had as early as 1814 expressed in no uncertain voice
his doubts and criticisms of this remarkable arrangement. "Is there a constitution", he asked in a letter
written to John Taylor, "more complicated with
balances than ours? In the first place, eighteen states
and some territories are balanced against the national
government. . . . In the second place, the House of
Representatives is balanced against the Senate, the
Senate against the House. In the third place, the
executive authority is, in some degree, balanced
against the legislative. In the fourth place, the judicial power is balanced against the House, the Senate,
the executive power, and the state governments. In
the fifth place, the Senate is balanced against the
President in all appointments to office, and in all
treaties. . . . In the sixth place, the people hold in
their hands the balance against their own representatives, by biennial . . . election. In the seventh

[1] C. Becker, *The Declaration of Independence*, pp. 40-47.
[2] Woodrow Wilson, *Constitutional Government in the United States*
(1908), pp. 54-6.

place, the legislatures of the several states are balanced against the Senate by sextennial elections. In the eighth place, the electors are balanced against the people in the choice of the President. Here is a complicated refinement of balances which, for anything I recollect, is an invention of our own and peculiar to us." [1]

Such were the principles on which the framers of the American Constitution sought to organise their Government. By these devices, soon to be copied in State and city governments throughout the union, they sought to create a political order which would resemble the Newtonian system of the universe, wherein the sun, the earth, the moon, each star and planet, is kept to its course in the heavens by the attraction of other bodies which move with equal regularity and restraint about them, the whole concourse being held in equilibrium by the balance of forces which gives the system its perfect symmetry and poise. There were, no doubt, good and sufficient reasons why the Founding Fathers should desire a constitution containing elaborate safeguards against tyranny or arbitrary action; it was demanded alike by the history of their connection with England, by the spectacle of the absolute monarchies which existed almost everywhere on the European continent, and by the vista of unlimited economic opportunity offered by the New World. But the fact remains that the system of checks and balances which they introduced was essentially Newtonian and mechanical. The trouble with the theory, as Woodrow Wilson complained, is that Government is not a machine and

[1] John Adams, *Works*, vi, p. 467. Cf. Woodrow Wilson, *Congressional Government*, p. 12.

cannot "be successfully conducted upon so mechanical a theory".[1] It is a living thing, said Wilson, and falls "not under the theory of the universe, but under the theory of organic life. It is accountable to Darwin, not to Newton. . . . No living thing can have its organs offset against each other, as checks, and live".[2]

The Darwinian theories in which Woodrow Wilson reposed so much confidence played, as a matter of fact, a part of considerable importance in the economic and social life of England during the latter part of the 19th century. In the earlier part of the century the classical economists, influenced no doubt by the rigid conceptions of mechanical law which dominated the scientific thought of the day, imported into political economy a more austere and severely disciplined approach than that which had so far prevailed. Publicists who either misunderstood the arguments of the economists or were unable or unwilling to become acquainted with their doctrines, grasped eagerly at the suggestion of inexorable and unchanging law which appeared to dominate the discussions. These popular exponents were for the most part ardent advocates of complete *laissez-faire* in the political sphere. It was, they declared, inevitably disadvantageous for Government to interfere in any way with the working of the inflexible laws of political economy, whose beneficent operation could most effectively be secured by leaving everyone free to pursue his own self-interest to the utmost possible extent.[3] The classical economists did not themselves explicitly take up this standpoint; but it seemed to

---

[1] Woodrow Wilson, *Constitutional Government in the United States*, p. 54.
[2] *Ibid.* p. 56.   [3] See *ante*, pp. 237-39.

follow from what they said.[1] Thus abstract freedom was associated with economic determinism. The essential paradox of the situation was not perceived.

Herbert Spencer epitomised the extreme individualism of the manufacturing and commercial classes, and gave it coherent and systematic form. Spencer was an engineer; his early training had been on the railways and he devoted a good deal of his time to mechanical inventions. He turned to biology after he had passed the formative period of his mental development; and although he spent much time in seeking to bring human society into relation with biological principle, he never overcame the difficulties arising from his early training.[2]

His first and most influential book was entitled *Social Statics*—a significant indication of the mechanical outlook which informed its philosophy. It was published in 1850, nine years before the appearance of Darwin's epoch-making work.[3] From *The Origin of Species* Spencer subsequently borrowed the conception of the struggle for existence and the survival of the fittest, but he never became a Darwinian in the true sense or even grasped the full social implications of biological science.[4]

In 1884 he published *Man versus the State*, in which the argument was put forward that the State must confine itself to the enforcement of contracts,

[1] J. M. Keynes, *The End of Laissez-Faire.*
[2] Cf. W. R. Inge, *Liberty and Natural Rights* (The Herbert Spencer Lecture, 1934), pp. 7-9.
[3] In 1852 Spencer published his *Development Hypothesis* in which he put forward the theory of organic evolution seven years before the *Origin of Species* appeared—a remarkable performance. And his *Principles of Psychology* also had an evolutionary basis.
[4] Cf. E. Barker, *Political Thought in England*, 1848-1914, pp. 92, 123 *et seq.*, 146.

any further activity being a violation of liberty. If the State attempts paternal government, the thesis runs, it is introducing family-ethics into a domain where they do not belong and in which they will do untold harm. Family-ethics applied to the State would stop "the beneficent struggle for existence" because it would give the weakling more than he deserved and thus perpetuate an undeserving life.

In this and similar ways, misconceptions derived from the work of Charles Darwin were used during the latter part of the century to reinforce the waning authority of the "iron law" and other popular conclusions drawn from the writings of the classical economists. Individualists attempted to shore up the crumbling structure of *laissez-faire* by asserting that any humanitarian effort on the part of Government, any assistance given to the weaker members of the community, the sick, the poor, the afflicted, was directly opposed to the beneficent struggle for existence and the survival of the fittest which Nature had provided as the only road to progress. Darwinism was also pressed into the service of militarists, who misapplied the ideas of the struggle for existence and the survival of the fittest as arguments to justify the selective agency of war.

The transformation of political thought which began about 1860 was thus intimately connected with the almost simultaneous appearance of new ideas in the study of organic nature. *Ancient Law* and *The Origin of Species* were both the fruits of the evolutionary movement.[1] It is difficult for us nowadays to appreciate the revolutionary change of outlook which

[1] Sir F. Pollock, *Comparative Jurisprudence* in *Essays in the Law*, p. 10-11.

was effected by that movement, or to recognise how many of our own ideas and assumptions are due to it.

In the ancient world and throughout the Dark and Middle Ages, it was thought that the universe, no less than the order of society, was fixed and immutable. The belief in change, in evolution and progress, is modern, and constitutes one of the fundamental differences between our own society and all the civilisations which preceded it. The very words by which we express the idea, such as development, improvement, evolution, progress, advance, amelioration, were unknown to the English language with their present meanings until comparatively recent times.[1]

The doctrine of evolution might have exerted a great liberating and humanising influence on social life from the outset, but unfortunately the publicists who applied it to economic and political questions used it to defend the harshest features of their philosophy and the world in which they lived, just as the doctrines of the classical economists of an earlier decade were used to justify the misery which resulted among the poor from the operation of *laissez-faire* and to oppose any attempt to ameliorate the social order in the interests of those who suffered from it most severely. It is the lingering memory of such abuses that leads Sir Arthur Eddington to say that "exact science invokes, or has seemed to invoke, a type of law inevitable and soulless against which the human spirit rebels".[2]

By a strange irony the department of science which has contributed most to the widespread acceptance of the doctrine that the different social

---

[1] Logan Pearsall Smith, *The English Language*, p. 233-4.
[2] A. S. Eddington, *The Nature of the Physical World*, p. 251.

classes in our society are distinguished by different biological characteristics is unconsciously exercising at least some part of its authority by virtue of borrowed plumes. I refer, of course, to biology. Both the word *inheritance* and its companion *heredity* are of legal origin, and so too are the ideas first implied by them. Yet "the legal conceptions of inheritance have no resemblance to the biological facts of heredity. Nevertheless, in the course of history, the legal conception has influenced the biological. Strange to say, biology has still not quite shaken itself free from this extraordinary misalliance. The power of words, terminology, over our scientific ideas is very much greater than most men of science are willing to admit." [1]

Scientists are, however, becoming increasingly aware of the difficulty of describing their theories, and even the facts on which they are based, without borrowing phrases and metaphors from other fields of experience, especially from the realm of jurisprudence and politics. Sir James Jeans, for instance, remarks that the series of concepts relating to the Quantum theory are difficult to grasp and still more difficult to explain, largely because our minds receive no assistance from our everyday experience of Nature. It therefore becomes necessary, he says, to speak mainly in terms of analogies, parables, and models which can make no claim to represent ultimate reality.[2] One wishes he had added that it also becomes important for the scientist to see that the metaphors and analogies which he borrows from other fields

---

[1] Charles Singer, *A Short History of Biology*, p. 539.
[2] Sir James Jeans, *The Universe Around Us*, p. 119. See also p. 124.

represent ideas or knowledge which are generally accepted in those other fields rather than outworn dogmas such as the Austinian theory to which I have already called attention.[1]

When we recall that scientific thought arose as a revolt against the anthropomorphic tendency which saw spirits and gods, and later a single deity, in every manifestation of Nature, it seems a strange destiny that in our own time the most eminent scientists should be impelled to seek refuge from the elusive complexity of Nature and the limitations of human language by describing the behaviour of inanimate matter in anthropomorphic terms borrowed from the social sciences. What are we to think of "a well-established law of nature" by which "no molecule is allowed permanently to retain more energy than his fellows", by which "a gas forms a perfectly organised communistic state" wherein the molecules are compelled "to share their energies equally and fairly"?[2]

It is a fact of immense social significance that contemporary men of science are talking and writing and thinking in this way. The theory of evolution which Darwin, Huxley, Wallace, and their colleagues disseminated in the second half of the 19th century suggested to the general public that changes in Nature take place very slowly and are spread over such enormously long periods of time that the effect on any individual member or particular generation of a species is almost imperceptible. This impression was greatly strengthened by the rise of geology, which not only immensely extended the vista of time during which the earth was shown to have been in existence,

[1] *Ante*, p. 296-7.   [2] Jeans, *op. cit.* p. 156.

but also revealed the extraordinary slowness with which geological processes take place through the long ages. The influence of this idea spread from biology and geology to the social sciences. Alfred Marshall placed in the frontispiece of his celebrated *Principles of Economics*, for decades the most widely read English treatise on the subject, the maxim *Natura non facit saltum* (Nature does not proceed by leaps). In anthropology a similar emphasis was laid on the extreme antiquity of cultures and the slow rate of change among primitive peoples. In the political sphere the apotheosis of the idea was reached in 1923 when Mr. Sidney Webb (now Lord Passfield) introduced into his Presidential Address to the Labour Party's Annual Conference his famous observation concerning the "inevitability of gradualness".[1] Mr. Webb subsequently explained that the first word rather than the last should be emphasised; but the phrase undoubtedly conveys the notion of the necessity for gradual change as opposed to rapid and perceptible breaks with the past. It is unmistakably derived from Darwinian theory.

The idea of gradual evolution no longer carries its former authority among men of science. "Gradualness is driven out of physics, and discontinuity takes its place"[2] declares Sir James Jeans. Even in biology the centre of gravity has shifted to the study of Mendelian genetics, which proceeds on entirely different assumptions. At the same time the old conviction previously held by most scientists that underlying all phenomena there exists a complete scheme of primary law governing the career of every particle or

---

[1] The address is reported in *The Times*, 27th June 1923.

[2] Jeans, *op. cit.* p. 121.

constituent of the world with an iron determinism;[1] has been undermined by the suggestion that many of the laws of Nature are statistical in character, and relate only to the behaviour of crowds or aggregates. In consequence, "much of the uniformity of Nature is a uniformity of averages" and the regularity of the average may well be compatible with "a great degree of lawlessness of the individual".[2] The result is that whereas it used to be said that the future of physics lay beyond the sixth decimal point, to-day the certainty of absolute laws shows signs of yielding to the suggestion that the universe is in important respects indeterminate and its behaviour not susceptible of prediction.[3]

These doubts and uncertainties are at present not widely known outside the relatively small circle of educated readers who attempt to keep abreast of the main lines of scientific enquiry. But it can scarcely be expected that they will remain confined within so narrow a sphere. Alfred Marshall may already have seen the cloud on the horizon, though it was no bigger than a man's hand in his day, when he wrote that "the best statement of tendencies that we can make in a science of human conduct, must needs be inexact and faulty".[4] There is a world of difference between Marshall's uneasy diffidence and the jaunty conviction of absolute certainty shown by Hume a hundred and fifty years earlier in his essay "Politics a Science".[5]

[1] A. S. Eddington, *The Nature of the Physical World*, pp. 75-6.
[2] *Ibid.* p. 244.
[3] Cf. John A. Fairlie, "Political Developments and Tendencies", xxiv, *American Political Science Review*, February 1930, p. 1.
[4] A. Marshall, *Economics of Industry*, p. 24.
[5] *Ante*, p. 316.

No one who has observed the political and economic events of the past twenty years can have much faith in the theory of gradual evolution as applied to social affairs. Yet no more appropriate scientific principle has so far taken its place to interpret the catastrophic events which have occurred during those decades or to illuminate those which appear likely to occur in the future if the present unstable condition of the world continues. It is at least within the bounds of possibility that discontinuity will be borrowed from physics to justify a rapid jump to "Socialism in our Time" or Medievalism, or Fascism; or the theory of the equipartition of energy be claimed as evidence of Nature's approval of Communism.

V

NATURAL LAWS AND HUMAN LAWS

In this concluding section I shall outline a synthesis which is intended to provide a possible interpretation of the phenomena surveyed in the foregoing pages.

In bygone ages, we have seen, it was believed that the conduct of natural phenomena was governed by causes which sprang from the same divine origin as that which gave birth, directly or indirectly, to the laws of human society. A period of secularisation set in, and eventually it came about that no relationship of any kind was recognised as subsisting between the laws of Nature on the one hand and the laws of man or the order of society on the other. The wheels of the universe were supposed to revolve in a purely objective and mechanical way, and it was felt to be a grave impropriety to suggest that the laws which described their movements had any relation to human life or thought. It is only in recent decades that a new tendency towards reintegration has appeared.

The new movement towards a reunion of man with the remainder of the universe, if it is to have a fruitful outcome, must start from an essentially simple yet reasonably certain basis: namely, that it is the human mind which both formulates the pattern of physical conduct we call natural law and also establishes the pattern of social conduct we call human

law. Human law, said Spinoza, is a plan of living
which men have laid down for themselves.[1] To which
one may add that science is a plan of knowing which
men have laid down for themselves.

The emphasis which contemporary men of science
now place on the creative power of the human mind
is undoubtedly one of the most significant tendencies
of the 20th century. Law in the scientific sense,
declares Professor Karl Pearson, is "essentially a
product of the human mind and has no meaning
apart from man. It owes its existence to the creative
power of his intellect. There is more meaning in the
statement that man gives laws to Nature than in its
converse that Nature gives laws to man."[2] Thus the
law of gravitation is not so much the discovery by
Newton of a rule guiding the motion of the planets
as his invention of a method of briefly describing the
sequences of sense-impressions termed planetary
motion.[3] It is rightly said, observes Professor Charles
Singer, that natural law is not absolute, that it exists
in our minds and not in things, and that even in our
minds it is subject to change.[4] "The mind", writes
Sir Arthur Eddington, "has by its selective power
fitted the processes of Nature into a frame of law of
a pattern largely of its own choosing; and in the discovery of this system of law the mind may be regarded as regaining from Nature that which the mind
has put into Nature."[5] It is the human intellect

---

[1] *Tractus Theologico-Politicus. Works*, ed. R. H. Elwes, vol. i,
p. 59.
[2] *Grammar of Science*, p. 87.
[3] *Ibid.* p. 86.
[4] Charles Singer,.*The Historical Relations of Religion and Science*
in *Science, Religion and Reality*, p. 147.
[5] A. S. Eddington, *The Nature of the Physical World*, p. 244.

which has eliminated chaos from the universe and unified its diverse elements.[1]

A similar doctrine is adopted by Mr. J. W. N. Sullivan in a recent work in which he surveys the present status of scientific knowledge. It is not at all clear, he says, that even the mathematical characteristics of Nature, on which we place so much reliance, are not also subjective. It may be contended with some plausibility that we inevitably arrange phenomena in a mathematical framework because of the structure of our minds.[2] What we have done, he suggests, is to read into Nature certain forms which govern our ways of thinking. "The scientific picture of the universe . . . is much more of a mental creation than we had supposed. The attitude of scientific men, before Relativity Theory, was comparatively naïve. They looked abroad on the universe and saw lumps of matter moving about in accordance with certain laws. Both the lumps of matter and the laws were supposed to move about quite independently of our minds. We simply saw what happened to be there. The lumps of matter we perceived "directly". The laws of matter were not so directly perceived—it was often a matter of considerable trouble to find them— but they were just as truly objective, they were just as truly independent of us."[3]

Sir James Jeans, in his Presidential Address to the British Association for the Advancement of Science in 1934, observed that in the older physics men imagined they were studying an objective Nature

---

[1] H. Dingle, *Astronomy and Scientific Ideas* in *Science To-day* (1934), p. 292.
[2] J. W. N. Sullivan, *Limitations of Science*, p. 228.
[3] *Ibid.* pp. 82-3.

which had its own existence independently of the mind which perceived it, and which had existed from all eternity, whether it was perceived or not. In the new physics "the Nature we study does not consist so much of something we perceive as of our perceptions; it is not the object of the subject-object relation, but the relation itself. There is, in fact, no clear-cut division between the subject and object; they form an indivisible whole which now becomes Nature."

The rise of the social sciences is one of the most striking intellectual developments of recent decades. But the efforts devoted to studying the various activities and characteristics of the human race (in such subjects as economics, political science, anthropology, psychology, and jurisprudence) have so far failed to disclose laws of Nature in any degree comparable in precision or certainty, at any rate so far as individual behaviour is concerned, with those prevailing in the universe of matter. Hence a great gulf has seemed to exist between social science and natural science. On one side of the gulf there were marshalled up the laws of the natural scientist, exact, meticulous, impeccable, utterly unassailable in the perfection of their ability to measure, describe, explain, predict, and yield practical service no less than intellectual comprehension. On the other side of this gulf were drawn up the miscellaneous collection of uncertain generalisations, doubtful conclusions, anecdotes, unreliable statements of vague tendencies, qualitative evaluations, and moral injunctions which had emerged from the social sciences. A more dissimilar and unequal array of forces could scarcely be imagined; and there seemed to be little chance of the gulf being bridged.

The situation has now changed almost beyond recognition. On the one hand the social sciences have advanced enormously in clearness of aim, objectivity of method, and clarity of statement, while natural science appears to have declined in these qualities. The one feature of the Newtonian outlook which is left, declares Sullivan, is the insistence on a mathematical formulation of Nature; [1] and that, he has previously admitted, is a purely subjective process. The conservation of energy, a corner-stone of 19th-century science, becomes "an article of faith. It is no longer an observed characteristic of Nature, based upon experimental evidence, but becomes, at best, a metaphysical doctrine." [2]

Even the traditional conception of cause and effect has undergone a radical transformation; and all the old assumptions relating to it have broken down. It might be supposed that so fundamental a relation as the causal connection between two successive events would be essentially independent of the mind which considers it. Yet Professor Max Planck assures us that this is not so. It is necessary in his view to attach the concept of causality to the human intellect, with reference to the ability to predict an event. Moreover, a physical world-picture created by our imagination has to be substituted in all such operations for the world-picture known to our senses. [3]

A further notable change which has occurred is that physicists, astronomers, and biologists frankly admit that the natural laws with which they are con-

[1] J. W. N. Sullivan, *Limitations of Science*, p. 253.

[2] *Ibid.* p. 250.

[3] Max Planck, *Causality in Nature* in *Science To-day* (ed. J. Arthur Thompson), p. 362; Guthrie Lecture delivered 17th June 1932, *Proc. Physical Society* (London, 44, Part V (1932).

cerned relate mainly to the behaviour of crowds.[1]
Once we enter the domain of aggregates and averages, it becomes far easier to link up the knowledge
we have of mankind drawn from the social sciences
with our knowledge of the external world derived
from the natural sciences. The jurist assumes the
physical characteristics of human beings, wrote
W. G. Miller in *The Data of Jurisprudence*, and also
that they possess the power of controlling their
actions by means of the will. "But while this is a
fundamental assumption with regard to the individual man, it is also true that as a body men are
subject to invariable laws like physical matter.
Suicide is an act of the will on the part of each
individual, and yet statistics show that a definite
annual percentage of the population commit the act;
it is induced by external circumstances, disease,
famine, calamity, and even the weather."[2] Human
life, echoes Eddington, is proverbially uncertain, yet
few things are more certain than the solvency of a
life insurance company. The average law is so trust-
worthy that we can predict the expectation of life of
the children now born with great accuracy. But that
does not enable us to foretell the span of life of a
particular child. "The eclipse of 1999 is as safe as the
balance of a life insurance company; the next quantum jump of an atom is as uncertain as your life and
mine."[3]

We have been chiefly concerned with jurisprudence in these pages; and jurisprudence resembles the
physical sciences perhaps less than any of the other
social studies. It is extraordinarily difficult to discover

[1] *Ante*, pp. 325-6.   [2] Pp. 16-17.
[3] *The Nature of the Physical World*, p. 300.

any trace of natural law in the scientific sense prevailing among the legal systems which exist or have existed in the world. The multitudinous laws which men have made for themselves are infinitely variegated; and it is seldom possible to ascribe the particular forms assumed by the flora and fauna of the juridical kingdom to specific causes of general and immutable validity. The forces which make the laws of a community what they are at any given moment seem usually without universal significance. It is true, of course, that modern legal institutions are for the most part the outcome of deliberate will and are therefore neither haphazard nor accidental creations. But to recognise this obvious fact does not necessarily imply the existence of any universal principles of cause and effect. It is possible that psychologists may one day be able to show that the conduct-sequences of human beings are everywhere the invariable, inevitable, and predictable results of particular predisposing causes; and that a specified cause always produces precisely the same results in the world of men, provided that the same operative conditions are present.

If that were to happen, the age-long discussion concerning free-will and determinism would be brought to a conclusive end; and it would be possible so to extend the realm of natural law as to include all the activities of human beings within its domain. It would be evident that the legal systems of the world are as much the inevitable product of cause and effect—whether considered subjectively or objectively—as the passing of the seasons or the behaviour of a gas at specified temperatures. It would be possible to assimilate completely our knowledge of mankind with our knowledge of the external world. It would be possible to formulate natural laws concerning the laws of man.

That day may never come, in the opinion of many of the most profound thinkers; and even those who hold the mechanistic view of life agree that its arrival must in any case be exceedingly remote. Therefore, whether we hold the mechanistic view that life is subject to the same laws as inanimate matter, and to none others, or whether we accept the vitalist doctrine that life in general, and particularly human life, possesses qualities which distinguish it from the world of matter and enable it to transcend all the limitations of natural law, or more precisely, to escape from its application, it is clear that these are only ultimate doctrines and that for present and practical purposes we have to contemplate a world in which natural phenomena appear to behave in an orderly fashion and man alone seems the creature of disorder.

In these circumstances what hope can there be of relating the laws of Nature to the laws of man?

A suggestive answer was given by Thomas Huxley, who sought to reconcile juridical law and scientific law by projecting them on to a common plane of function or purpose. When we have observed that a particular cause always produces the same effect, or that the same sequence of events invariably takes place, then, said Huxley, the truth thus discovered is termed a law of Nature. Thus it is a law of Nature that if a heavy object is unsupported it will fall to the ground. But, he continued, it must be remembered that the laws of Nature are not the causes of the order of Nature, but only our way of stating as much of that order as we have managed to discern. The laws of Nature resemble in this respect the laws of man. There are laws requiring the payment of taxes and those which aim at preventing murder and theft. But the juridical law is not the cause which makes a man pay his taxes or abstain from one of these crimes. The law is no more than a statement of what will happen to a man who does not pay his taxes or who commits theft or murder. "The cause of his paying his taxes or abstaining from crime (in the absence of any better motive) is the fear of consequences which is the effect of his belief in that statement. A law of man tells us what we may expect society will do under certain circumstances; and a law of nature tells us what we may expect natural objects will do under certain circumstances. Each contains information addressed to our intelligence. . . ." [1]

Huxley thus regarded juridical laws as statements of conduct-sequences in human society involving a coherent relation of cause and effect corresponding to the sequences of natural events described by the laws of science. He expressly declared that human law is not rendered null or void by being "broken", for the individual is free to adopt whichever course of action he may prefer. The idea of obedience is, indeed, irrelevant to Huxley's conception of human law as a statement of conduct-sequences. What is important is to preserve the accuracy of the statement, and this is achieved as effectively when the civil remedies, penal provisions, or other enforcement arrangements prescribed by the law are called into operation, as when the conduct of the persons affected

---

[1] T. H. Huxley, *Science Primers*, Introductory, pp. 13-14.

by the law enables the intervention of the Courts, judicial officers or administrative officials to be dispensed
with entirely. It follows from Huxley's conception,
observes Sir Frederick Pollock, that only those cases
of "disobedience" which escape punishment or the
prescribed consequences can be regarded as exceptions to the uniformity of conduct which it is the aim
of the law to ensure, whereas according to the commonly held view all cases of "disobedience" violate
the uniformity. Thus, Huxley's view strengthens the'
resemblance between the laws of Nature and the laws
of man.[1]

That resemblance, declares Sir Frederick Pollock,
is a true one despite all the criticism which has been
levelled at it. For juridical law aims with more or less
success at producing uniformity of conduct within its
sphere of operation, while in the processes of Nature
we observe uniformities which are perfectly constant.
This constancy has at all times presented itself to
men as the perfect fulfilment in another region of
that which the law-giver can only strive to attain.[2]
If this was an acceptable view in the days before the
physicist had begun to cast doubts on the determin-
acy of the atom and before the statistical law of averages was recognised as the mainstay of the scientific
household, it must be far more tenable to-day. For
now the constancy of man no longer compares so
unfavourably with the constancy of Nature. The
average human being appears to be a more law-
abiding creature than the modern Schrödinger atom,
with its waves in multi-dimensional space.[3]

[1] Sir F. Pollock, *Essays in Jurisprudence and Ethics*, p. 47.
[2] *Ibid.* p. 42. Cf. R. M. Maciver, *Community*, p. 12.
[3] J. W. N. Sullivan, *op. cit.* p. 251.

I believe, however, that in the last resort we must regard the legislative activity of the human mind as the most significant phenomenon in any attempt to relate jural law to natural law. The attempt may seem far-fetched and even absurd when one contrasts the intractable material of the physical universe with the malleable stuff of human nature. The physicist, the chemist, the astronomer, are confronted with the "stubborn and irreducible facts" of the world of matter, and they can, it would seem, "make" law only within the narrowest limits, whereas the legislative assembly of every minor State or the most short-lived dictator can and often does radically transform the entire juridical system under which a particular community lives.

It may be said, of course, that the laws of Nature have been changed as frequently and as fundamentally as the laws of man during the past two or three centuries, and it is possible or even probable that the existing body of scientific law is highly ephemeral.[1] It is also urged by a distinguished modern thinker that since the laws of Nature depend on the individual characters of the things which comprise Nature, then as these things change so too must the laws which refer to them change also. Thus an evolutionary view of the physical universe should conceive of the laws of Nature as evolving concurrently with the things which constitute the environment. Hence the conception of a universe evolving subject to fixed eternal laws should be abandoned.[2]

But this demonstration of the transitory character of scientific law does not meet the point that although

[1] A. N. Whitehead, *Nature and Life*, pp. 67-8 (English ed.).
[2] A. N. Whitehead, *Adventures of Ideas*, p. 143.

it may be true that man gives laws to Nature as well as to himself, the purpose and character of the laws which are given in the one case are different from those in the other. The laws of Nature are essentially descriptive statements of causal relations which exist regardless of human choice or volition; they are, as it were, announcements of what actually exists, mere rules of succession. Juridical laws, on the other hand, presuppose a voluntary element in the activities to which they relate and are to some extent designed for the express purpose of producing in the real world relations which would not otherwise exist. Their object is often not to describe the operation of forces but to set them in motion.[1] They are therefore the result of judgments as to what values are desirable rather than, or in addition to, judgments as to what facts actually exist. In jural law ultimate aims loom in the background such as justice or equality, or the protection of property, the safety of the community, social welfare, or some other goal; and these operate explicitly or by implication as norms or ideal standards. Hence it is said that in human law the conditions in a given situation are connected with its consequences by the idea of *ought*, whereas in the system of Nature the link prevailing between condition and consequence is the causal one denoted by the word *must*.[2]

The Austrian jurist Kelsen has rested a substantial part of his philosophy on this distinction between a normative (or jural) law and a causal (or natural) law.

---

[1] John Dickinson, *The Law behind Law*: xxix, *Columbia Law Review*, p. 287.

[2] *Ibid.* pp. 289 n., 290 n., 292-3; Kelsen, *Die Idee des Naturrechts* (1928), 7 Zeitschrift für Offentliches Recht, p. 222.

For Kelsen's system of jurisprudence proceeds on the basis that every concrete law in the domain of natural science is a specific application of the general law of causality: it shows a particular event to be the necessary consequence of a preceding one, and explains the actual processes of Nature. In a normative science such as jurisprudence, on the other hand, the word law has an entirely different meaning. It lays down rules which prescribe right conduct.[1]

This rigid dichotomy is not in harmony with recent advances in scientific thought. As I have already shown, men of science no longer claim for natural laws the inexorable, immutable, and objective validity they were formerly deemed to possess. On the contrary, emphasis is now laid on the subjective element contributed by the human mind in formulating the laws of Nature, on their applicability to aggregates and averages rather than to individual cases, and on the difficulty of establishing an objective relationship of cause and effect. Professor Max Planck tells us that the impossibility of accurately predicting in even one single case, either from the standpoint of classical physics or from that of quantum physics, is a natural consequence of the fact that man with his senses and his measuring instruments is a part of Nature. He is subject to her laws and cannot escape from her.[2]

In these circumstances a new significance is given to the conception of man's place in the universe put

---

[1] H. Lauterpacht, *Kelsen's Pure Science of Law* in *Modern Theories of Law* (1933), pp. 108-9; Kelsen, *Hauptprobleme*, pp. 3-33; *Staatsbegriff*, pp. 75-81; H. Kelsen. *The Pure Theory of Law*, 50 *Law Quarterly Review*, pp. 474-98 (tr. C. H. Wilson).

[2] Max Planck, *Causality in Nature* in *Science To-day* (1934), p. 364, Guthrie Lecture, *Proc. Physical Soc. of London*, 44, Part V. (1932).

forward by Immanuel Kant a hundred and fifty
years ago. Kant drew a clear distinction between the
laws of Nature in the physical sense and the natural
law or natural rights which had for long formed the
basis of political, legal, and social thought. But
having done this, he did not then contrast the involuntary subjection of the world of matter to causal
law with the unrestricted power of human beings to
behave as they choose, to follow or depart from the
hypothetical norm. It is true that men are free; and
the notion of freedom is fundamental to Kant. But
to him freedom did not mean chance or arbitrariness,
but the highest realisation of the idea of law in the
universe. Man is an ethical subject governed by a
universal system of laws. Yet he is free as an ethical
subject; for the system is not imposed on him through
the impersonal compulsion of things or through the
command of an external authority, but is one that he
has conferred upon himself. The concept of freedom
thus coincides with the principle of self-legislation or
autonomy.[1]

Reflections of this kind are, of course, highly
speculative in character. Recourse to them is justifiable only when it becomes difficult or impossible to
continue the argument on more substantial grounds.
That point has now been reached in the present
discussion.

The analysis so far pursued has enabled us to trace
the origin of both jural laws and the laws of Nature to

---

[1] Ernst Cassirer, "Immanuel Kant" in *The Encyclopaedia of the
Social Sciences* (ed. E. R. A. Seligman and Alvin Johnson), viii, p. 540.
Cf. I. Kant, *Idee zu einer allgemeinen Geschichte in weltbürger-
licher Absicht* (1784).

the human mind. Hence, we can reunite natural law with the laws of man by acknowledging the legislative power and creative ability of the human intellect to be the source of both. At the same time it is evident that in the juridical sphere the element of will, of voluntary activity, is a dominant factor which so far as we can see is entirely absent from the domain of natural law; and it is obvious that immediately we introduce the voluntary element, we are no longer in the region of natural science.[1]

That, however, is a conclusion we should gladly accept. For in the present state of knowledge science can find neither aim nor creativity in Nature: it finds but mere events in succession,[2] whereas aim, directive of the creative process, is an inherent characteristic of life. The spectacle of existence would be almost unendurable were this otherwise; if, let us suppose, we were confronted with a system of human laws and activities devoid of aim and purpose, mere rules in succession as empty of meaning and significance as the laws which science now offers us. The discovery of the power to aim at ideal ends freely chosen by his own will and intelligence is the supreme achievement of man, and in that, more than in any other single fact, lies the hope of the future.

I have attempted to suggest in earlier chapters what human life was like during the long ages when the belief was held, in one form or another, that both human existence and the physical universe were alike subject to unpredictable and inscrutable interferences on the part of magical and supernatural forces and various divine powers against whose omnipotence

---

[1] J. Dickinson, *op. cit.* p. 285.
[2] A. N. Whitehead, *Nature and Life* (English ed.), p. 66.

all opposition was in vain. In such conditions dogma, rite, and fear were the ultimate masters of every situation. Not only was the mind crippled, but the will of mankind was in fetters.

Such was the condition of the human race for by far the greater part of its existence. With the doubtful exception of a short period in the ancient world, it is only during the past three centuries that the clouds which darkened our vision have begun to lift, and we have been able to perceive that the fetters which imprisoned the will were the bonds of superstition and ignorance. Man is at last coming to realise that the troubles and misfortunes which afflict him are for the most part due to human causes rather than to divine or supernatural visitations, and are therefore curable by human intelligence and human will. The art of law-making and the practice of government are in consequence becoming at once distinctly easier and much more difficult. They have become easier in that the problems with which they have to deal are more malleable, more susceptible of rational treatment than formerly; more exacting in that the sufferings of mankind can no longer be conveniently ascribed to supernatural forces or divine punishment.

A new freedom and a new responsibility have thus been attained by the human race. It is painfully clear that so far mankind has not learned how to make intelligent use of its newfound liberty; and in much of our public and private life there is a puerile and dangerous irresponsibility. But even a misused freedom has a certain educational value, and the potential opportunities of our present condition are at least as important as the misdeeds and stupidities of which we are guilty. It is not absurd to suppose that the confusion and conflict, the lack of coherent purpose, the misery and cruelty and unnecessary suffering, which at present disfigure human society will eventually pass away. They are at bottom mainly due, in their particular manifestations, to a denial of the belief that man is free to choose, to an assertion that he is rooted in an unchangeable social mould. This refusal to recognise our ability to aim at the creation of whatever type of society we desire belongs to the old order of things. As such it is doomed to give way before a more hopeful attitude.

INDEX

345

THE END